D1553438

PYRAMID ODYSSEY

PYRAMID

by WM. R. FIX

ODYSSEY

MERCURY MEDIA, INC.
Urbanna, Virginia

Mercury Media, Inc.
P.O. Box 54
Wake, Va. 23176

Mercury Media books are available at
special discounts for bulk purchases. For
details contact the publisher at the above
address.

Library of Congress Cataloging in
Publication Data

Fix, William R., 1941-
   Pyramid Odyssey.
   Bibliography: p. 287
   1. Giza. Great Pyramid of Cheops
   2. Atlantis
I. Title.
DT63.F55   932   78-14540
ISBN 0-932487-00-9

A Mercury Media Book
Printed in the United States of America

To my parents

For nothing is secret, that shall not be made manifest; neither any thing hid, that shall not be known and come abroad.

Luke 8:17

CONTENTS

The Reckoning

Appendix

1

DISCOVERIES AT THE GREAT PYRAMID

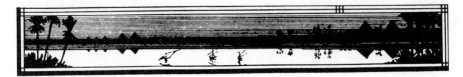

Beginning at the Center

The geographical center of the land mass of the earth is located where the Sahara Desert meets the Valley of the Nile in a district called Gizeh in the land of Egypt. In this district on the edge of the desert is a limestone plateau that rises about one hundred feet above the delta to the east. On and surrounding this plateau is the most important archaeological site on earth. Here is the largest, oldest and last remaining wonder of the Seven Wonders of the ancient world – the Pyramids of Gizeh. And here is the most remarkable single ancient monument on our planet – the Great Pyramid – the largest stone building ever constructed.

The Great Pyramid has fascinated men for thousands of years. It is mentioned in documents going back thirty-five centuries and has inspired hundreds of books and a myriad of articles, theories, speculations and comments. It commands the interest of millions and the fascination grows as new theories and books continue to appear every year. In the fourth quarter of the twentieth century the fascination of the Pyramid is reaching extraordinary proportions. It is almost as if, by some universal instinct, men expect a great light to come from Gizeh – a light which will reveal the secrets of its origin and purpose.

This is a travelogue of an odyssey through fields of ignorance and knowledge surrounding the Seventh Wonder of the World and from there into the depths of the past and to the brink of the future. Although we will explore recent scientific discoveries about the Pyramid, this is not a scientific document in the sense that our journey will not be confined to the boundaries of a particular discipline. We will freely trespass into areas long shunned by the academic community.

With the great acceleration of scientific knowledge in the nineteenth and twentieth centuries, interest in the Great Pyramid has also accelerated. The more sophisticated we have become, the more men have realized what an astounding accomplishment the Pyramid is. New discoveries which have never been published before show that the Pyramid builders measured the earth as precisely as has been done in the 1970s with satellite surveys from space. All that was necessary to make these discoveries – or to understand them – was a knowledge of arithmetic. The basic dimensions of the Pyramid incorporate three key measurements from which the earth's size and shape can be calculated in a clear and simple manner with extreme precision. As if the Pyramid builders were aware that languages and alphabets would change, they recorded their message in the universal language of numbers.

These discoveries imply that the Pyramid is far older and more exotic than has generally been supposed. We will look at many sources – some never before examined – indicating that the Great Pyramid was built by a high scientific civilization sometime before the Great Flood, possibly as many as 10,500 years before Christ. Certain sources connect the Pyramid with the fabled lost continent of Atlantis and indicate that this ancient civilization knew it was doomed, and that it would be followed by a great age of intellectual darkness in which the very existence of that vanished age of the world would be forgotten, until its remains would again be perceived for what they are. In the light of these findings, the primary purpose of the Pyramid can be seen to have been to record the knowledge and abilities of that ancient world in such a way that that record would last 12,500 years – until the present day. If one wishes to follow the implications further he could interpret the message of the builders: "Here are the measures, that you may know there was once another order of the earth as able and exalted as yourselves, and it vanished in the passing cycles of time."

But the message doesn't end there. We cannot yet say where it ends. The Pyramid may reveal to us as much of the future as of the past, and only time will tell if all the earth may not be touched by its terrible and wonderful implications.

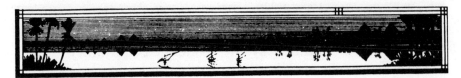

2

The Wonder of the World

The difficulty in attempting to convey anything both novel and significant about the Great Pyramid is that it has been described thousands of times before and many statements about it are either misleading or simply inaccurate. It seems that practically everyone interested in archaeology wants to decipher the Pyramid. Unfortunately, greater claims are often made for it than there is evidence to support, and the abundance of misinformation and false claims naturally tends to confuse the issue.

For instance, a long line of writers will tell you that in its original state the Pyramid was 760 feet at the base and 484 feet high. Using these figures they construct elaborate theories as to the significance of these measurements. But these figures are derived from inaccurate surveys performed in the nineteenth century when the base of the Pyramid was buried under piles of debris. After the debris was cleared away, the most accurate survey ever performed shows that the perimeter of the Pyramid was 3023.13 feet (921.453 meters).[1] The average side was thus 755.78 feet (230.36325 meters).[2] This may seem a small difference, but it is substantial enough to destroy the theories based on the older figures, so their proponents simply ignore the more current information.

Writer after writer will tell you that the Pyramid's height relates to its perimeter as the radius of a circle does to its circumference. They will tell you that if you divide the perimeter by twice the height you get the value of *pi*,

3.1415926+. Some writers shade the figures a bit, claiming *pi* as expressed in the Pyramid is 3.1416 or some other nearly perfect figure. However, the original height of the Pyramid was not 484 feet but 480.95 feet (146.59 meters),[3] and if we divide the perimeter by twice this figure we do not get the mathematically perfect value of *pi*, but its value approximated as 22/7, or 3.1428. This is a working approximation of *pi* still used by contemporary engineers, as it is very near the "true" value.

In the introduction to *Secrets of the Great Pyramid* Peter Tompkins writes: "It is, in fact, a scale model of the hemisphere, correctly incorporating the geographical degrees of latitude and longitude."[4] Tompkins has sound data to show that the perimeter of the Pyramid equals a half minute of equatorial latitude but does not give a valid demonstration of how the longitudinal value is incorporated.

It is now becoming the vogue for writers to declare that, contrary to what Egyptologists have been teaching for a century and a half, the Pyramid is not a tomb. But aside from pointing out that no burial was ever found inside the Great Pyramid, they do not examine the Egyptological data upon which the tomb theory is based. It would take a fat book to debunk all the misleading, inaccurate, or superficial information put out about the Great Pyramid. As we have seen, simply because someone says something is a fact does not make it a fact, and this applies to the scientist as well as the layman. Checking the sources, the following is the most important and most interesting information about the Great Pyramid published to date.

Gizeh is at the center of the land mass of the earth, which means that if one identifies the lines of latitude and longitude which pass over more of the earth's land surface than any other such lines, they cross near Gizeh. The Great Pyramid is built on the closest suitable site to that intersection. This was first pointed out in 1864 by Charles Piazzi Smyth, then Astronomer Royal for Scotland.[5] Because he believed the Pyramid was a temple built by a people of the Judeo-Christian tradition, Smyth has been widely regarded by Egyptologists as a crackpot. Nevertheless, he was an excellent mathematician and astronomer and no one has challenged this fact of the Pyramid's geographical position.

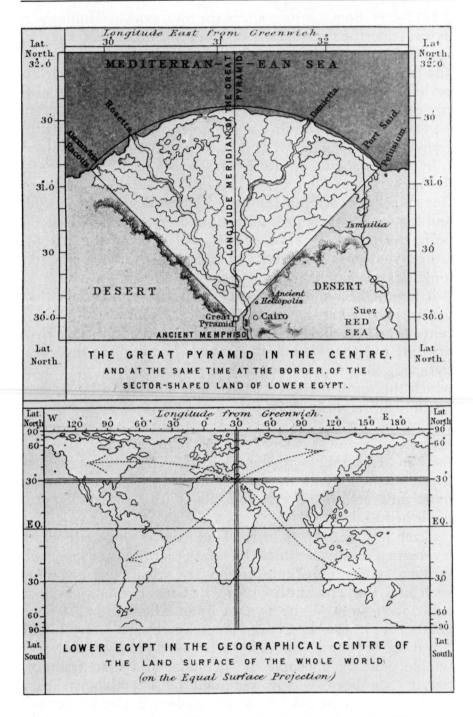

Above: The diagonals of the Great Pyramid define the delta of the Nile.
Below: The Pyramid is located at the center of the earth's land mass.

Of course, the intriguing question is whether the Pyramid builders were aware of this fact and placed the Pyramid in Gizeh for that reason, or whether it is pure coincidence. If they intentionally chose Gizeh as the center of the earth's land mass, they must have had an advanced science of geography and known the size, shape and position of all the continents. It further suggests that the builders were accustomed to thinking on a global scale and attached great importance to the buildings they erected at Gizeh. If it is a coincidence, then this is the first extraordinary coincidental fact among an amazing array of others.

The Pyramid is also located at the geographical apex of the delta of the Nile. The extension of the Pyramid's diagonals northwest and northeast define the delta.[6] Its four sides face the cardinal points of the compass with such precision that this cannot be accounted for by the use of any instruments which were likely available to a primitive agrarian civilization. Instruments of adequate precision have been developed in modern times only in the last two centuries.[7]

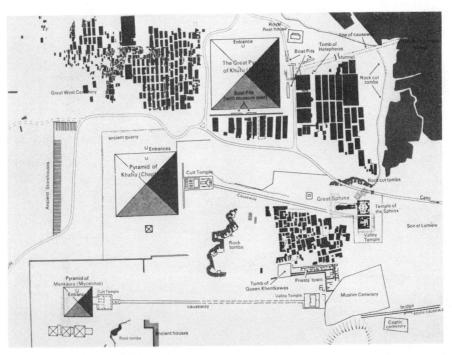

Modern map of the Gizeh Plateau.

Early aerial photograph of the Gizeh Plateau.

The Great Pyramid.

The Great Pyramid.

The tripod on top of the Great Pyramid indicating its original height and center.

The Pyramid today is significantly smaller, shorter and cruder in appearance than it was in its original condition. What is visible now is merely the stepped, yellow limestone core of the building. Originally the four sides were covered with huge blocks of fine-grained white limestone. The outside surfaces of these blocks were pitched so that each side of the Pyramid was one smooth continuous shining surface. This white finishing stone was ripped off in the fourteenth century and used to build palaces and mosques in Cairo. A few original casing stones are left at the base on the north side. (The Second and

Third Pyramids at Gizeh were also stripped of their casing stone except for some at the top of the Second and at the bottom of the Third.) With the remaining casing stones, there is enough left of the Great Pyramid for surveyors to calculate precisely the building's original dimensions. Until recently, the most remarkable fact to emerge from these dimensions is the apparently odd coincidence that the original perimeter of the Pyramid exactly equals a half minute of latitude at the equator.[8]

There is also enough left of the building for archaeologists, engineers and surveyors to have produced some astounding figures and comparisons. The Pyramid originally covered an area of 13.11 acres. Some of its stones weigh 70 tons[9] – as much as a railroad locomotive. The total Pyramid weighs about six million tons. There is more stone in the Great Pyramid than in all the churches, chapels and cathedrals built in England since the time of Christ.[10] If all the stone in the Pyramid were sawed into blocks one foot on an edge and these were laid end to end, they would stretch two thirds of the way around the earth at the equator.[11] Together with the Second and Third Pyramids, there is enough stone at Gizeh to construct a wall one meter thick and three meters high around France.[12] The Great

The Second Pyramid from the top of the Great Pyramid.

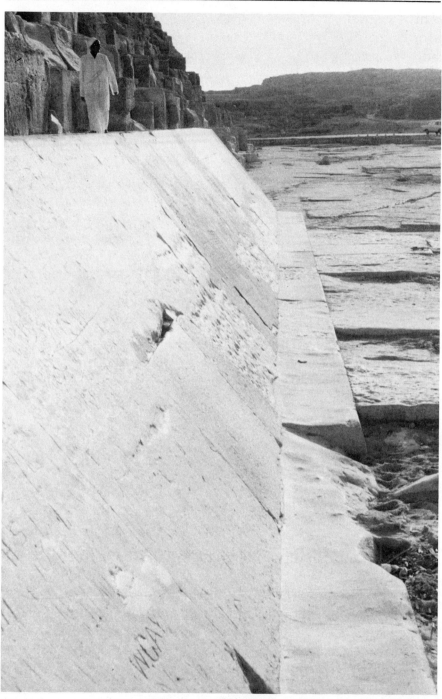

The last remaining casing stones glisten in the sunlight. The entire Pyramid was once covered with giant white casing stones such as these. The stones seen here weigh about 16 tons each.

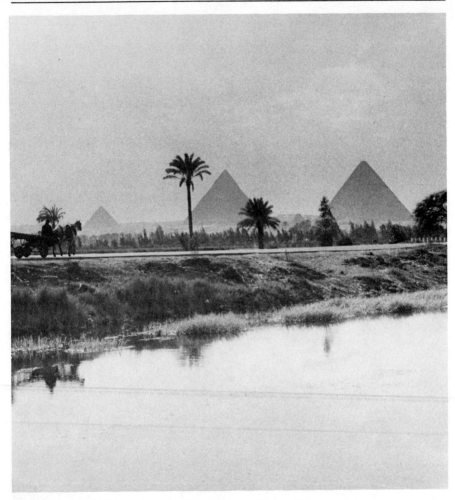

Gizeh: (from left) Third, Second and Great Pyramid.

Pyramid alone contains enough material to build thirty Empire State Buildings.[13]

The precision with which all this material was assembled presents evidence of an advanced and almost unbelievable engineering skill. The Pyramid rests on a square and level platform of carefully cut slabs of stone 21.6 inches (55 cm) thick. This platform protrudes from the edge of the Pyramid's base an average of 15 or 16 inches (40 cm) on each side. Despite earthquakes and thousands of years, this platform is still dead level to within .8 of an inch (21 mm) over a distance of 758 feet (231 meters) on a side.[14]

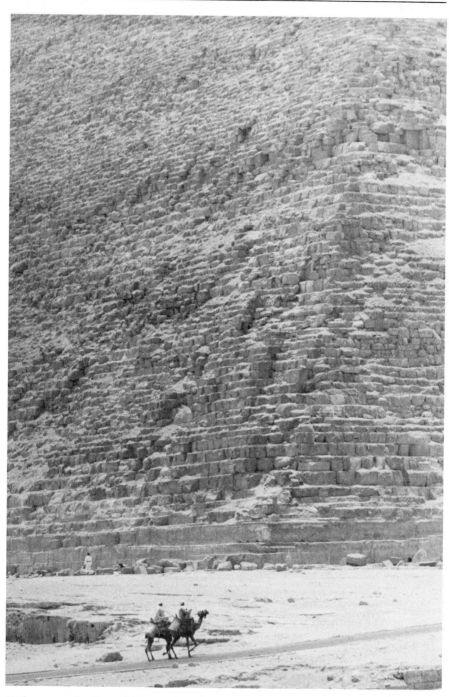

Riders pass the Second Pyramid.

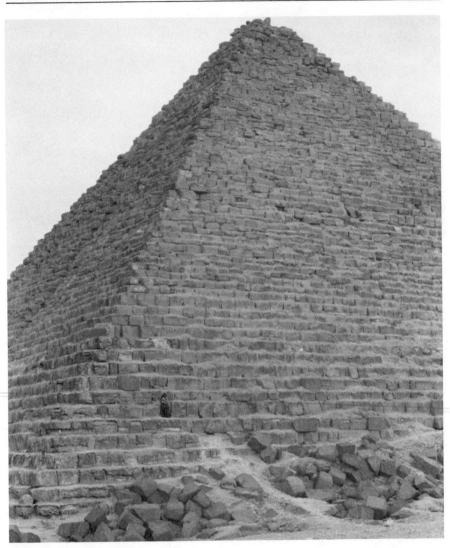

The Third Pyramid.

This detail is almost insignificant in comparison with the archaeologist Flinders Petrie's observations about the remaining casing stones on the Pyramid's north side. He found that the faces and butting surfaces of 16 ton stones were cut to within 1/100 of an inch of mathematical perfection. He reports that in the joints between the blocks:

> the mean variation of the cutting of the stone from a straight line and from a true square is but .01 inch in a length of 75 inches up the face, an amount of accuracy equal to most modern

opticians' straight edges of such a length. These joints, with an area of some 35 square feet each, were not only worked as finely as this, but were cemented throughout. Though the stones were brought as close as 1/500 of an inch, or, in fact, into contact, and the mean opening of the joint was 1/50 of an inch, yet the builders managed to fill the joint with cement, despite the great area of it, and the weight of the stone to be moved – some 16 tons. To merely place such stones in exact contact at the sides would be careful work, but to do so with cement in the joints seems almost impossible. [15]

Each of the Pyramid's four faces is about 5.25 acres in area and together were covered with 21 acres of white limestone casing blocks which gradually became smaller as they approached the top. Each block had six surfaces. The top, bottom, outer face and the two sides were precision cut and the back was left comparatively rough. If the same quality of precision cutting was employed throughout the Pyramid, it seems that the builders cut approximately 80 acres of casing stone within 1/100 of an inch of perfection. They built a man-made mountain as meticulously as we cut gems.

Nearly invisible seam in the pavement on the east side of the Great Pyramid. The coin is a piaster, about the size of a U.S. quarter (.9 inches or 2.3 cm in diameter).

Another intriguing aspect of the quality of the masonry is that the technology does not exist today either to build the Pyramid or even to repair it to its original specifications. This is not to say that we could not invent adequate machinery if we had sufficient money, time and motivation. But there are other lost arts that have not been rediscovered and even after having gone to the moon, modern man has no guarantee that he could duplicate the Seventh Wonder of the ancient world.

The extraordinary engineering precision lavished on the Pyramid's exterior was more than "skin deep"; it extended as well into the heart of the building. A shaft, called the Descending Passage, enters the Pyramid's north face and penetrates the bedrock under the building. This passage consists of two parts. The first section passes through built masonry, the second through solid rock. Petrie measured the straightness of this shaft using observations of Polaris, the North Star. He was amazed to discover that the average error from a mathematically perfect straight line in the first section was 1/50 of an inch in 150 feet (.5 mm in 45.72 meters). Over the entire length of 350 feet (106.68 meters) he found the sides were one quarter of an inch (.635 cm) from perfection.[16]

The dimensions of the King's Chamber inside the Pyramid express the ratios of the two most basic "Pythagorean" triangles: $2:\sqrt{5}:3$ and $3:4:5$.[17] The builders evidently were familiar with these special triangles thousands of years before Pythagoras was supposed to have invented them. These basic geometric principles are in addition to the incorporation of *pi* as 22/7 already mentioned.

The King's Chamber is completely lined with hard granite and contains a large lidless box called the sarcophagus, which is also cut from granite.[18] It is hollowed out so that the volume of its external dimensions is twice that of its internal measurements. Assuming drills with fixed cutting points of hard jewels were used to hollow out the sarcophagus, Petrie estimated that a pressure of two tons would have to be placed on the drills in order to cut the granite. He did not understand how this could have been done and wrote: "Truth to tell, modern drill cores cannot hold a candle to the Egyptians . . . Their work shows the marks of such tools as we have only now reinvented."[19]

Some would add scores of additional facts about the Pyramid,

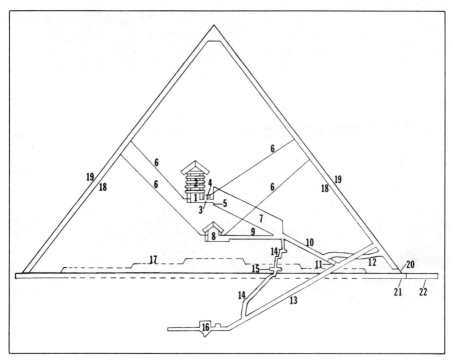

Cross section of the Great Pyramid, looking west.

1. The King's Chamber
2. The Relieving Chambers
3. The Antechamber
4. The Granite Leaf
5. The Great Step
6. The air vents
7. The Grand Gallery
8. The Queen's Chamber
9. The passage to the Queen's Chamber
10. The Ascending Passage
11. Granite plug
12. Al Mamoon's forced passage
13. The Descending Passage
14. The "well shaft"
15. The "grotto"
16. The "pit"
17. Possible level of natural rock
18. Present outline of the Pyramid, disregarding the steps
19. Original outline of the Pyramid with the white limestone casing blocks in place
20. The casing blocks on the north face
21. The platform beneath the Pyramid
22. The pavement

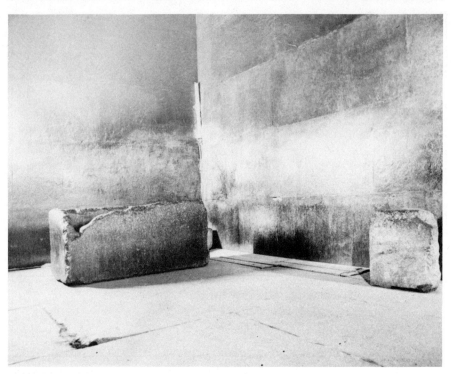

The King's Chamber and granite sarcophagus.

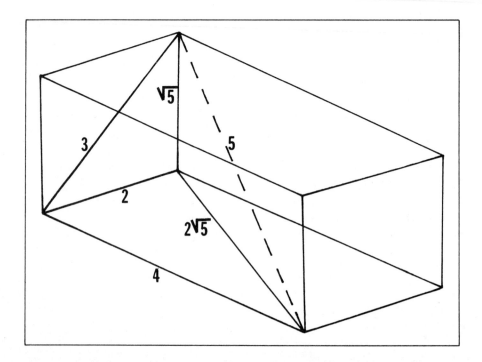

but these I have mentioned are well documented, regardless of how they are interpreted. What is the explanation for these extraordinary features? Egyptologists do not explain them. They simply ignore them. Of course, the familiar story, repeated in most history books and encyclopaedias, is that the Pyramid is the tomb of a pharaoh. There is much that can be said about this idea, but even at the outset one thing is obvious: none of these extraordinary features is necessary to build a tomb. If one is really happy with the tomb theory, he must suppose that most or all of these features are the result of coincidence or whim. That is a possibility. But there are several more facts which deepen this mystery. The first is that there is no reliable record that any burial or mummy was ever found in the Great Pyramid. Secondly, there is no record that any original burial has ever been found in *any* pyramid in Egypt. And the last fact is this. Despite the protestations of those who accept the tomb theory, there has never been a clear and comprehensive explanation for the Great Pyramid. If there were such an explanation, sooner or later it would be noticed and largely agreed upon. But the truth is that, in addition to all its other superlatives, Gizeh remains the most controversial archaeological site on the planet. Men of many nations continue to sift and explore its nature and to write yet more books with yet more possible explanations for this enormous, impossible ancient pile of stone situated at the crossroads of the earth.

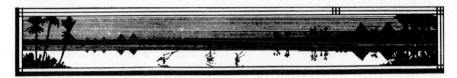

Recent Discoveries

In order to appreciate the discoveries I am about to relate, it is necessary to understand a few basic concepts of geography. Geography is among the most fundamental of all branches of knowledge and is as basic to civilization as numbers and language. Without geography we don't know where we are or where we are going. The definition of national and domestic boundaries, military maneuvers, trade and commerce are all dependent upon geography. Today the basis for geography around the earth is the system of latitude and longitude. Most people think of this as an invention of the modern world, but the concepts behind this are extremely simple and there is mounting evidence they were also known and used by the higher civilizations of antiquity.[1]

Here are the basic concepts of the system:

—The equator of the earth is divided into 360 degrees of longitude. These degrees are measurements of distance, east and west of the prime meridian – an imaginary north-south line which runs through Greenwich, England. At the equator, each degree of longitude is about 69.17 miles (111.32 km).[2] Going north or south from the equator, a degree of longitude gradually becomes shorter. The imaginary meridians or lines of longitude converge as they approach the North and South Poles, so that exactly at the poles a degree of longitude has zero length.

—Latitude is the measurement of distance north and south of the equator. From the equator to either of the poles there are

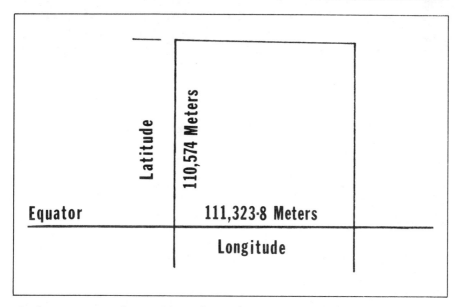

At the equator one degree of latitude equals 110,574 meters or 68.7 miles. One degree of longitude equals 111,323.8 meters or 69.17 miles.

90 degrees of latitude. In the northern hemisphere one degree of latitude is defined as the distance a traveler must go due north in order to make the pole star rise one degree above the horizon.

—Degrees of longitude vary in length from 69.17 miles to zero. Degrees of latitude are roughly equal. But the earth is not a perfect sphere. It is flatter at the poles and bulges out around the equator. The earth is 26.57 miles (42.77 km) thicker through the equator than it is through the poles. This means the surface of the earth is curved more sharply at the equator than at the poles and because of the way a degree of latitude is defined, there are in fact small but significant differences between the various degrees of latitude. Where the earth is curved more sharply a traveler will have to go less far to make the pole star rise one degree than where the earth is curved more gently. The distance from the equator to one degree north is 68.7 miles (110.57 km). The distance from 89 degrees north to the North Pole is 69.4 miles (111.7 km).[2] Each degree of latitude and longitude is divided into 60 minutes and each minute into 60 seconds, so that 30 minutes represents a half degree and 30 seconds a half minute.

One of the curious facts mentioned earlier is that the perimeter of the Great Pyramid is exactly equal to a half minute of latitude at the equator. The distance around the Pyramid or a half minute of equatorial latitude is 3023.13 feet (921.453 meters).

This apparently freakish bit of information is the most important fact to emerge from one of the countless interpretations of the Pyramid. Surprisingly, the idea that the Pyramid incorporates a fraction of a geographical degree goes back to certain ancient Greek historians. Some of the scholars who went to Egypt with Napoleon in 1798 resurrected this idea and measured the Pyramid to test it.

They had trouble getting an accurate measurement because the Pyramid's base was covered with huge piles of rubble and gravel as much as 50 feet (15 meters) high which had accumulated hundreds of years earlier when the casing blocks were removed and rolled down the sides of the building. Surveyors had to burrow down to the corners of the building and make their measurements as best they could. But no two measurements agreed. In addition, they did not know if they

Photograph taken about 1860 showing debris around the Sphinx and the Great Pyramid.

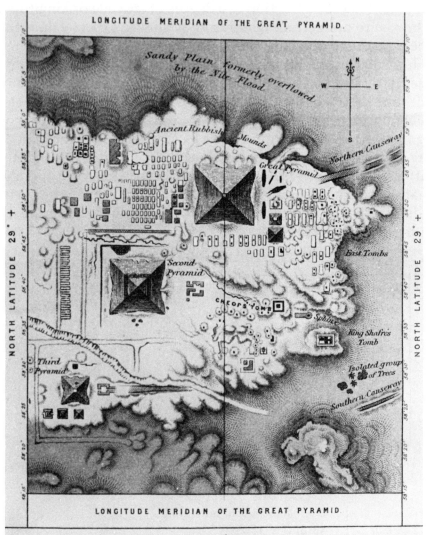

Smyth's illustration of the Gizeh Plateau around 1865, showing mounds of rubble at the base of the Great Pyramid.

were looking for a fraction of a degree of latitude or longitude. They were not certain whether they should expect values for the equator or the latitude of Egypt.

Incredibly, for the next 125 years men developed vast theories based on the dimensions of the Great Pyramid without really knowing its exact size. Finally, in 1925 the rubble and gravel were removed and an English surveyor named J.H. Cole determined the exact size and orientation of the building. He found that each of the four sides was slightly different in length. The greatest difference between them is that the south side is 7.9 inches (20.3 cm) longer than the north side. The total of the four sides produces a half minute of latitude at the equator.[3]

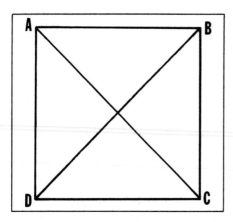

A-B-C-D-A = *Perimeter of the Pyramid on the platform*
        = *921.453 meters*
        = *1/2 minute of equatorial latitude*
1/2 minute = *1/43,200 of 360°*

There has been almost no reaction to this peculiar fact on the part of archaeologists and scholars up to this time. Few Egyptologists are aware of it. As far as they are concerned, the Pyramid is a tomb and nothing more. They merely disregard information which does not support this idea. If anyone points out the equivalence of the Pyramid's perimeter to a half minute of equatorial latitude, many Egyptologists will shrug their shoulders and postulate that the Pyramid builders were very simple people, that it is absurd to think they could have known such things, and that it is a coincidence.

But not everyone thinks so. L.C. Stecchini, a professor of ancient history specializing in the study of measures and ancient geography, sees it as a major verification that there was an advanced science of geography in ancient Greece, Babylon and Egypt. Stecchini tells us that the front of the Parthenon in Athens is equal to one second of equatorial longitude, that the famous renegade pharaoh Akhenaten (or Ikhnaton, formerly Amenophis IV, who reigned about 1375-1358 B.C.) deliberately placed his new and short-lived capital city of Tell el-Amarna in the geographic center of Egypt, midway between its northern and southernmost points, in accord with the concept that the capital should be the center and at the center of the country, and that many other similar indications of an understanding of latitude and longitude are found in ancient remains and documents.[4] Stecchini has pages and pages of calculations to support his conclusions.[5] According to Stecchini, many academic archaeologists reject the possibility of advanced geography in antiquity because of nothing more than their groundless assumption that these civilizations were primitive.

Whether or not it is a coincidence that the Pyramid's perimeter equals a half minute of equatorial latitude, two more

The Parthenon. The front of the temple is equal to one second of equatorial longitude.

curious facts can now be added to it. While in Egypt in 1975, I discovered that there were two additional such measurements, even more dramatic and important than the value for latitude. They are the clearest, simplest and most solid indication ever found that the Pyramid builders had measured the earth. They imply more strongly than anything else yet discovered that beyond the historical horizon there was a very high civilization that vanished long ago. Yet the story of how I made these discoveries is not exactly an epic adventure. Basically, all I did was look at the Pyramid, notice certain features, check out previous surveys and reports – and do a bit of arithmetic.

As has been said, there are 360 degrees in a circle, 60 minutes in a degree, and two half minutes in one minute. The equivalence of the Pyramid's perimeter to a half minute of equatorial latitude implies that the Pyramid incorporates key measurements of the earth on the scale of 1:43,200.[6] In other words, 360 x 60 x 2 = 43,200. If there are any more measurements incorporated in the Pyramid relating to the size of the earth, they should be on this same scale. What other measurements could there be? I had read Stecchini's remarks suggesting that the Pyramid builders could have been expected to incorporate a value for equatorial longitude since the measurement of the equator is more basic than that of latitude, but he has no figures to show that they did so. I had also worked out that a half minute of equatorial longitude is about 20 feet (6 meters) longer than a half minute of equatorial latitude. Therefore, if a value for equatorial longitude is involved, it must be incorporated in some measurement larger than the Pyramid's perimeter.

Now it happens that a little outside the four original corners of the Pyramid there are four roughly rectangular shallow holes called "sockets" cut into the bedrock, one at each corner. At one time it was thought that these marked the corners of the Pyramid itself, but it was later discovered the corners ended a bit short of the outside corners of these sockets. As with everything else about the Pyramid, men have been arguing about the significance of these sockets for hundreds of years. Most have thought that they marked the position of neatly cut stones adjoining the corners of the Pyramid.

I hunted up all the surveys and reports giving measurements

of these sockets that I could find in the library of the Cairo Museum. Whatever these shallow depressions held, and however this fitted into the architecture of the Pyramid, it is a simple fact that the distances between the outside corners of these four sockets add up to an extremely exact value for a half minute of equatorial longitude, or 1/43,200 of the equatorial circumference of the earth.

	Feet	Meters
Distance between the outside corners of the sockets	3043.7	927.72161
Length of 1/2 minute of equatorial longitude	3043.51	927.66571
Difference	.19	.0559

Even this insignificant difference of about 2.28 inches (5.59 cm) overall, or .57 of an inch (1.3975 cm) on a side, can be accounted for if it is assumed that the cornerstones that rested in these sockets had surfaces that tapered upwards, consistent with the style of masonry from the same age found elsewhere at Gizeh. (See Part I of Appendix for detailed figures.) The simplicity of the scheme is stunning. All we have to do to get an extremely accurate figure for the equatorial circumference of the earth is to multiply by 43,200.

3043.7 feet x 43,200 = 131,487,840 feet = 24,903 miles
927.72161 meters x 43,200 = 40,077,573 meters = 40,077.573 kilometers

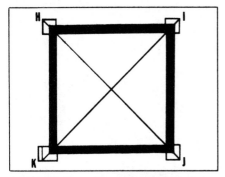

H-I-J-K-H = Perimeter reckoned from the outside corners of the sockets
= 927.72161 meters or 3043.7 feet
= 1/2 minute of equatorial longitude
= 1/43,200 of the earth's equatorial circumference

Current estimates of the equatorial circumference vary between 24,901.5 and 24,902.45 miles (40,075.159 and 40,076.688 km).

The second discovery I made involves the Pyramid's height. Several writers have suggested that the height of the Pyramid should correspond to the polar radius of the earth (the distance from the center of the earth to the North Pole). The polar radius is 3949.9081 miles (6356.774 km), but if we take the Pyramid's height of 480.95306 feet (146.59479 meters) and multiply it by 43,200, we get a figure that is short by some 14 miles (23 km).

	Miles	Kilometers
Expected figure	3949.9081	6356.774
Calculated figure	3935.0704	6332.8949
Difference	14.8377	23.8791

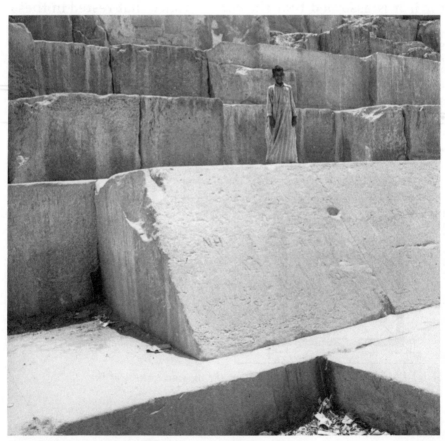

Casing blocks and the platform beneath them.

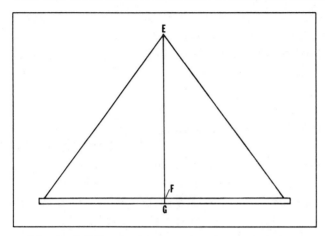

E-F = *Height of the Great Pyramid from the top of the platform*
= *146.59479 meters or 480.95306 feet*
F-G = *Thickness of platform*
= *55 cm or 21.6535 inches*
E-G = *147.14479 meters or 482.75751 feet*
= *1/43,200 of the earth's polar radius*

However, looking at the Pyramid one day, I noticed the man-made square and level platform under the structure which is 21.6535 inches (55 cm) thick. If we add the thickness of the platform to the height of the Pyramid above it, the height becomes 482.75751 feet (147.14479 meters). Multiplying this new figure we get an extraordinarily close approximation to the best modern estimates of the polar radius.

	Miles	*Kilometers*
Expected figure	3949.9081	6356.774
Calculated figure	3949.834	6356.6549
Difference	.0741	.1191
		or 391 feet

The difference is negligible – only 391 feet (119 meters) on a distance halfway through the earth! Even today, depending on the definition of what is being measured, figures for the earth's polar and equatorial dimensions may vary a couple of hundred yards or more. Because we are multiplying by 43,200 it would take the addition of only one ninth of an inch (2.75 mm) to the height of the Pyramid to have the figures coincide perfectly with those used today. (See Part I and Part III of Appendix.)

Extraordinarily enough, men have been looking for geodetic measurements (measurements which relate to the size and shape of the earth) in the Pyramid since 1798 and yet, as far as I know, this is the first time these correspondences to the equator and polar radius have been pointed out with figures to back them up. The results of Cole's 1925 survey had been largely forgotten until they were resurrected by Tompkins and Stecchini in a book published in 1971, and neither they nor anyone else had ever analyzed the dimensions of the building including the platform underneath it or the sockets at its corners in search of geodetic values. My discoveries came about simply because no one else had taken the platform and sockets into account. I was astonished that something so fundamental and of such importance could have been overlooked for decades. Perhaps it was a case of: "Thou hast hidden these things from the wise and understanding and revealed them unto babes."

No doubt some wise and understanding Egyptologist will come along wagging his head sagely and tell me that the Pyramid builders were very simple people, that it is absurd to think they could have known such things and that it is all coincidence.

People may believe what they wish, but there are several curious things about these measurements which argue against their being coincidental: these are the three basic external measurements of the Great Pyramid; they are all on the same scale; they are simple lineal measurements recorded in stone. Calculating with these measurements to find the dimensions of the earth involves only arithmetic and does not require higher mathematics. The calculations using these measurements are extremely accurate. These three measurements (a half minute of equatorial longitude, 1/43,200 of the polar radius, a half minute of equatorial latitude) correspond to *the* three key geodetic measurements of our planet, defining the circumference, the polar radius and the equatorial bulge. Calculating from only these three measurements it is possible to form a very accurate image of the size and shape of our planet, including the flattening at the poles and the equatorial bulge, which were not rediscovered until the eighteenth century of our era.

These discoveries fit into a larger pattern of other geographic facts about the Great Pyramid – its placement at the center of the earth's land mass, its position at the apex of the Nile's delta, its orientation to the points of the compass – all of which point to the same expression of a high geographic science.

Finally, these discoveries are paralleled by additional evidence, documented by men like Stecchini and Hapgood, of an ancient and advanced science of geography pertaining to Egypt and surrounding areas. When all these factors are weighed, the question of coincidence becomes ridiculous.

The three key geodetic measurements recorded in the dimensions of the Great Pyramid show that whoever built it had measured the earth with incredible accuracy – an accuracy comparable to what has been achieved in the 1970s with satellite surveys from space.

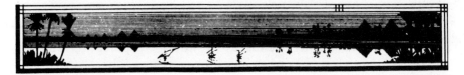

The Madness

Thousands of years before Christ, someone measured the earth with extreme precision and recorded this information in the dimensions of the Great Pyramid.

Here is the greatest mystery in all archaeology and one of the great mysteries of the earth. What civilization possessed the means to do this thousands of years ago? What happened to that civilization? When was this message recorded and why? What has this to do with the commonly held belief that the Pyramid was a king's tomb? This new information raises so many questions that in attempting to answer them we must separate all that is known about the Pyramid from what is unknown.

The first thing to be noted is that, quite apart from its size and age, there is something extraordinary, something almost magical about the Great Pyramid in terms of the way men react to it. Anyone who becomes really involved with the Great Pyramid must face a unique hazard: the Pyramid takes possession of the mind. There is another hazard: men are capable of perceiving the Pyramid in an astonishing number of ways. Some have thought the Pyramid was an astronomic and astrological observatory. Some have thought it functioned as the equivalent of a theodolite for surveyors in ancient times when the valley and delta of the Nile had to be re-surveyed annually after the seasonal floods. Some think it performed as a giant sundial by which an exact yearly calendar could be kept. Some think it records the mathematics and science of a

The Great Pyramid.

civilization which vanished thousands of years before pharao-
nic Egypt. Some think it is a huge water pump. Others have
thought it was filled with fabulous treasures, the repository of
jewels the size of eggs. One early investigator came away
convinced it was the remains of an extinct volcano. Another
thought the pyramids were Joseph's granaries. Some thought
they were heathen idols which should be destroyed. Some
believe the Pyramid captures powerful cosmic energies which
were used to rejuvenate or mummify the elect. Some think it is
a tomb. Some think it is a Bible in stone with prophecies built
into the scheme of its internal passages announcing the Second
Coming of Christ. Some think it was a mammoth public works
project which consolidated the position of the pharaoh and
unity of the nation. Some think it was built by beings from
outer space. Some say it was a temple of initiation. Some hold
that it was an instrument of science. Some believe it is an altar
of God built through direct Divine Revelation. And today,
judging by the uses to which it has been put, some apparently
think it is an outhouse.

If one looks hard enough and uses his imagination, it is
possible to conjure up evidence for most of these opinions. The
behavior of those who have attempted to explain this
monument is as interesting and extraordinary as the Pyramid
itself. From the dawn of recorded history there have been
innumerable conflicting explanations. Time and again serious
investigators have completely lost their sense of perspective in
searching for and advancing the explanation which suits them.
This has happened with even the most sober and scientific of
men. Flinders Petrie, the dean of modern archaeology and one
of the most fruitful men ever to have worked in Egypt,
declaimed his contemporary Piazzi Smyth as "hallucinating"
because Smyth attempted to find significance in the measurements of the sockets.[1] Petrie claimed that the sockets had no
significance because they did not match the locations of the
Pyramid's corners in its original state. Although it is now
established that the sockets do not match the corners, the
sockets seem to be significant anyway. This is but a single
instance among hundreds. Virtually everyone who has
committed his thoughts on the Pyramid to paper has
subsequently been shown to have serious "blind spots". There

are several major theories about the Pyramid which appear to have a good deal of evidence to support them but are convincing only at the cost of completely ignoring other evidence. The proponents of these theories dismiss conflicting information as "fantasy", or "coincidence", or denigrate those who believe it significant. Some archaeologists are aware of these hazards. Maragioglio and Renaldi, contemporary authors of a comprehensive survey on the architecture of the pyramids of the Memphis area, which includes Gizeh, have this to say:

> We have often noted an almost total absence of critical spirit as regards the interpretation of data obtained from excavation, so that the excavator's conclusions, which are often questionable, have never been discussed, but almost always accepted as *verba magistri*, [words of the master]. In some cases, moreover, to sustain a given theory, incontrovertible excavation data have been neglected, or in fact deliberately ignored. In other cases again, what were only hypotheses in need of confirmation have been repeated by everyone who has taken a superficial interest in the problems (often without having visited the monuments) and thus assumed the appearance of acquired facts.[2]

It is not just excavation data to which these remarks apply, however, but to measurements, engineering data, astronomic data, geographic and mathematical data, and data in general. Livio Stecchini, in an article entitled "Notes on the Relation of Ancient Measures to the Great Pyramid" (1971), states that until he had done so, no one had ever used the last major survey of the Pyramid, made by J.H. Cole in 1925, to interpret the architecture of the building – and this in spite of the fact that it was the first and only survey made once the base had been completely cleared of rubble and it is more precise than any other. He elsewhere states that Egyptologists ignore scientific geography and brush aside any evidence suggesting an advanced geographic science in ancient Egypt.

There is another peculiar thing about most theories and explanations of the Pyramid: the key evidence is missing. In the sundial theory, the ground markings are missing. In the pump theory, the valves and drains are missing. In the tomb theory, the bodies are missing. In the cosmic energy accumulator theory, controlled experiments demonstrating such forces inside the Pyramid are missing. (Food preservation experiments conducted by Stanford Research Institute inside the Pyramid in February 1977 showed entirely normal deterioration of samples.) In the outer space theory, the beings from outer space are missing. In the stone Bible theory, a well-founded construction date and a consistent chronology derived from the passageways are missing. In the public works theory, evidence of the nation-state supposed to have built it is missing.

The fact is that the key evidence for all of these theories is simply not there. In hundreds of books authors attempt to explain why it is missing, *assume* that what the theories require actually existed, and then *invent* detailed descriptions of the missing evidence, surrounding and supporting the descriptions with masses of circumstantial evidence and conjecture.

Understanding this unusual behavior associated with the Pyramid is part of understanding the Pyramid itself. It has changed the lives and altered the consciousness of many. Men feel *compelled* to explain it and to account for it on their own terms, regardless of the evidence, or lack of it. This compulsion

The Great Pyramid.

to account for it on our own terms arises from the overpowering presence of the Pyramid: it is enormous; it is ancient; it is legendary; it is sophisticated; it is the result of a great enterprise; it is here for all to see at the crossroads of the earth – and it does not seem to belong to our world.

That is the crux of it: the Great Pyramid does not seem to belong to our world, and because of this it is challenging and vaguely threatening. Much Pyramid literature is filled with strange emotions, with impatience and anger for conflicting ideas. Many hold their theories about it at the level of religious conviction. It is almost as if those who have sought to explain the Pyramid have said to themselves: "I must make this thing fit into what I *believe* about the history and the nature of the world."

If we are to rise above yet another partisan interpretation of the Pyramid, we must not exclude any significant body of information simply because it is unfamiliar or because it is not what we expect or want. We must keep asking what solid evidence exists for each explanation. If we are to be truly detached and open-minded, we must accept the unsettling possibility that the Great Pyramid simply may *not* fit into what we believe about history and the nature of the world.

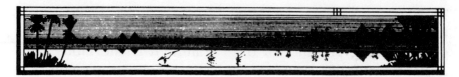

An Impossible Building

Another unsettling thing about the Great Pyramid is that we do not know how it was built. Erecting a structure with the size, precision and finish of the Pyramid is not merely a matter of piling one stone upon another. Some of the stones in the Great Pyramid weigh 70 tons. In the walls of the large temples immediately east of the Second and Third Pyramids 200 ton blocks are common. One block is estimated at 468 tons. But a few especially large blocks at Gizeh present the least of the engineering problems that had to be met. The standard suggestion is that in building the pyramids great teams of men harnessed to the stones pulled them up enormously long ramps. In building some of the smaller and later pyramids which used smaller blocks, ramps and men may have been employed, but this idea applied to the Great Pyramid creates more problems than it solves – especially with the time scale currently accepted.

How the Pyramid was built has occupied many thoughtful minds, and the more that men have studied the question, the more mysteries they have uncovered. The Greek historian Herodotus (484-425 B.C.) wrote that the Pyramid was built with 100,000 men in 20 years. At first glance this may seem plausible enough, but it is really quite impossible and a little arithmetic shows why.

In 20 years there are 7305 days. There are about 2,300,000 blocks of stone in the Pyramid, averaging 2.5 tons each. The current academic theory requires at least 315 2.5 ton blocks to

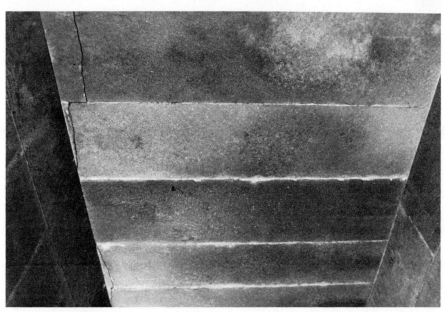

Seventy ton granite beams in the King's Chamber. Note cracks due to an earthquake.

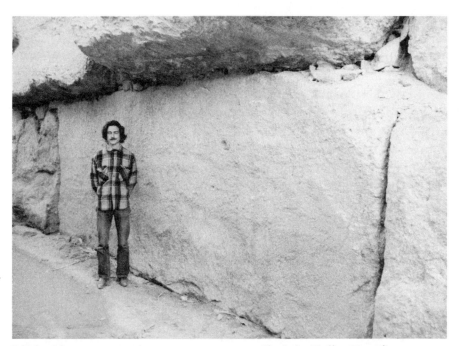

Block of limestone weighing 170 tons in a wall of the Valley Temple.

These giant limestone blocks forming the core of the walls in the Valley Temple were originally covered with polished granite.

be placed in the Pyramid every day. But with each and every course of masonry completed, it would have been necessary to heighten and lengthen the entire ramp in order to service the next layer. To carry an inclined plane to the top of the Pyramid at a grade of one in ten requires starting the ramp 6000 feet (1828 meters) away in the Nile Valley.[1] The volume of such a ramp would have been 75,000,000 cubic feet, or nearly the volume of the Pyramid itself – some 88,000,000 cubic feet. Since the Pyramid would have been built more carefully than the ramp, it may be supposed that only one third of the total time was used in building the ramp. If we proportionally decrease the number of working days allotted to the Pyramid by one third, only 4870 days remain, and this implies that 472 blocks (averaging 2.5 tons each) were placed in the structure each day when work was not taking place on the ramp. Assuming they worked 12 hours a day, this means that between 39 and 40 blocks were positioned each hour, a rate of one block every 91.5 seconds!

The workmanship in the Great Pyramid is far too careful for this to have been possible, and the organizational problems implied by the numbers of people required to maintain this rate are overwhelming. At the same time, the companion problems of quarrying, transporting and finishing this vast volume of material also had to be solved.

As for those who hold to theories involving wooden wedges, copper chisels, ramps and human muscle to do all this work, it would be extremely interesting to see them put such a theory into practice by repairing the existing structure and replacing the 21 acre layer of white Tura limestone casing blocks to the original specifications of the monument. It might be even more enlightening to see how much time, expertise, money, men, special tools and techniques it would take to perform such repairs with the best scientific minds and resources of the twentieth century employed in an unrestricted manner.

Simple arithmetic shows that either the Pyramid took an incredibly long time to build and/or that it must have been built

Remains of the temple east of the Third Pyramid. Its walls contain 200 ton blocks of stone.

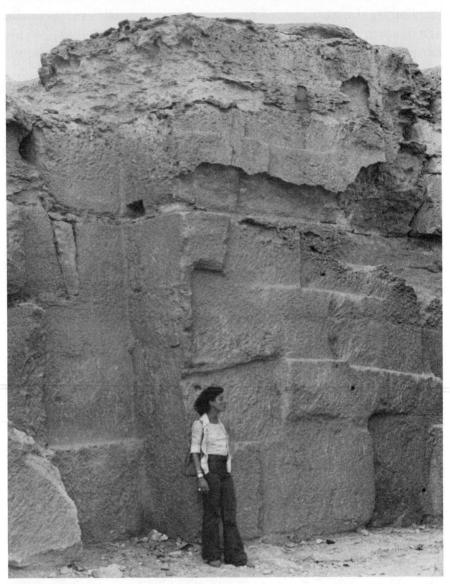

Multifaceted 468 ton limestone block in an inner wall of the temple east of the Second Pyramid.

by a very technologically advanced society. But the mystery doesn't end there. There is strong archaeological evidence that the casing blocks were put in place from above.

A number of Egyptologists have commented on the problem of how the casing stones were placed in the building. Assuming the Pyramid was finished layer by layer from the bottom up, all theories so far suggested boil down to two possibilities: (A) The casing stones were brought to the truncated top of the partially finished Pyramid, were given their final touches, and were then put into position. (B) The casing stones were finished on the ground, were brought up the side of the Pyramid by a ramp (or other means) and then put into position.

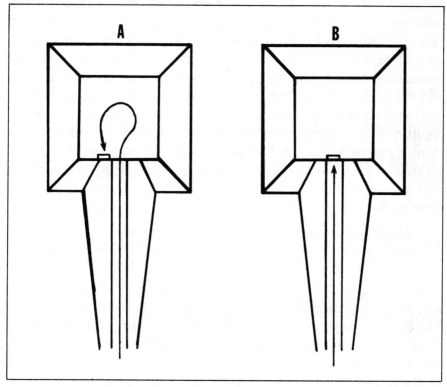

Case "A" shows a casing stone brought up a ramp to the top of the partially completed Pyramid and put into position from "inside". Case "B" shows a casing stone brought up a ramp and put into position from "outside" the Pyramid.

It is interesting that different Egyptologists have pointed to details which render each of these alternatives virtually impossible. Case "A" is impossible because it requires that on any particular layer of blocks the casing stones would have to be laid first, otherwise there would be no room to maneuver them into position. (They would have to be brought to the edge and dropped from the top of the layer of backing stones – which would surely result in many chipped and damaged blocks.)

However, archaeologists Maragioglio and Renaldi have pointed out that because of the way the blocks are cut and fitted into each other, it seems certain that the backing stones (the yellow limestone blocks behind the casing blocks) were laid first.[2]

Case "B" is even less likely. Several Egyptologists have pointed out that it would have been impossible to bring the finished casing blocks up the side of the building and into position without chipping and scratching them and the layer below.[3] Thousands of multi-ton stones could not have been moved in this way without marring quite a few. But the remaining casing stones and the platform edge on which these and the others rested show no sign of chips or scratches. It might be thought that once the Pyramid was complete, masons could have retouched the entire exterior surface, removing a thin layer of stone and thus smoothing out the chips and scratches. However, archaeologists have carefully studied the remaining casing stones and fragments of them found in the rubble. According to Petrie:

> There is a small difference of angle between the [casing] blocks at their juncture, proving that the faces have not even been smoothed since being built together.[4]

If the casing blocks had been touched up after being put into position, they should all have the same angle at their junctures. The minute differences of angle at the junctures indicate these blocks were not refinished after being laid and therefore were not damaged.

There are, then, some well-attested details in the remains which suggest that it was impossible to put the casing blocks into position using either of these methods. This seems to allow for the possibility that the casing blocks were in some way individually lifted up over their intended positions in the Pyramid and lowered into place by means of a controlled descent.

All of this, of course, assumes that the entire Pyramid was finished layer by layer from the ground up. Another suggestion is that the Pyramid was finished except for its casing stones, leaving exposed the yellow stepped core more or less as it is today. Then the white finishing blocks with one

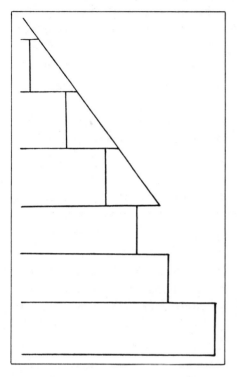

*Casing blocks placed from
the top down.*

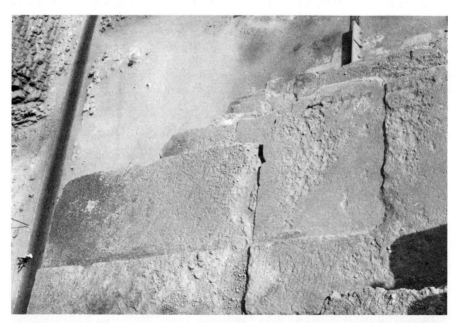

*Carefully worked backing stones on the southeast corner of the Great Pyramid near
the top, showing surfaces which were precisely leveled to receive the casing stones.*

slanted face were added last from the top down. This suggestion may not seem likely, but it is not physically impossible. The large well-squared blocks and the neat rows of steps in the core would have allowed the blocks to be placed from the top down, once they had in some way been brought up to the necessary level.

The contemporary Egyptologist J.-P. Lauer also believes this was possible and has illustrated how rows of wooden derricks and cranes resting on the steps and operated by ropes and men could have lifted the blocks several layers at a time. One weak point in this theory is that the sharp lower edge of each casing block would have stuck out to be easily chipped or broken.[5] Secondly, this situation seems to rule out the use of ramps entirely since if only one ramp were used, the blocks, once at the right altitude, would have to be taken all the way around the Pyramid along the high narrow steps to get them to the other side. (If the Pyramid were finished from the bottom up, they could have simply carried the casing blocks across the truncated top, but finishing it from the top down eliminates this possibility.) If we assume four ramps were used, one for each side, the size of the ramp problem is merely multiplied four-fold and the feasibility of the operation collapses in a heap of huge numbers.

Lauer's idea of derricks and cranes is more plausible, except that hundreds of derricks and cranes would have been needed in simultaneous operation if the project were not to take forever. We are also faced with questions about the availability and strength of lumber and ropes, and the nightmarish dangers of swinging multi-ton stones around the side of a pyramid 400 feet (121 meters) above the ground. The amount of damage dealt by a one ton block falling from this height upon the masonry and men below is enough to produce serious reservations about this idea as well.

There are numerous possibilities as to how the Pyramid was built and numerous difficulties with each possibility. In the end the mind cries out for some simpler, cleaner, swifter method. Physicist William Tiller of Stanford Research Institute has suggested levitation as an explanation of how the Pyramid was built. Indeed, according to legend, the priests of Heliopolis and ancient Babylon were able to levitate stones that a thousand men could not have lifted. This would certainly have helped solve some extraordinary engineering problems. Whether the casing blocks were put into position from the bottom up or the top down, levitation seems a necessary ingredient for the project to have been finished at all, and even with levitation, or some other advanced technique, it was still no easy task to produce the precision and care evident in the building. Of course, the levitation theory has its weakness too – sceptics will want a demonstration.

The more closely we look at the Great Pyramid, the more its mystery multiplies. Even if we seek to increase our knowledge about it by looking at the traditional sources of Egyptology, the darkness becomes deeper at every turning.

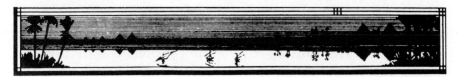

6

Legends and the Mistress of the Pyramid

Egyptian papyri and inscriptions are for the most part strangely silent about the Great Pyramid. There are no documents from the time of the building of the Pyramid that describe either its origin or its purpose. The earliest major sources concerning the Pyramid are the historian Herodotus (484-425 B.C.) and ancient Arabic legends. Herodotus reports that it was built by an extremely unpopular king called Cheops who, he was told, reigned for fifty years. He says 100,000 men labored constantly for twenty years in its construction. Herodotus describes the Pyramid as a monument to Cheops' memory and not, as so often reported, as his tomb. He noted that the body of Cheops was said to lie on an "island" under or near the Pyramid and that this island was surrounded by water from the Nile, supplied through an "artificial duct".[1]

In evaluating the account of Herodotus it should be kept in mind that he was separated from the time of the Pyramid's construction by thousands of years and wrote on the basis of what he was told by unidentified informants. Herodotus' report is valuable because it is the most extensive ancient writing that mentions Cheops, thought to be a Greek version of Khufu – the name of the pharaoh most Egyptologists now believe built the Pyramid. Unfortunately, his report includes inaccurate statements about the size of the pyramids and the size of the stones they contain, and is questionable on many other grounds. He claims the middle subsidiary pyramid east of the Great Pyramid was built by Cheops' daughter who prostituted herself for a stone per man to acquire the materials Estimates of the number of stones in this small pyramid reach 20,000. He is also notorious for reporting:

> There is an inscription in Egyptian characters on the Pyramid which records the quantity of radishes, onions and garlic consumed by the laborers who constructed it; and I perfectly well remember that the interpreter who read the writing to me said that the money expended in this way was 1600 talents of silver. [2]

It seems hardly likely that the Great Pyramid would have been embellished with such inconsequential information. Nevertheless, many take seriously Herodotus' estimate of the number of men involved and the time required, with no direct evidence for these. Nor is there any evidence so far of the island, the duct or Cheops' body. Diodorus Siculus, another Greek writer who lived after Herodotus in the first century B.C., also reported that the Pyramid was built by Cheops, but that Cheops was not buried there.

Completely different accounts are found in Arabic legends. Although the writers who recorded these legends lived after Herodotus, they evidently used sources which go back before the time of the Greeks. The ancient Arabic *Akbar Ezzeman Manuscript* states that the Pyramid contains:

> ... the wisdom and acquirements in the different arts and sciences, especially the sciences of arithmetic and geometry, that they might remain as records for the benefit of those who could afterwards comprehend them ... [It indicates] the positions of the stars and their cycles, together with the history and chronicle of time past [and] of that which is to come. [3]

In about A.D. 390 Ammianaius Marcellinus had this to say:

> Inscriptions which the ancients asserted were on the walls of certain underground galleries of the pyramids were intended to prevent the ancient wisdom from being lost in the Flood. [4]

A number of researchers, including Robert Ballard, Ahmed Fakhry, Egerton Sykes, Peter Kolosimo and Baron de Cologne, have all come to the conclusion that there are extensive underground galleries and chambers beneath the Pyramid. [5]

In about A.D. 870 Abou Balkh wrote:

> Wise men, previous to the Flood, foreseeing an impending judgement from heaven ... which would destroy every created thing, built upon ... a plateau in Egypt pyramids of stone in order to have some refuge against the calamity.[6]

Another version has it that the pyramids were not only intended to preserve knowledge but to memorialize the cataclysm from which it was to be preserved.

Masoudi, who died about A.D. 943, wrote in *Fields of Gold-Mines of Gems*[7] that:

> Surid ... one of the kings of Egypt before the Flood, built two great pyramids ... The reason for building the pyramids was that the king ... who lived 300 years before the Flood, once dreamt that the earth was twisted around, the stars fell from the sky and clashed together with a great noise and that all mankind took refuge in terror.[8]

The king, Masoudi then relates, summoned his interpreters of dreams. The best of them reported that he had had a parallel dream about a year earlier and was told in it that after the disaster the firmament would return to its former site. Then the king ordered the position of the stars to be examined and was told that first a great flood and then a great fire would come from the direction of the constellation Leo. Upon being told that afterwards Egypt would flourish again, the king ordered the pyramids to be built. According to Masoudi they were filled with the knowledge of the secret sciences, everything known of mathematics, astronomy and geometry, and other wonders and treasures. Masoudi also refers to automata – monstrous idols of stone and metal that were animated by spirits – protecting the sacred precincts and destroying anyone who violated them.[9]

In addition to these reports, the most persistent story found in old Arabic sources is the legendary association of Hermes with the Pyramid. The historian Al Makir (c. A.D. 672) wrote that Hermes built the pyramids. Ibn Batuta (1304-1378), one of the most traveled men of his time, recorded the widespread tradition that Hermes was the architect of the Great Pyramid, built to preserve science during the Flood. Other early Arabic writers such as Watwati, Makrimi, Sorar and Al-Dimisgi all recorded substantially the same tradition.[10]

If we extract the common elements from all these sources the picture that emerges is this: at some unspecified time in deep antiquity, some wise man or king perceived that a great world disaster was impending, a disaster described most often as "the Flood". This leading figure caused the Pyramid or pyramids to be built to preserve the knowledge, and to act as a record, of that world. This figure may have been either a king called Surid or the god or demi-god, Hermes.

These legends, however, are not the only sources linking the Pyramid with Hermes. Nor are they unique in the idea that the Pyramid was built before a great disaster to preserve the knowledge of another order of the earth.

The references in some of these accounts to fabulous treasures inside the Pyramid are apparently fantasies. These tantalizing references probably inflamed the imagination of Al Mamoon, the adventurer who in about A.D. 820 hired a crew of men to burrow through the solid stone into the heart of the Great Pyramid. Al Mamoon and his men eventually tunneled into one of the passages inside the building and gained access to the King's Chamber. There are no reliable indications that they found anything other than what is still found there: a large room with granite walls, and a lidless stone box large enough to hold a man.

The oldest intact document mentioning the Pyramid is a controversial piece of engraved, yellow-gray limestone called the "Inventory Stela", currently in the Cairo Museum. This stela is about a foot and a half high. The engraving is not good; it is only barely legible. Archaeologists are uncertain of its age. It is very unlikely that it is older than the Eighteenth Dynasty (about 1500 B.C.) because certain titles are given the Sphinx on this stela which have not been found on earlier documents. Some scholars believe it may have been produced as recently as 700 B.C.

The stela was found by the French Egyptologist August Mariette (1821-1881) in a minor temple dedicated to Isis just east of the Great Pyramid. This stela is remarkable because it purports to have been made at the command of Khufu himself – the Cheops of Herodotus. It describes an inventory of the statues of the gods Khufu is supposed to have found in the little temple of Isis when he came to repair it. It reads in part:

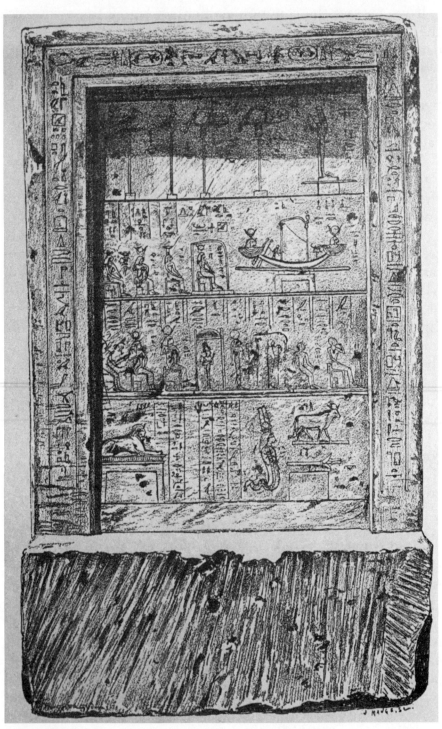

The Inventory Stela.

Live Horus the Mezer, the King of Upper and Lower Egypt, Khufu, given life. He made for his mother, Isis, the Divine Mother, Mistress of the Western Mountain, a decree made on a stela; he gave to her a new offering and he built her temple of stone, renewing what he had found, namely these gods in her place.

Live Horus the Mezer, the King of Upper and Lower Egypt, Khufu, given life. He found the House of Isis, Mistress of the Pyramid, by the side of the cavity of the Sphinx, or on the northwest of the House of Osiris, Lord of Rosta, and he built a pyramid for the King's daughter, Henutsen, beside this temple.

The place Hwran Horemakhet [the Sphinx] is on the south side of the House of Isis, Mistress of the Pyramid, and on the north of Osiris, Lord of Rosta ... He [Khufu] restored the statue all covered in painting, of the Guardian of the Atmosphere [the Sphinx], who guides the winds with his gaze. He made to quarry the hind part of the nemes headdress, which was lacking, from gilded stone, and which had a length of about 7 ells [12.1 feet or 3.7 meters].[11]

The stela goes on to say that the king came on a tour to see the Sphinx and a great sycamore which had both been struck by

The face of the Sphinx.

lightning. It was this stroke of lightning which had removed part of the Sphinx's nemes headdress.[12]

There are two main schools of thought on the Inventory Stela. Some believe that at least in part it was copied from an older memorial which had fallen into decay. Others think it is a complete ancient "forgery" created for the benefit of an already considerable tourist trade a thousand years before Christ.

Some of the statements the stela contains reflect actual conditions. As Egyptologist Selim Hassan noted, the tail of the nemes headdress of the Sphinx is certainly missing. Its destruction by lightning may be the best explanation since it could not have been easily broken off except by a terrific force from above. A scar of the length mentioned in the stela can actually be seen on the back of the Sphinx, and traces of old mortar used to repair it are detectable. At least until recently, there was also a sycamore tree of great age to the south of the Sphinx.

This stela raises more questions than it answers and, like everything else associated with the Pyramid, is extremely controversial. The problems it raises are these:

Egyptologists are now uniformly of the opinion that Khufu lived in the Fourth Dynasty, which is commonly dated at 2700 B.C. Why does the stela, which cannot be older than 1500 B.C., mention Khufu as if he were alive at the time it was engraved? Why does the stela refer to the Pyramid as already in existence at the time of Khufu? Why, if Khufu built the Pyramid, does the stela refer to Isis as Mistress of the Pyramid?

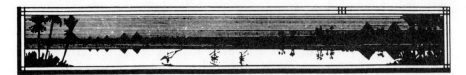

7

The Tomb Theory

For many people there is no mystery at all about the Great Pyramid. Any recent edition of an encyclopaedia or history of Egypt will assert that the Pyramid was built by the Fourth Dynasty pharaoh Khufu about 2700 B.C. and that it served as his tomb. This is often stated with a good deal of confidence. In *The Pyramids* Ahmed Fakhry declares:

> Archaeological research has proved beyond doubt that the Great Pyramid is nothing more or less than a tomb for King Khufu.

Moreover, the Pyramid has Khufu's name on it and the tomb theory has the great virtue of being short and simple. It is also somehow familiar and comforting. It puts the Pyramid in a recognizable context. It is as if we were describing the remains of any old city in the world: "People first came here in such and such a year. Their first prince was so and so. Here are the remains of their palaces and temples. Here is the royal graveyard. In such and such a year they fought with their neighbors and a few years later the kingdom fell."

If one is unaware of those curious geographical facts mentioned earlier, there is on the surface of things considerable reinforcement for the tomb theory. For example, here is what a visit to the Great Pyramid entails today. First, it is nearly impossible to avoid hiring one of the countless itinerant "guides" who frequent Gizeh. He will lead you up a flight of modern steps which have been built on the north face of the

Pyramid until you are about thirty feet above the ground. Then, passing a guard at the entrance, you enter the cavity known as Al Mamoon's Tunnel, the passage forced into the building by the ninth century explorer. It is crude and winding, about six feet (two meters) high and lit by naked light bulbs.

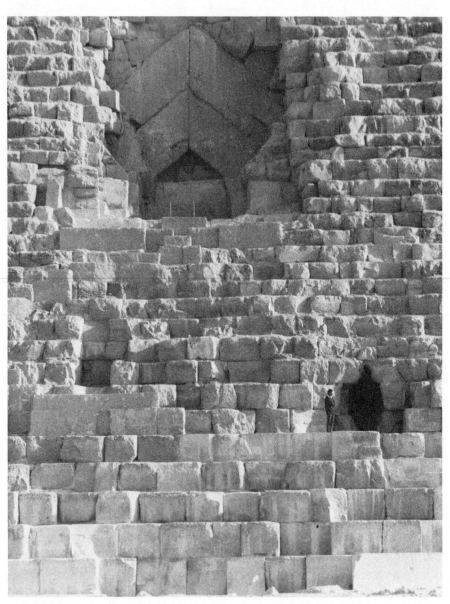

Al Mamoon's tunnel, below and to the right of the original entrance, is used for access to the Pyramid's interior.

The entrance to Al Mamoon's tunnel from inside the Pyramid.

After a hundred feet or so, this tunnel intersects one of the original shafts in the Pyramid, this one known as the Ascending Shaft. It is 3 feet 11 inches (1.19 meters) high and pitched at an angle of some 26 degrees. Uncomfortably bent over, you must climb this rather steep shaft for about 129 feet (39.3 meters) before you come out into a long, high gallery, pitched at precisely the same angle. This, the Grand Gallery, continues upward for another 153 feet (46.6 meters). At the upper end of the Grand Gallery there is a high step, called the Great Step, which has been made easier to climb by the modern addition of metal rungs. Mounting this step, you rest on a small platform. Beyond this is a small curious antechamber; passing through it you finally enter a moderately large, high-ceilinged room of elegant proportions lined in polished granite.

The Ascending Passage.

The other end of Al Mamoon's tunnel, where it meets the granite plugs and the bottom of the Ascending Passage.

The Grand Gallery.

Looking from the edge of the Great Step into the Antechamber and the entrance to the King's Chamber.

Here you are in the King's Chamber of the Great Pyramid. It is poorly lit by two weak blue fluorescent bulbs hissing malevolently in the corners. The room is empty except for a large stone box at the far end. Your guide lights his cigarette lighter above it. The box has no lid and in the gloom you discover it is completely empty. The typical guide will then proclaim with great drama: "Here is the tomb! Mummy in Cairo Museum."

This, of course, seems perfectly logical. The stone box looks like a coffer or sarcophagus and has been referred to as such for hundreds of years. There is a similar sarcophagus in the Second Pyramid and the whole site of Gizeh is honeycombed with graves which date from thousands of years before Christ to the present time. It is in fact a necropolis – a city of the dead – and a modern Muslim cemetery on the southeast corner of the site testifies that Gizeh is *still* a working graveyard.

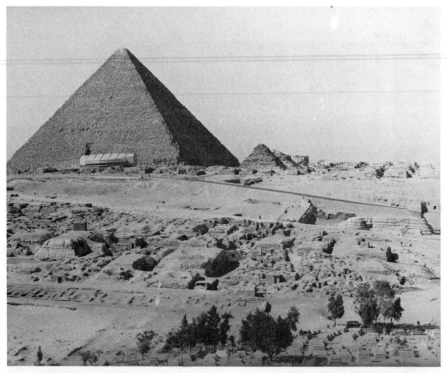

The necropolis south of the Great Pyramid with contemporary Muslim cemetery in the foreground. The modern building next to the Pyramid houses one of the "solar boats" found in the vicinity.

The necropolis west of the Great Pyramid.

Ancient tombs on the eastern edge of the Gizeh Plateau.

But whatever you may have been told, or whatever you may have read, there is no mummy from the Great Pyramid in the Cairo Museum. There is absolutely nothing from the Great Pyramid in the Cairo Museum or in any other museum. There is no proof that anything more than what is presently visible was ever found inside the Pyramid. For that matter, no original burial has ever been found in the Second or Third Pyramids either. Some bones, a sarcophagus and part of a coffin lid were found by Col. Howard-Vyse in 1837-1838 in the Third Pyramid. Even though the lid bore the cartouches of Menkaura, supposedly the builder of the Third Pyramid, because of the style of the engraving Egyptologists judged this to be an intrusive burial placed in the building thousands of years after its completion. According to Mendelssohn, when these bones were eventually carbon-dated, the test showed they came from the early Christian era.

So much is not difficult to discover. But one boiling day in April 1975, while walking around the Gizeh Plateau with a friend, I unexpectedly learned something which I suspect very few people know. My companion was Mark Lehner, a researcher from North Dakota who had been studying Egyptology in Cairo for a couple of years. As we walked, we debated points of view about the pyramids, trying to find a pattern which made sense. We were discussing the tomb theory when he said: "Of course you know, *no* original burial has *ever* been found in *any* pyramid in Egypt."

The idea that the pyramids were tombs has been repeated by so many eminent men, that I looked at him as if the heat of the day had gone to his head. But Mark had studied the matter thoroughly and knew what he was talking about. There are thirty to eighty pyramids in Egypt, depending on what is considered a pyramid. Many were small, poorly built, and now so completely ruined that it takes sharp eyes and considerable knowledge to be able to tell even where they stood. But regardless of whether the count is thirty or eighty, it seems remarkable that an original burial has not been found in a single pyramid.

The standard explanation for this is that every single pyramid was emptied by grave robbers in search of treasure. Grave robbery is undoubtedly one of the archaeological facts of life, and so is the later expropriation of some of the pyramids for burial purposes – a practice which at first misled archaeologists and seemed to support the tomb theory. During the Saite period (663-525 B.C.) there was an intense revival of interest in the pyramids and it became a "fad" to use them as tombs. It is generally agreed that the coffin lid fragment found in the Third Gizeh Pyramid was stylistically a product of the Saite period, although the bones appear to be even more recent.

In 1837 no less than sixty mummies were found in a large gallery under the Step Pyramid at Saqqara, another major ancient pyramid field about fifteen miles south of Gizeh. The Step Pyramid is usually dated around 3000 B.C. and the mummies were first thought to be the retainers of Zoser, the supposed builder of this pyramid. It was later discovered that not only did the mummies come from the Saite era, but that the gallery itself had been excavated then.

In another gallery under the Step Pyramid the bones of a child were found in a wooden coffin inside a stone sarcophagus and the skeleton of a young woman was discovered in a small granite sarcophagus in the central subsidiary pyramid south of the Third Gizeh Pyramid – but everything suggests these were also later, intrusive burials. Finally, bones from a human foot were unearthed in another chamber under the Step Pyramid, and while some writers refer to this as "Zoser's foot" they cannot, of course, tell to whom it belonged. Approximately 35,000 broken stone jars and dishes were also found in the galleries under the Step Pyramid and some of these seem to have come from *before* Zoser's time. The remains at the site are complex and confusing, and little can be established on the basis of those few foot bones.

If only a few intact burials had been discovered, it would be easier to accept grave robbery as the fate of the others. But without so much as a single original burial, the tomb theory seems to have a large hole in it. Why would thieves seeking gold and jewels also take the corpses?

Not only are the bodies missing – most pyramids don't even have a sarcophagus. In fact, many of the supposed "burial chambers" in the smaller pyramids are not even large enough for a sarcophagus. In all Egypt only three major pyramids (The Great and Second Gizeh Pyramids and the Pyramid of

Sekhemket at Saqqara) *have* sarcophagi which can be presumed original with the building. We know that the sarcophagus in the Great Pyramid was built into the King's Chamber before it was roofed over because it is too large to pass through the entrance passage. This sarcophagus would have to be smashed to be removed. Others could be removed intact only with great difficulty. As Kurt Mendelssohn has pointed out in *The Riddle of the Pyramids*, if grave robbery is the explanation for all these empty chambers, it is difficult to explain why anyone would want to steal a broken sarcophagus. And, in spite of careful search, no chips of broken sarcophagi have been found in any of the pyramid passages or chambers. If the pyramids were built as tombs to protect the remains of dead kings, they were certainly miserable failures.

Not only is there no direct solid evidence for the tomb theory, I next discovered that there is solid evidence against it. Of the thousands of graves at Gizeh, only *one* undefiled "tomb" has been excavated that is thought to date from the Old Kingdom – the first dynastic era of Egyptian history that is believed to have lasted about 1000 years and to have included the Pyramid Age. This Old Kingdom relic is also one of the most mysterious sites in Egypt and suggests a remarkable solution to the mystery of the empty stone boxes.

In 1925 a vertical shaft cut into the limestone of the plateau was found about a hundred yards east of the Great Pyramid. This 99 foot (30 meter) shaft led to a tomb tentatively identified as the tomb of Hetepheres, thought by some to be Khufu's mother – though this is very questionable. The shaft was completely filled in with carefully fitted, cut stonework and was not marked by a small pyramid, chapel or mastaba (a flat topped, rectangular stone construction with sloping sides) as might be thought appropriate to a person of high rank. The stones in the shaft were painstakingly removed and at the bottom was a chamber containing furniture, jewelry, pottery, personal effects and a compartmentalized alabaster box with the internal organs of some person in a preservative solution. There was also a large, well-made stone box or sarcophagus, with a lid, intact and *sealed* – which was found perfectly empty.

This empty sarcophagus is not the only one which has been found in such circumstances. In the 1950s the remains of a buried pyramid at Saqqara – now called the Pyramid of Sekhemket – were excavated by archaeologist Zakaria Goneim. The "burial chamber" was found intact and unviolated. Inside was another sealed stone sarcophagus which even had a wreath on it. This discovery caused much excitement since it appeared to be the first original burial ever found in a pyramid in Egypt. The opening of this sarcophagus was accompanied by considerable publicity. It too was found to be perfectly empty. In addition to these two cases, Mendelssohn reports that a third empty sarcophagus which had also been undisturbed since remote antiquity was found in a shaft under the Step Pyramid.

The only intact "tomb" from the Old Kingdom at Gizeh, and the only pyramid with an unviolated burial chamber both had an empty sealed sarcophagus. This is positive evidence suggesting that whatever these large stone boxes were used for, they were not used to hold a corpse.

Where do the mummies come from if not the pyramids? They have been found at a number of sites. The most important royal graveyard is in the Valley of the Kings, a sterile

Gizeh from the desert to the southwest. The subsidiary pyramids of the Third Pyramid are in the foreground.

desert valley across the Nile from modern Luxor, 450 miles south of Gizeh. It is there that the famous tomb of Tutankhamen was found, the only intact burial of a pharaoh ever uncovered. Yet this was a pharaoh of the New Kingdom, an era of Egyptian history long after the building of the pyramids.

Although there is no evidence for the tomb theory, and direct evidence against it, there are other considerations involved. How much is known about Khufu and the times in which he lived must also be considered. If we study the records of the man and his times more closely, the information should have a strong bearing on his relation to the Great Pyramid.

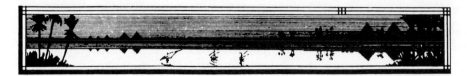

Searching for Khufu

Most contemporary Egyptologists put Khufu's date and that of the Pyramid at about 2700 B.C. A standard academic outline of Egyptian monarchy is as follows:[1]

Old Kingdom (1st to 6th dynasties)	3100-2181 B.C.
First Intermediate Period	
(7th to 10th dynasties)	2181-2040 B.C.
Middle Kingdom (11th and 12th dynasties)	2040-1786 B.C.
Second Intermediate Period	
(13th to 17th dynasties)	1786-1567 B.C.
New Kingdom (18th to 20th dynasties)	1567-1085 B.C.
Late Period (21st to 30th dynasties,	
includes Saite Period 663-525 B.C.)	1085- 332 B.C.
Greek (Ptolemaic) Period	332- 30 B.C.

This chronology is derived from ancient lists of kings which have survived to the present time, the works of early historians such as the Egyptian priest Manetho (early Ptolemaic Period) and Herodotus, the correlation of this information with the remaining identifiable monuments and tombs, and the synchronization of the derived dates with events in other lands of which there is independent record.

Naturally, where there is much information it is possible to describe reigns and events with some precision. But generally speaking, the great bulk of Egyptian historical materials applies to the Middle Kingdom and the more recent eras of Egyptian history. If we examine how much is actually known about the

Pyramid Age – the Third to Sixth Dynasties when all the chief pyramids of Egypt were supposedly built – then a considerably different state of affairs is found.

In attempting to date the reign of Khufu, the natural process is to try to establish a full chronology of kings back to Menes, traditionally thought to be the first pharaoh of upper and lower Egypt, to date his reign, and then count the length of the reigns forward to the Fourth Dynasty. The method is straightforward enough, but the results vary greatly from one expert to another. The problem is the meager amount of available data and the questionable nature of the little that does exist.

For example, some of the major documents that apply to the chronology and identity of the kings of the Pyramid Age are the Tablet of Karnak, the Tablet of Abydos, the Tablet of Saqqara, the Papyrus of Turin and the chronology of Manetho, but each has its limitations.

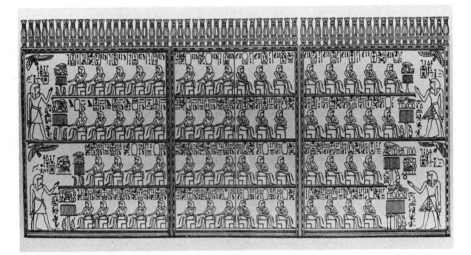

The Tablet of Karnak.

The Tablet of Karnak dates from the Eighteenth Dynasty. It contains a representation of Thothmes III paying homage to sixty-one of his ancestors whose names are recorded in cartouches (hieroglyphs enclosed with an oval) above their images. Half the kings face one way on the tablet and half the other. The cartouches are not arranged in chronological order and do not give a complete series of names.[2]

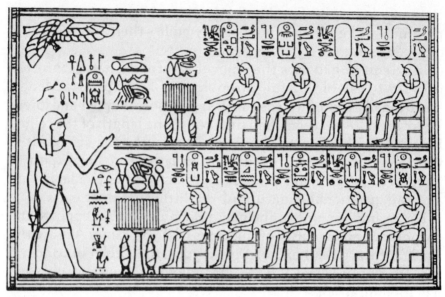

Detail from the Tablet of Karnak, showing erased cartouches.

The Tablet of Abydos (first part).

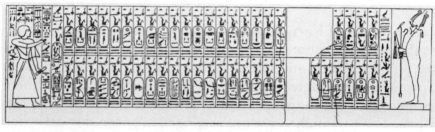

The Tablet of Saqqara.

The Tablet of Abydos, Nineteenth Dynasty, shows Seti I and his son Ramses II addressing seventy-five of their predecessors. Here the order is apparently chronological, but again only a selection of names is given with no information about the individual length or total number of years of their reigns.[3]

On the Tablet of Saqqara which dates from the time of Ramses II (1304-1237 B.C.) forty-seven names are given. It contains more or less the same order as the Abydos Tablet, except that the first name on the list is not Mena or Menes, the supposed first king of upper and lower Egypt, but one Merbapen, whose name is sixth on the Abydos Tablet.

These tablets are of great value in that taken together they supply the names of over a hundred kings who preceded the New Kingdom, but they are clearly selections rather than complete lists; they are sometimes contradictory; they give no idea of the length of the reigns; and they have in places suffered erasures of data. It is clear that even the Egyptians of 1300 B.C. had only indistinct ideas of their history 1500 years before. Wallis Budge wrote of these tablets:

> Until we have more evidence of a definite character on the general facts of Egyptian history, and a more accurate means for finding the date of the starting point of Egyptian civilization, we shall have to be content with a system of chronology which contains several gaps and a series of minimum dates for the greater number of the reigns of the kings, and for the beginning of which an exact date cannot be assigned.[4]

The most complete native list of kings known is (or was) contained on the Royal Papyrus of Turin. This document listed the names of over 130 kings, but when it was shipped to Turin in the early nineteenth century, it disintegrated into thousands of tiny pieces. A restoration was attempted by a gentleman named Seyffarth in 1826, but his knowledge of hieratic character was extremely limited and his efforts have since been termed "worthless".[5] This papyrus is apparently capable of yielding bits and pieces of information, as it were, but cannot be used to establish the larger facts of Egyptian chronology.

Perhaps the most important single source of all is the history of Egypt in both legendary and dynastic times written by the priest Manetho in the early Ptolemaic Period. He named over a hundred kings and his division of these into thirty dynasties is still employed. Unfortunately, his history itself is lost and elements of it survive only as they have been quoted by others. The two most complete versions of his list, quoted by Julius Africanus and by Eusebius,[6] differ in the arrangement of the dynasties, the lengths of the reigns of the kings, and in the number of kings assigned to different dynasties. According to Julius Africanus, 561 kings reigned in about 5524 years. According to Eusebius, 361 kings reigned in 4480 or 4780 years. It is said that the version of Africanus is "clearly the more accurate of the two".[7]

These discrepancies in the versions of this important source obviously present a major problem. Some authorities declare that "Manetho's work, as handed down to us, is short of useless".[8] And yet Manetho's scheme of thirty dynasties is still employed.

Specifying dates and events for the Nineteenth Dynasty with some precision is one thing, but if we ask when the Great Pyramid was built, the answers from Egyptological sources show remarkable variation. For instance, if we take Africanus' figures and add to his 5524 years for the length of the thirty dynasties the 332 years from Alexander the Great to the birth of Christ, we arrive at 5856 B.C. for the reign of Menes. Calculating further, the reign of Khufu, sometimes also called Souphis, is put at 5058 B.C.[9] which is a long way from the conventional date of 2700 B.C.

This extraordinary discrepancy of over 2000 years is not the product of a forced or isolated approach to the problem. Egyptologists themselves have long held the widest variety of opinions on the duration of the dynastic period. In dating the beginning of Menes' reign, nineteenth century estimates ranged from 5867 B.C. to 2320 B.C. with every variable in between.[10] Since the last century no significant information has emerged to alter the picture. Today there is more unanimity of opinion, but the dating and attribution of the Great Pyramid are still matters of convention and not items of indisputable knowledge.

The chronological problem is further compounded by the presence of two major "dark periods", the First and Second Intermediate Periods on either side of the Middle Kingdom. James Henry Breasted said of the first of these feudal eras:

It was a period of such weakness and disorganization that neither king nor noble was able to erect monumental works which might have survived to tell us something of the time. How long this unhappy condition may have continued it is now quite impossible to determine.[11]

Other authorities echo this evaluation. A similar gap in the chronology followed the Middle Kingdom. Around the end of the Thirteenth Dynasty a foreign invasion is thought to have poured in through the delta. Breasted said of these invaders, usually called the Hyksos:

[They] left so few monuments in Egypt that even their nationality is still the subject of much difference of opinion; while the length and character of their supremacy, for the same reason, are equally obscure matters.[12]

In the conventional version of Egyptian chronology 141 years are allotted to the First Intermediate Period, and 219 years to the Second. These remarks by Breasted, however, allow for the possibility that these eras may have spanned many centuries, which would push the Pyramid Age into a more remote and possibly a very great antiquity.

In attempting to date the Fourth Dynasty, we get some idea of how very slight the knowledge of this period is. The popular conception of the pyramids as tombs of the pharaohs and the Great Pyramid as the tomb of Khufu has been proclaimed for so long by so many educated men and has appeared in so many encyclopaedias and histories, that one would imagine there must be clear evidence for this somewhere. But incredibly, not only is the date of the Fourth Dynasty impossible to specify – *there are no historical records of any kind for the reign of Khufu!*

Perhaps the single most important collection of Egyptian historical materials is a work called *Ancient Records of Egypt*. This is a five-volume, 1500 page catalogue of the historical documents of ancient Egypt, translated and commented upon by J.H. Breasted. It is arranged by dynasty and pharaoh. In Volume One, under the Fourth Dynasty, the records (translations of inscriptions on stones) which supposedly pertain to this era occupy just thirteen pages, which consist as much of the notes, interpolations and comments of Breasted as they do of the documents. This seems scant indeed. But what is truly extraordinary is that of these thirteen pages the documents for the entire reign of Khufu occupy only three, and these are taken up by the controversial "Inventory Stela", which Breasted flatly declares does not belong to the Fourth Dynasty at all! Other than that, the entire documentary remains from the "reign of Khufu" consist only of the names Khufu and Khnum-Khuf which have been found inside the Great Pyramid and written in a few other places.

In terms of solid evidence, we know absolutely nothing about the times in which Khufu lived nor is there clear evidence of any kind to support the dating of the Great Pyramid and the Fourth Dynasty at 2700 B.C. That dating is only a convention, an agreed-upon estimate – more simply, only a guess. And because we are left with nothing from the reign of Khufu except a few symbols which have been translated as Khufu and Khnum-Khuf, we know virtually nothing of Khufu either. Many Egyptologists have said as much.

> Ahmed Fakhry:
> It is astonishing that we know so little about King Khufu.[13]

> James Henry Breasted:
> Khufu's name has been found from Desuk in the northwestern and Bubastis in the eastern Delta, to Hieracoupolis in the south, but we know almost nothing of his other achievements.[14]

> Gaston Maspero:
> All we know of them [Khufu, Khafra and Menkaura, thought to have built the Great, Second and Third Gizeh Pyramids, respectively] is made up of two or three series of facts, always the same, which the contemporary monuments teach us concerning these rulers.[15] [Maspero might more correctly have stated that it was a case of "two or three series of *conjectures*, always the same ..."]

There is another thing about Khufu that is very curious. The ancient Egyptians were extremely adept in working both soft and hard stone and were a great image-making people. Many of their statues were designed to glorify their important men. The size and quantity of the statues representing a person or king appears to have been a direct expression of power and prestige – so much so that it became the custom of kings to appropriate the idealized statues of their predecessors, to erase the identifying cartouches, and to supply their own instead. Specialists in Egyptian art believe the artists were reaching a

Red granite statue of Panejem in the Temple at Karnak.

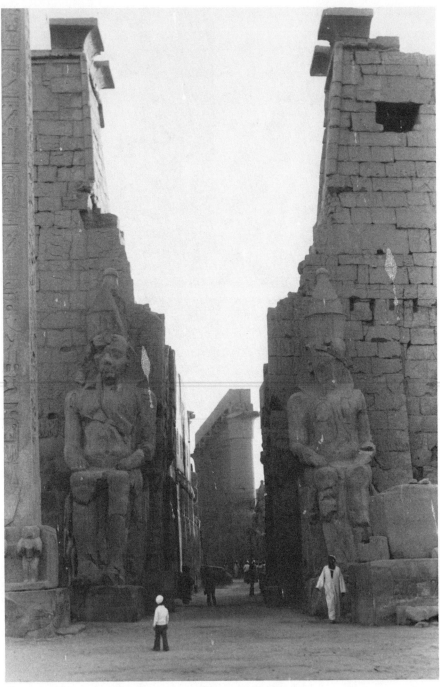

Statues of kings at the entrance to the Luxor Temple.

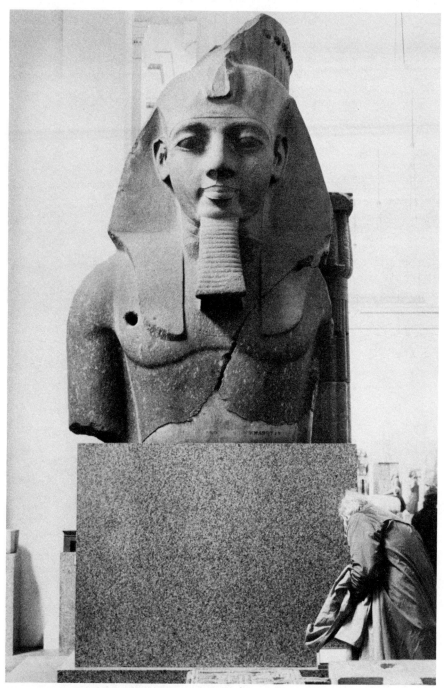

Statue of Ramses II in the British Museum.

The Colossus of Memnon on the west bank of the Nile at Thebes, the modern Luxor. The statue was carved from a single block estimated to weigh 1000 tons.

The only surviving statue purporting to represent Khufu.

peak of creative ability during the Fourth Dynasty.[16] But where are the statues of the mighty Khufu?

The only preserved statue supposed to represent Khufu is a tiny ivory seated figure found by Petrie, not at Gizeh, but in the temple at Abydos, approximately 300 miles to the south. It is now in the Cairo Museum. Contrasted to the many beautiful and often giant statues still in Egypt, it seems both humorous and pathetic that this four-inch figurine is purported to be the only surviving image of the man alleged to have commanded sufficient power to build the Great Pyramid. Moreover, its size and level of execution, the place in which it was found, and the material of which it is made all suggest that this was a votive figurine of a much later era than the Pyramid Age.

In searching for Khufu, after centuries of explorations all that has been found that can be considered contemporaneous with him are those few cartouches translated as Khufu, Souphis, or Khnum-Khuf. There is nothing else. It seems extraordinary that we know absolutely nothing of the man said to have caused the greatest monument on earth to be built and that, in truth, we are not even certain of his name. If the Pyramid was built around 2700 B.C., as many Egyptologists accept, by a hundred thousand men who labored continuously for twenty years, then it seems obvious that this reign would have involved an unparalleled coordination and control of the state, and the affairs of the royal house would have permeated every village and district in the land. In spite of the thousands of years and countless eras of destruction which have intervened, it is quite incredible that virtually all the images and records of this king and his reign should have been destroyed and that all we are now left with are a few cartouches, the controversial Inventory Stela, the two thousand year old reports of Herodotus and Diodorus Siculus, and an ivory figurine of questionable date.

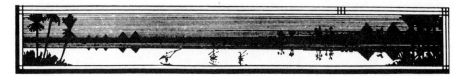

9

The Marks in the Hidden Chambers

In terms of direct and solid evidence, the association of Khufu with the Great Pyramid rests entirely on the apparently straightforward fact that there are cartouches reading "Khufu" painted on the walls of hidden chambers inside the building. However, the general controversy surrounding the Pyramid extends even to the meaning of these marks, and the evidence is not as straightforward as it may seem.

Above the King's Chamber inside the Pyramid are five low chambers one on top of the other whose function is unknown. Some speculate that they were designed to relieve the thousands of tons of pressure upon the main chamber below. It is for this reason they are called "relieving chambers". The Pyramid was not constructed with an entrance to these chambers, except perhaps for the lowest one to which a small crude passage at the top of the Grand Gallery was discovered by a traveler named Davison in 1765. There are no markings in this chamber. The other chambers were discovered in 1837-1838 by Col. Howard-Vyse and J.S. Perring when they broke a tunnel through to them with chisel and gunpowder while seeking secret rooms. On the walls of these upper chambers crude masons' marks and hieroglyphs are daubed in red paint. Among them is a mason's mark one Egyptologist has translated as reading "year 17", meaning, according to his thinking, that the Pyramid had reached that level in the seventeenth year of

VERTICAL SECTION /*Looking West*/ of KING'S CHAMBER; ALSO OF
ANTE-CHAMBER, SOUTH END OF GRAND GALLERY, AND VYSE'S HOLLOWS OF
CONSTRUCTION, ABOVE KING'S CHAMBER. CROSSED LINES INDICATE GRANITE.

Scale of British Inches

The relieving chambers above the King's Chamber.

the king's reign. Some of the hieroglyphs are enclosed with an oval, forming a cartouche. It is some of these cartouches that have been translated Khufu or Souphis. Since some of the hieroglyphs are upside down, these blocks were apparently marked before they were placed in the Pyramid.

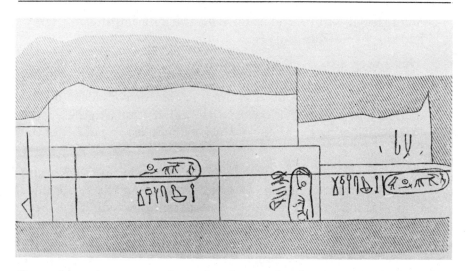

Cartouches and quarry marks in the relieving chambers.

These marks are the only original inscriptions or writing of any kind inside the Pyramid and constitute the only hard evidence for attributing the Great Pyramid to a "king" called Khufu. In terms of direct evidence, the entire case linking the Pyramid with Khufu comes down to these few cartouches. As the Egyptologist Maspero put it, without them "we should not know to whom it belonged".[1]

Here is the complication: the cartouches reading Khufu are not the only cartouches in the relieving chambers. There are others, more numerous, which read Khnum-Khuf. The problem is that Egyptologists do not know who or what Khnum-Khuf was.

As Breasted has explained, the writing from these early dynasties "is in such an archaic form that many of the scanty fragments which we possess from this age are unintelligible to us".[2] The meaning of the cartouches translated as Khufu and Khnum-Khuf falls into this category. In addition, these cartouches are found together in a few other places. The second most important place is an inscription on the rocks of Sinai. Here is what Flinders Petrie wrote about these cartouches:

> The only great royal inscription [of Khufu], like that of Sneferu [his immediate predecessor, according to most Egyptologists], is on the rocks of Sinai. There are two tablets: one with the name

and titles of Khufu, the other with the king smiting an enemy, and the name Khnum-Khuf.

This raises a difficult question, to which no historian has yet given a satisfactory answer. Who was the person designated as Khnum-Khuf? That he was not a successor is evident by the name being used indifferently with that of Khufu in the quarry marks inside the Pyramid, and by his not appearing in any of the lists ...

The name is found in five places ... The addition of Khnum cannot be merely a flight of orthography ... The two names being placed in succession in one inscription cannot be mere chance variants of the same. Either they must be two distinct and independent names of one king, or else two separate kings. If they were separate kings, Khnum-Khuf must have been the most important ...[3]

Ancient inscription on the rocks of Sinai with cartouches of Khufu, Khnum-Khuf and the figure of Thoth.

On this same problem Gaston Maspero wrote:

> The existence of the two cartouches Khufui and Khnumu-Khufui on the same monuments has caused much embarassment to Egyptologists: the majority have been inclined to see here two different kings, the second of whom, according to M. Robiou, would have been the person who bore the prenomen of Dadifri[4] [or Dedefra, another Fourth Dynasty king who according to some scholars immediately followed Khufu].

However, Maspero also noted that another scholar, Max Müller, thought Khnum-Khuf indicated a god, the words "Khnumu-Khufui" signifying "the god Khnumu protects me". Contemporary Egyptologists have swung around to the opinion that Khufu and Khnum-Khuf are two different names for one king, but this has merely shelved the problem without really solving it. There has been no new evidence since the time of Petrie, Maspero and Müller to support this opinion. On the contrary, several clues have emerged which make it all the more questionable and raise the distinct possibility that such quarry marks and cartouches as have been used to attribute pyramids to kings, and numbers or dates to years of their reigns, have been completely misinterpreted.

The first clue comes from the Northern Stone Pyramid at Dashur, another pyramid field south of Gizeh and Saqqara. This very large pyramid also has what seem to be construction dates inscribed in red ink on two of its casing blocks. According to I.E.S. Edwards:

> One of these blocks bears a date which has been read as the twenty-first year of the reign of Sneferu [the king who is supposed to have built it] and, being situated at the northeast corner, it should indicate the year in which the work of construction was begun; the other block, seen by Richard Lepsius halfway up the face of the pyramid, was dated in the following year.[5]

Unless they built the entire pyramid and put the casing on last, (a practice which is highly unlikely except in the three major Gizeh Pyramids which used very large casing blocks), this would seem to imply either that the ancient Egyptians could build a pyramid 719 feet square at the base in a couple of years – or that something is awry in the understanding of these quarry marks.

Another clue comes from Dashur. Although the dates arrived at by Egyptologists for the Fourth Dynasty vary greatly, they are generally agreed that the succession of the pharaohs of the period was Sneferu, Khufu, Dedefra, Khafra and Menkaura. A further complication is that some of these pharaohs (if that is what they were) seem to have built more than one pyramid. Petrie found inscriptions linking Menkaura with two different pyramids.[6] In the case of Sneferu, the problem is still more acute – quarry marks seem to attribute no less than three major pyramids to him. These are according to Edwards: the Meydum Pyramid with a side of 473 feet (144 meters); the Bent Pyramid at Dashur, side of 620 feet (189 meters); and the Northern Stone Pyramid at Dashur, side of 719 feet (219 meters).[7]

At this point many Egyptologists, Edwards included, begin to have misgivings, since it would be quite extraordinary if one king were to have built these three giant structures – the more so if it is assumed that they were each to be his tomb. The usual answer to this problem is to speculate that Sneferu might have finished one of these pyramids for his predecessor who died before he could complete it. In the other case, he seems to have built an entire pyramid and then changed his mind.

Attempting to account for the Fourth Dynasty monuments through a chronology of kings results in one puzzle after another. There are the remains of another pyramid at Abu Roash, roughly seven miles northwest of Gizeh, which Egyptologists now attribute to Dedefra, generally agreed to be the immediate successor to Khufu. But as the Second and Third Gizeh Pyramids were supposedly not in existence when the Abu Roash Pyramid was built, some experts have resorted to fabricating "a family quarrel" to explain why Dedefra built his pyramid at Abu Roash and not at Gizeh. Yet this does not explain why Dedefra is the only "royal name" occurring on the roofing stones of the recently discovered boat pit in front of the Great Pyramid.

These problems indicate that the cartouches and quarry marks on these early monuments are simply not understood. This is not to question the entire grammar of hieroglyphics but to recognize that language changes over thousands of years and that lacking a context of solid evidence all that Egyptologists or anyone else can do is speculate upon their meaning. Students naturally tend to accept the assumptions of their teachers and to parrot their speculations, and over the last century these speculations have tended more and more in the same direction until today they have assumed the appearance of acquired facts – for example that the Great Pyramid is the tomb of a king called Khufu.

But the truth of the matter is that Egyptological descriptions of the Fourth Dynasty are little better than fantasies built up by decades of conjecture and groundless assumptions. No one knows what that history was. There are just not enough historical materials for anyone to describe that era. There is no clear and solid evidence of any kind that there ever was a pyramid building Fourth Dynasty king called Khufu – nor, for that matter, that there ever were Pyramid Age kings called Sneferu, Dedefra, Khafra or Menkaura! The entire pattern of evidence suggests, on the contrary, that if there ever was a King Khufu he lived long after the Pyramid was built and *was named after the Pyramid* – not the other way around.

Then, we are left to wonder, who or what was the "original" Khufu? Scholars have put forward three different explanations for Khufu and Khnum-Khuf: these are two different names for the same king; these are names of two different kings; one is the name of a king and one is the name of a god. To these may be added two additional possibilities: these are names of two different gods; these are two different names for the same god.

The last two are strong possibilities because cartouches reading Khufu are found not only on remains attributed to the Fourth Dynasty, but on dozens of tombs and monuments, some of which have been dated at only a few centuries before Christ. Egyptologists explain that Khufu's name had become "a powerful charm", and was put on monuments as a sign of sanctity and protection. In other words, it was used in later times as the sign of the cross has been used in Christian countries for nearly two thousand years. Of course, we do not assume that every representation of a person bearing the symbol of a cross is Jesus Christ, nor that every building with a cross was personally ordered to be built by Jesus. Neither do we assume that every person named Jesus is the original Jesus

Christ. Yet in assuming that these ancient cartouches represent men instead of gods, they have been treated as personal names instead of symbols.

If there is evidence that the cartouches of Khufu were "powerful charms" over thousands of years after the Pyramid was built, how do we know that they were not powerful charms, or sacred symbols, at the time it was built – and that they do not represent a king, but something more than a king? The answer is that we do not know. It has simply been assumed that Khufu was an actual king, as believed by Herodotus' informants, although they lived thousands of years after the building of the Pyramid and there is no guarantee they knew any more about it than do many contemporary Arab guides.

If the cartouches of Khufu as well as of Sneferu, Dedefra, Khafra and Menkaura were sacred symbols identifying different sects, schools, branches or cults, a multitude of problems would be solved. It would explain why the cartouches of one king are found on more than one pyramid, why some cartouches are found in unlikely places, and why there are no historical records of these Fourth Dynasty kings.[8] It could even explain the Inventory Stela as something other than a forgery, since it was standard practice for later kings to bear the names of the deities they represented. And in hypothesizing that these cartouches represent something other than what has been thought, we might surmise that present interpretations of the accompanying quarry marks are also questionable and discount the suggestion that a pyramid 719 feet (219 meters) square at the base may have been erected in a couple of years.

Finally, this interpretation of the cartouches of Khufu also puts into a new perspective the vast necropolis surrounding the Gizeh Pyramids. If the pyramids were temples instead of tombs, it would help to explain why burials were performed at the site thousands of years after the Pyramid was built. Men might have been buried there for the same reason they still desire to be buried in the sanctified ground near churches and cathedrals. A hypothesis that solves so many problems and fits so neatly into what little evidence there is may have something going for it.

There is a final curious twist in searching out the meaning of these old cartouches. Working on the hypothesis that Khufu

Eroded cartouche of Khufu from a tomb east of the Great Pyramid.

and Khnum-Khuf were gods, or two names for a single god, the question naturally arises: who were these gods? Are they known by other names?

The names of the gods varied from country to country in antiquity, and even within certain countries, much as they do today. For instance, Hermes, Mercury, Thoth, Tehuti and Enoch are all names of the same god. Ancient Egypt was notorious for the number of different names it gave to the

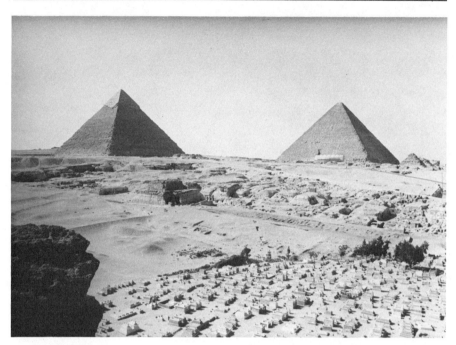

Gizeh is still used as a cemetery. A modern Muslim cemetery is seen in the foreground.

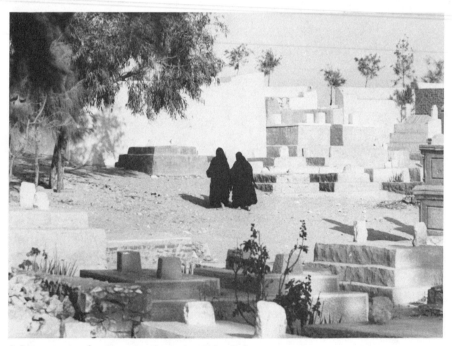

Mourners in the graveyard south of the Sphinx.

same deity. In the royal tombs in the Valley of the Kings, the god Ra is invoked under seventy-five different names.[9] Khufu and Khnum-Khuf are not the only interpretations of the cartouches in the relieving chambers. Standard variations of Khufu are Cheops, Souphis and Saophis.

One scholar says there was a god in Egypt called Khnemu who was the embodiment of intellect itself. Alternative names for Khnemu were Khnum, Knef, and Chnuphis or Chnouphis.[10] The attributes of this god are not as broad but are very close to those of Thoth. Another scholar writes that Khnum or Khnoum became the Khnoubis of the pagan and Christian Gnostics.[11] Yet another says that Khnoubis and Chnouphis are the same god and that Chnouphis became known as the Christos of the Gnostics.[12] The symbol of Chnouphis was a giant serpent which stood for genius. Thoth-Hermes, this writer says, was later a generic name given to great initiates who were "all serpents of wisdom".[13] A giant serpent guarded the legendary book of Thoth sunk in the Nile at Koptos and the caduceus or staff of Hermes is still portrayed as entwined with one or two serpents.[14] Moses, taught in all the ways of the Egyptians, held a staff entwined with a brass serpent during the Exodus.[15]

According to these symbols and interpretations, Chnouphis was a figure or power the equivalent of Hermes or Thoth. But Chnouphis is simply an alternate form of Khnoum or Khnum and is etymologically similar to Souphis. There are relationships and patterns of symbolism, then, suggesting that Khnum, Khnoum, Khufu, Souphis, Khnoubis, Chnouphis, Tehuti, Thoth, Mercury, Enoch, Hermes, and possibly "Christos" are simply different representations of the same figure and power that finds remarkably similar expression in cosmologies extending over many thousands of years.

Why then hasn't the relationship between Hermes and Khufu been pointed out long ago? Most Egyptologists dismiss the Arab legends as fantasies, just as archaeologists once dismissed legends of Troy, and few, if any, students of ancient Egyptian religion have been interested in the cartouches of Khufu or the Arabic legends. The connection between Hermes and Khufu may not have been seen before for the simple reason that no one looked for it.

10

Adventures in Wonderland

Who built Gizeh? When? How? Why? We are separated from the building of Gizeh by the desolation of unnumbered centuries. Our ignorance is enormous, shrouding the ancient secrets like a cloud. Yet sifting information from the debris of the ages we find faint glimmerings in the darkness.

We have seen that there is nothing to support the tomb theory or the existence of a Pyramid Age king called Khufu; that Arabic legends state that the Pyramid was built to record the knowledge of an ancient world in order to preserve it from a great disaster; and that multiple sources associate the legendary name Hermes with the Pyramid. We know that whoever built it incorporated the three key measurements of our planet in its dimensions. But other than these hints, we still have no answers to our guiding questions.

Where else can we look? Not all the theories and ideas about the Pyramid attempt to answer these questions. Aside from the chronologies and theories of Egyptology, there are only a few major bodies of literature about the Pyramid. Among the most controversial is a British hypothesis that the Pyramid contains a scheme of prophecy. The prophecies are supposed to be indicated by the pattern of the passages inside the Pyramid. Proponents of this idea believe that key events in the Christian cosmology such as the birth of Christ and the Second Coming are signified. Many in this school of interpretation refer to the Pyramid as "a Bible in stone". Its disciples start from two peculiar scored lines in the Descending Passage near the original entrance to the Pyramid and measure the distance along the passageways, counting each inch as a year, looking for significant dates at those points where the passages change shape. Events are not recorded in British inches, however. These are "Pyramid inches", said to measure 1/1000 of an inch more than the conventional inch. These ideas are so far removed from the world of academic Egyptology that some of the orthodox denigrate those who believe in a prophetic scheme as "Pyramidiots". I prefer the term "Inchers".

The prophetic concept has been put forward by a surprising number of men. It was first developed back in 1859 and 1864 by John Taylor and Piazzi Smyth, who noted some of the Pyramid's mathematical properties and its central geographic position. These gentlemen knew of no ancient civilization advanced enough to have had such knowledge and concluded, in line with their own beliefs, that this knowledge must have come directly by Divine Revelation. They saw the Pyramid as the work of a God-fearing man of the chosen people.

The Pyramid inch came into being because there were indications (and still are) that the inch and other British units of measure are very ancient. Secondly, Smyth thought the Pyramid's base measured 9140 British inches or 9131.05 Pyramid inches. He also believed (erroneously) that the base

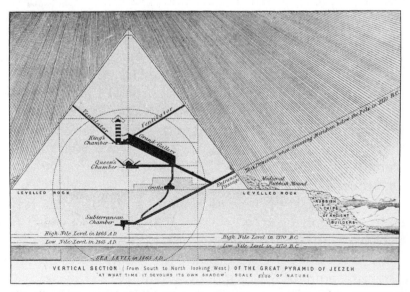

Smyth's illustration of the Pyramid, indicating his construction date of 2170 B.C.

was exactly square, so that its perimeter was 36,560 British inches or 36,524.2 Pyramid inches. This last figure is exactly 100 times the number of days in the year, or the number of days in 100 years. Smyth further believed that the Pyramid inch was a sub-unit of a larger ancient unit called the sacred cubit, with 25 Pyramid inches to one sacred cubit. Thus each side of the Pyramid was 365.242 sacred cubits, exactly equal to the number of days in the year.

This was a sign to Smyth and his many followers that the Pyramid inch must have been used in the construction of the building. As far as he was concerned, it was further proof that the Pyramid was built through Divine Revelation since he thought no one thousands of years ago could have measured the length of the year so precisely.

There are several problems with the Inchers' theories. What Smyth actually measured was the perimeter of the sockets, not of the Pyramid, which is some yards shorter. (This was when the base was still covered with mounds of rubble, and even as a measurement of the socket distances, Smyth's figures are inaccurate.) Their entire case for the inch, whether British or Pyramid, is dependent upon this single measurement. Since it is of key importance many writers who adhere to Smyth's school of thought have found it convenient to overlook the later, more accurate surveys of the Pyramid.

As we have seen, the perimeter of the sockets equals a half minute of equatorial longitude. Now it is a very curious "coincidence" that if the perimeter is expressed in inches the result is within an inch or two of 36,524.2, and there is some room to argue that it may have been exactly that figure.[1] The figure of 36,524.2 is just what Smyth was looking for – but these are regular British inches, not slightly longer Pyramid inches – and even if the inch were employed to record astronomic information, this does not help the Inchers out of their other difficulties.

Two other major problems remain. First, in order for the system of prophecy to work, a starting date is needed from which to count the unfolding prophecies and years. Some Inchers favor 2170 B.C. as the date the Pyramid was begun and the starting point of the prophetic scheme. Others start at 4000 B.C. But, other than that these dates fit their theories, the

Inchers have no more basis than anyone else for determining when the Pyramid was built. The second problem is that the passages inside the Pyramid can be measured and interpreted in many ways and different Inchers have come up with various dates for the Second Coming. One advocate declared it would be in 1953 and a contemporary writer has picked 1979.

It is obvious that the prophetic chronology theory has some wrinkles in it and despite the large and venerable body of literature built around it, there is not much in it that can be used to answer our guiding questions. The most interesting things about this theory are that it has attracted the sympathy of so many men, that they have seen a Christian connection in the Pyramid, and that it has been around for such a long time. Indeed, some Inchers point to the *Akbar Ezzeman Manuscript* (quoted earlier) which says that the Pyramid indicates "the position of the stars and their cycles, together with the history and chronicle of time past [and] of that which is to come". The antiquity of the idea and of prophecy itself cannot be forgotten. Even if no one has so far succeeded in nailing down the scheme, the basic idea is unlikely to die, and someone may yet prove its validity. There are in any case many paths to the prophetic question other than through the passages of the Great Pyramid, and they may all come to much the same thing.

Like the prophetic interpretation, the concept that the Pyramid encodes geographic information dates back a long way. Agatharchides of Cnidus, a second century B.C. geographer and historian, wrote that the Pyramid incorporated fractions of geographical degrees.[2] Since the 1798 French campaign in Egypt, a substantial scientific tradition has developed attempting to verify the concept that the Pyramid records key dimensions of the earth. This has attracted scholars of several nations and the history of this tradition is long and intricate.[3] Until now however, although numerous claims have been made, no one has produced figures to substantiate this theory that are as clear, simple and well-founded as those reported earlier. But while it is reassuring to have 2200 years of tradition behind this concept, the writers and scholars who have explored the earth-measurement idea have been concerned mostly with establishing the principles and measurements involved and not with the questions who?

when? how? and why?

However, there is another extensive and almost unknown source of information concerning early Egypt and the Pyramid which has not been investigated in a scientific manner. These detailed verbal pictures came through the famous American psychic Edgar Cayce (1877-1945), sometimes called "The Sleeping Prophet".[4] Cayce had the ability to go into a self-induced hypnotic trance and while in this condition could answer practically any question. Over a period of forty years everything he said while in trance was stenographically recorded and preserved. He is popularly known for the thousands of psychic medical diagnoses and suggested remedies he produced for ailing clients and is reputed to have had an accuracy of 85 to 90 percent in this area.[5] In a time when increasing numbers of people claim psychic abilities, Cayce remains in a class by himself because of the remarkable extent to which his descriptions have been verified.

The most controversial "discovery" Cayce made while probing patients' problems occurred in 1923. Answering questions from a man with philosophical interests, Cayce's psychic faculty informed the gentleman that reincarnation was a fact and that he had lived on earth before. When Cayce woke up from his trance and was told what he had just said, (he had no conscious recall of his psychic pronouncements), he was less than happy. He was a conservative orthodox Protestant and had never shown the slightest interest in teachings he did not recognize as contained in the Bible. Faced with the dilemma of denying his own psychic credibility or accepting the possibility of reincarnation, he eventually chose the latter.

During the remainder of his career, Cayce produced approximately 2500 psychic descriptions of previous lives for individuals who came to him for counseling. Among these descriptions, over 700 mention lives in legendary Atlantis and over 1100 refer to early Egypt around the time the Great Pyramid was supposedly built. At least 300 different transcripts describe early Egypt in detail. They contain a cast of dozens of leading characters and are remarkable for their internal consistency, even though they were produced over a twenty-year period. In his normal conscious state, Cayce was absolutely uninterested in Atlantis, the Great Pyramid and ancient Egypt, and seems never to have read a single book about any of them. Even though Cayce's psychic descriptions of the Pyramid and early Egypt are now thirty to fifty years old, very few people know of them. No one attempted to compile and edit the Egyptian transcripts until Mark Lehner did so in a work called *The Egyptian Heritage,* first published in 1974.

According to Cayce, the Great Pyramid was built by a consortium of emigré Atlanteans, native Egyptians and wandering Caucasians who came from the vicinity of southwest Russia. These groups were headed by a high priest called Ra or Ra Ta, an architectural genius called Hermes, and a counselor or adviser named Isis. Cayce states that the Pyramid was built between 10,490 and 10,390 B.C. and that the builders knew how to effect levitation or the neutralization of gravity. It was by this means that they transported and raised the giant blocks of stone. The transcripts further relate that the Pyramid was a sacred temple with multiple functions. There was an exact science of prophecy in this early age and the Pyramid builders supposedly knew that the final destruction of Atlantis was impending and would be followed by other great disasters. The Pyramid was built to record and preserve knowledge, to encapsulate a scheme of prophecy, and to function as a temple of initiation. According to Cayce, thousands of years later Jesus went to Egypt with John the Baptist during the "missing years" of his life and underwent a final initiation inside the Great Pyramid before embarking on his public career.[6]

Obviously, there are elements in this outline that coincide with legend, scientific tradition and even with the theories of the Inchers. Of course, if one imagines that men were primitive barbarians in 10,000 B.C., this version of the origin and function of the Great Pyramid sounds utterly fantastic. Some will say that this is to be expected since it comes from such an unconventional source. But if we are even to pretend at scientific detachment, the source of an hypothesis is not important. Einstein derived the equation for the conversion of mass to energy from a dream. If an hypothesis is valid or false, it is valid or false regardless of who has announced it or how he got his ideas. What counts is whether it can be verified. Surprisingly, there are some statements in Cayce's Egyptian transcripts which can be examined in detail for their accuracy.

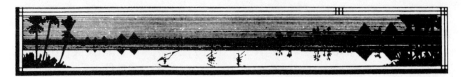

Checking Out the Sleeping Prophet

In his trance state Edgar Cayce described the multinational civilization in lower Egypt around 10,500 B.C. as very advanced. They had a monotheistic religion which was a holistic marriage of mysticism, nature, science and art.[1] Much of the science and technology seems to have come from Atlantis. They had air travel,[2] "chariots driven by gases",[3] electricity,[4] advanced metallurgy and chemistry,[5] an understanding of geothermal energy,[6] archaeology,[7] hospitals or temples of healing,[8] anaesthesiology,[9] an electric knife for bloodless surgery,[10] group insurance plans,[11] an advanced geography employing latitude and longitude,[12] and standard units of measurement.[13]

Among the many large structures supposedly built during this period was one Cayce called "The Temple Beautiful". He described this as a long, low pyramid with a large oval floorplan in the interior. He gave the dimensions of this temple in "mir cubits", a unit he specified as "twenty-seven and one half inches" (.6985013 meters).[14] Cayce did not specifically say that this was the unit used to build the Great Pyramid, but that it was a standard unit of length used at the time.

Because so little is definitely known about the pyramid era, historians have hoped that by identifying the unit of measurement used, they might better identify the people who built the Great Pyramid and the date of its erection. Since the time of Isaac Newton (1642-1727), scholars have been arguing about the unit of measurement involved. Tompkins and Stecchini have shown that a variety of ancient units fit the building reasonably well. Egyptologists currently believe that the Pyramid was built with an ancient Egyptian unit called the "royal cubit of Memphis", about 20.6 inches (.524 meters) in length.

In terms of arithmetic, the basic test scholars apply is to divide the side and height of the Pyramid by the length of the unit being tested. Any unit which might have been employed is expected to fit the Pyramid in round even numbers. For example, the Pyramid is frequently reported to be 440 royal cubits at the base and 280 of these units high. However, the royal cubit does not fit the Pyramid perfectly; 440 royal cubits produce a length that is 10.3 inches (.261 meters) longer than the average side of the Pyramid.

Returning to the mir cubit, there is no historical record outside the Cayce transcripts of a unit by this name or of this length. However, there was an ancient Egyptian word "mir", which referred both to the pyramids and to their height, but no one knows why.[15]

The most basic quantitative test which can be applied to the Egyptian transcripts is to determine how well the mir cubit fits the Great Pyramid. A detailed analysis shows this unit fits the

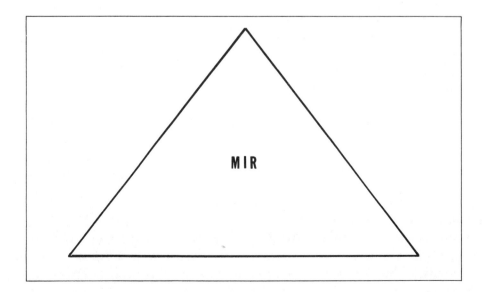

Pyramid more exactly and more organically than any other unit of measure ever suggested, but it does not fit perfectly.

Using the figures of J.H. Cole's 1925 survey, the most accurate survey of the Pyramid ever performed, we find the mir cubit goes into the average side 330 times and into the height 210 times. 330 mir cubits of 27.5 inches (.6985013 meters) produce a length that is 5.5 inches (.139 meters) longer than the average side of the Pyramid. This is about half the error of the royal cubit. However, the mir cubit is not historically determined. Archaeologists have not found measuring sticks showing exactly how long it was. All we have is Cayce's description, and we do not know on what level of detail he was speaking. If the mir cubit were 27.483 inches (.6980704 meters – only .017 inch or .43 mm shorter), it would fit the Pyramid perfectly.

The most intriguing verification for the mir cubit is this: the Pyramid is 210 mir cubits high, and although the capstone and top layers are missing, it has been estimated that it originally contained 210 layers of stone (including the capstone or pyramidion). Most people count 201 or 202 presently existing layers, which vary in thickness. Thick layers of stone were used at the bottom of the building for stability, gradually becoming thinner at higher levels. If the mir cubit were used to build the Great Pyramid, it stood one cubit high for each layer of stone, which may have aided the builders in regulating the thickness of the layers. This organic relationship does not exist with any other unit of measure. If the Great Pyramid was the first pyramid built or one of the earliest, and was designed with the mir cubit, it might also explain why the ancient word "mir" refers both to the pyramids and their height.

The mir cubit also fits the King's Chamber better than the royal cubit. This room is now 34 feet, 4.54 inches long and 17 feet, 2.27 inches wide (10.478 meters by 5.239 meters). A length of 20 royal cubits and a width of 10 produce dimensions which are a little too large for the chamber. In mir cubits 15 and 7.5 produce dimensions which are a bit short. The crucial difference here is that it is known that an earthquake seriously shook the Pyramid in antiquity, causing the King's Chamber to expand slightly. Thus, in the room's original condition, the royal cubit would have produced dimensions even more excessive, whereas the mir cubit may then have fitted perfectly.

These verifications of the mir cubit are of considerable importance. One of the few ways we can test theories about the Pyramid involves measurements, for the simple reason that it is still there to be measured. Numbers, it is said, do not lie and, improbable as it may seem, in this instance the Cayce information is more accurate than that of any other source. (See Part III of the Appendix for a detailed examination of the mir cubit and ancient units of measure.)

In the light of this, it is worth examining the Egyptian transcripts in more detail to see if there is further evidence to support them. According to Cayce, before the nomadic Caucasians migrated to the Nile they were counseled by a man who was to become the high priest of Egypt, Ra Ta or Ra. One transcript explains why Ra Ta and his followers decided to settle in Egypt.

> Why Egypt? This had been determined by [the priest Ra Ta] as the center of the universal activities of nature, as well as [of] the spiritual forces, and where there might be the least disturbance by the convulsive movements which come about in the earth through the destruction of Lemuria, Atlantis and – in later periods – the Flood ... When the lines about the earth are considered from [the standpoint of] the mathematical precisions, it will be found that the center is nigh unto where the Great Pyramid, which was begun then, is still located. Then there were [factors of] the mathematical, the astrological and the numerological indications, as well as the individual urge.[16]

And, somewhat later, while Ra Ta was in temporary exile in Nubia, the transcripts state:

> The priest then began ... reckoning the longitude, as termed now, latitude, and the activities of the planets and stars ...[17]

Cayce never read anything about Egypt or the pyramids, yet the first transcript states that the priest who led these people was very much aware that the Gizeh area is the geographic center of the land mass of the earth, and that this was a major reason why they built the Pyramid there. This fact was first publicized by Piazzi Smyth in 1864 and has been almost totally ignored ever since. Nevertheless, Smyth's discovery is a verification of the psychic description. The second transcript specifies that the concepts of latitude and longitude were known and studied by the priest, which dovetails with the discoveries described earlier.

Cayce states that responsibility for building the Great Pyramid was divided up as follows:

> Hence [the Pyramid was built] under the authority of Ra, and Hermes as the guide, or the actual ... construction architect, with the priest or Ra giving the directions – and [with] Isis ... the adviser.[18]

We already know that Isis was identified in the Inventory Stela as the "Mistress of the Pyramid", a reference that no one has otherwise been able to account for. Of course, this does not conclusively "prove" the transcripts' accuracy in this case, but it is certainly interesting that the oldest intact document mentioning the Pyramid reaffirms the Cayce description. It is also intriguing that Hermes is again associated with the Pyramid, corroborating both the Arabic legends and a possible interpretation of the cartouches in the relieving chambers.

There are additional indications that the transcripts describe actual people and events which left their marks on later Egyptian history. If there were a high priest called Ra Ta or Ra who played a key role at a crucial juncture in history, one might expect to hear some echoes of this, even if only in myth and legend. Of course, the name Ra is still the most popularly recognized name in the ancient Egyptian pantheon. Interestingly, the names Rosta, Ra-sheta, Re-stau, and Re-stew occur often in dynastic religious literature and are all variations of one name which is phonetically the equivalent of Ra Ta.[19] Ra Ta or Rosta is associated with Gizeh and with Sokaris, the god of geodetic orientation.[20] On the Inventory Stela the phrase "Lord of Rosta" occurs several times in connection with the "House of Osiris".

According to the transcripts, Ra Ta, when in Egypt, was seduced by a maiden named Isris which led to their temporary banishment in Nubia. While there, the priest deteriorated physically. They were eventually recalled to Egypt to deal with a difficult political situation. (Atlanteans had begun to move in and threatened to take over the country.) When they returned they used the names Ra and Isis. Ra, who is credited with a profound knowledge of healing, repaired to the Temple

Beautiful and was rejuvenated. As it happens, there is a religious story from dynastic Egypt in which the goddess Isis attempted to learn the secret name of the god Ra in order to increase her powers. Ra had become old and feeble and to accomplish her purpose Isis poisoned him with a serpent. Ra was beyond the help of the other gods and so was forced to reveal his secret name. In possession of new powers, Isis then restored him to health and life. These two accounts bear more than a passing resemblance to each other, especially as the serpent symbol is traditionally associated with sexuality and knowledge.

The transcripts relate that when the Caucasians invaded Egypt around 10,506 B.C. they used trained animals to destroy their foes.[21] "Projections" were fastened to some of the beasts which included bulls, bears, leopards and hawks. Apparently, the training of animals for war continued in Egypt after the invaders had established themselves. Finely carved slate palettes have been found which come from the earliest dynastic or predynastic eras. On one of these, a hawk is portrayed slightly above and facing the figure of a king, as if the hawk were his symbol or protector. On the other side of this palette is depicted an encounter between two stylized leopards held on leashes, and below this is an image of a bull chasing or trampling a man. These palettes seem to reflect the transcripts' descriptions.[22]

Of considerably more importance is whether there is any evidence to support the transcripts' dating of the Pyramid. Unfortunately, the carbon-14 dating test cannot be employed to determine the age of the Pyramid since it can be used to date only organic materials, and no organic remains have yet been found which can be considered clearly contemporary with that building. The transcripts' date for the beginning of construction, 10,490 B.C., is long before any recognized historian believes there was any civilization advanced enough to undertake such an enormous project.

Of course, evidence is only evidence when it is perceived as evidence. There may be more support for the Cayce dating than one might think. The date of 10,490 B.C. does not rest upon a single reference in the transcripts; dates of 10,506, 10,500, 10,490, 10,390 and 10,300 B.C. are given for events of

Front: Prehistoric green slate palette attributed to Narmer.

The back of the green slate palette.

the same era. Plato, Manetho and Herodotus each provide dates which are generally consistent with these. Although we have seen that even ancient writings by famous authors should be approached with caution, in this case several sources draw together to reveal a clear pattern.

The transcripts tell us that the Pyramid was built with Atlantean assistance shortly before the final destruction of Atlantis and the Arabic legends state that the Pyramid was built before the Flood – an event that could have been easily associated with the Atlantean destruction. Plato dates the destruction of Atlantis 9000 years before the time of Solon, who lived 638-559 B.C., or at about 9600 B.C. This dating is consistent with the transcripts' chronology.

About 300 B.C. the scribe Manetho gave an outline of Egyptian chronology which reached back to a similar order of antiquity. Manetho's report, as it has come down to us, is considered in some circles as slightly "short of useless", but as he is the sole basis for the system of thirty dynasties still employed in Egyptology, there is reason enough to look at his larger chronology.[23]

MANETHO'S CHRONOLOGY

Reigns of the Gods		13,900 years
Heroes	1255	
Other kings	1817	
30 other Memphite kings	1790	
10 Thinites	350	
Menes and demigods (30 dynasties)	5813	
	11,025	11,025
		24,925 years

From the Age of Heroes until his time, Manetho counted some 11,000 years, a figure in good agreement with 10,500 B.C. Herodotus reported that from the first king of Egypt until a certain monarch, thought to have reigned about 700 B.C.,[24] there was a span of 341 generations or, according to his calculations, 11,340 years. The transcripts do not state that the first king of Egypt reigned at the time the Pyramid was built, but imply that a centralized monarchy with the ability to carry out great projects began about that time.[25]

Air vent inside the King's Chamber.

There are also physical indications that the major Gizeh monuments date from a completely different era than the rest of the pyramids attributed to dynastic Egypt. The Great Pyramid is unique in a number of respects. It is singular in its size, the precision of its orientation, the incorporation of mathematical and scientific data, and it is the only pyramid with air vents. Moreover, it is the only pyramid with a great ascending passage and with its principal chambers elevated so considerably within the structure.

All the other pyramids may well be later "copies" of the Great Pyramid. No graffiti from the dynastic Egyptians or from Greek and Roman times were found in the Ascending Passage, the Grand Gallery, the Queen's Chamber or the King's Chamber, but only in the Descending Passage and the "Pit".[26] Until A.D. 820 access to the upper chambers (except via the "Pit" and "well shaft") was blocked by the granite plugs in the bottom of the Ascending Passage. It was not until Al Mamoon tunneled around these plugs that the upper rooms could be reached easily. This suggests that the dynastic Egyptians' knowledge of the interior consisted only of the descending elements, which may be why the other pyramids have only descending passages. That the pyramids were roughly

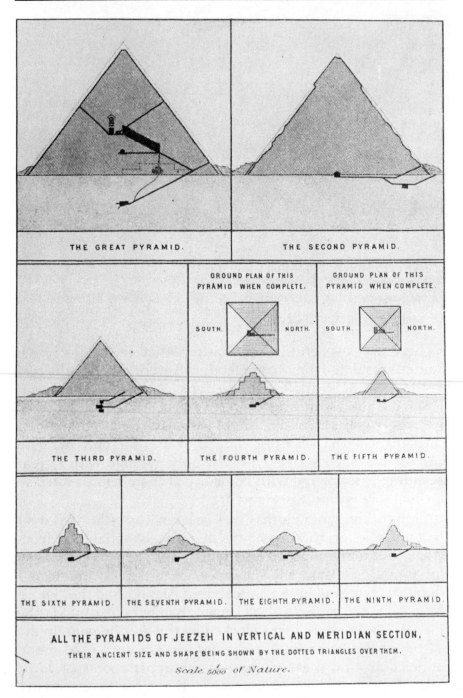

THE GREAT PYRAMID.

THE SECOND PYRAMID.

THE THIRD PYRAMID.

GROUND PLAN OF THIS PYRAMID WHEN COMPLETE.

SOUTH.   NORTH.

THE FOURTH PYRAMID.

GROUND PLAN OF THIS PYRAMID WHEN COMPLETE.

SOUTH.   NORTH.

THE FIFTH PYRAMID.

THE SIXTH PYRAMID.

THE SEVENTH PYRAMID.

THE EIGHTH PYRAMID.

THE NINTH PYRAMID.

ALL THE PYRAMIDS OF JEEZEH IN VERTICAL AND MERIDIAN SECTION,

THEIR ANCIENT SIZE AND SHAPE BEING SHOWN BY THE DOTTED TRIANGLES OVER THEM.

Scale 5000 of Nature.

Smyth's illustration comparing the Egyptian pyramids.

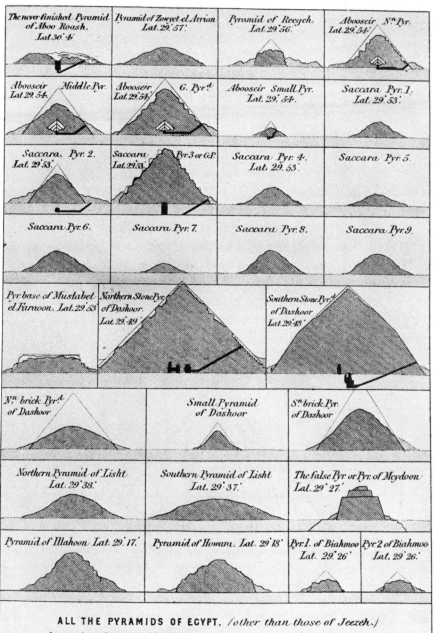

The never finished Pyramid of Aboo Roash. Lat. 30° 4'

Pyramid of Zoryet el Arrian Lat. 29° 57'

Pyramid of Reegeh. Lat. 29° 56'

Abooseir N.n Pyr. Lat. 29° 54'

Abooseir Middle Pyr. Lat. 29° 54'

Abooseir G. Pyr.d Lat. 29° 54'

Abooseir Small Pyr. Lat. 29° 54'

Saccara Pyr. 1. Lat. 29° 53'

Saccara. Pyr. 2. Lat. 29° 53'

Saccara Pyr. 3 or G.P. Lat. 29° 53'

Saccara Pyr. 4. Lat. 29° 53'

Saccara Pyr. 5

Saccara Pyr. 6.

Saccara Pyr. 7.

Saccara Pyr. 8.

Saccara Pyr. 9.

Pyr. base of Mustabet el Faraoon. Lat. 29° 53'

Northern Stone Pyr. of Dashoor. Lat. 29° 49'

Southern Stone Pyr.d of Dashoor Lat 29° 48'

N.n brick Pyr.d of Dashoor

Small Pyramid of Dashoor

S.n brick Pyr. of Dashoor

Northern Pyramid of Lisht Lat. 29° 38'

Southern Pyramid of Lisht Lat. 29° 37'

The false Pyr or Pyr. of Meydoon Lat. 29° 27'

Pyramid of Illahoon Lat. 29° 17'

Pyramid of Howara. Lat. 29° 18'

Pyr.1. of Biahmoo Lat. 29° 26'

Pyr 2 of Biahmoo Lat. 29° 26'

ALL THE PYRAMIDS OF EGYPT, *(other than those of Jeezeh.)*
beginning from the North and going to the South of the country.

SCALE = $\frac{1}{5000}$ OF NATURE.

designed after the same architectural model is otherwise attested to in that virtually all of them have their entrances on the north face.

However, those at Gizeh stand out in this important respect. According to George Reisner in *The History of the Gizeh Necropolis,* all the Gizeh Pyramids, including the subsidiary pyramids, are unique in having subterranean passages and chambers carved out of the underlying solid rock.[27] The general pattern in other pyramids is that the descending passages were dug out as open trenches and the chambers were excavated as open pits.[28] The trenches and pits were then roofed with stone and the pyramids were built on top of them. The Pyramid at Abu Roash, which supposedly was constructed immediately after the Great Pyramid, reverts to the trench and pit technique.

The Great, Second and Third Pyramids of Gizeh, the large temples immediately east of these and the Valley Temple immediately south of the Sphinx, have other characteristics separating them from everything else in Egypt. These characteristics reveal a general excellence of workmanship and

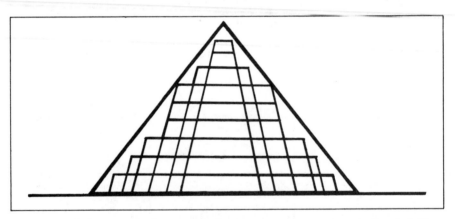

A cross section of a typical pyramid showing its structure as a series of shells.

also imply a much higher technological capability than that employed elsewhere. In these structures, massive blocks of granite were used as building materials on a scale not seen elsewhere in Egypt. The blocks of stone in these buildings, whether granite or limestone, are much larger than those found in other pyramids and temples. Because the other pyramids consist of much smaller blocks, they were built as a series of shells with multiple internal retaining walls to give cohesiveness. The three large Gizeh Pyramids do not have these internal casings. The very size of the blocks produces the necessary stability.[29]

These Pyramids and the large Gizeh temples are further separated stylistically from the rest of Egyptian antiquities in their general lack of ornament and inscription. At Gizeh the walls and chambers of these major structures are blank, but the walls and columns of the temples and tombs at Luxor and the chambers of the pyramids at Saqqara are literally covered with carved symbols and inscriptions.

The traditional motifs in dynastic Egyptian art, architecture and inscription remained remarkably stable over great periods of time. The many fundamental differences between the major

Largest of the three subsidiary pyramids east of the Great Pyramid, an example of "shell" construction.

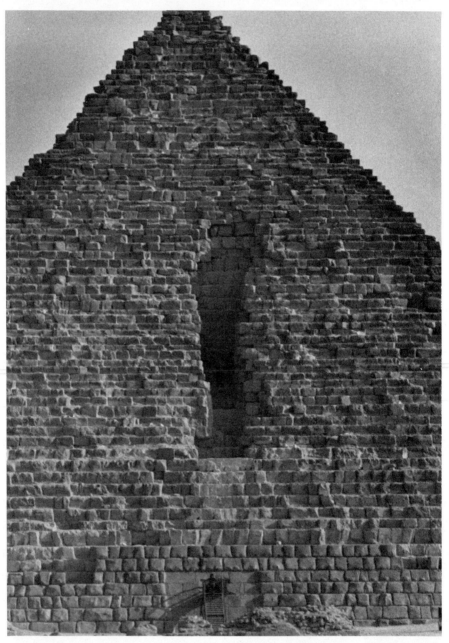

The north face of the Third Pyramid. The large blocks ensure stability without retaining walls. The cavity resulted from an attempt to destroy the pyramid in the thirteenth century.

Ruined mound of the Pyramid of Unis at Saqqara, testifying to the inferior construction methods used at the site.

East face of the Valley Temple with some of the giant granite casing blocks in place.

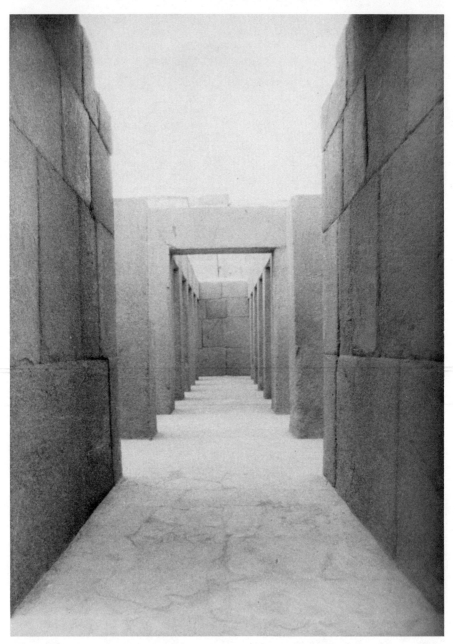

Undecorated granite lined interior of the Valley Temple.

Blank granite wall in the King's Chamber.

Remarkable granite masonry in a corner of the Valley Temple.

Inside the Temple of Karnak.

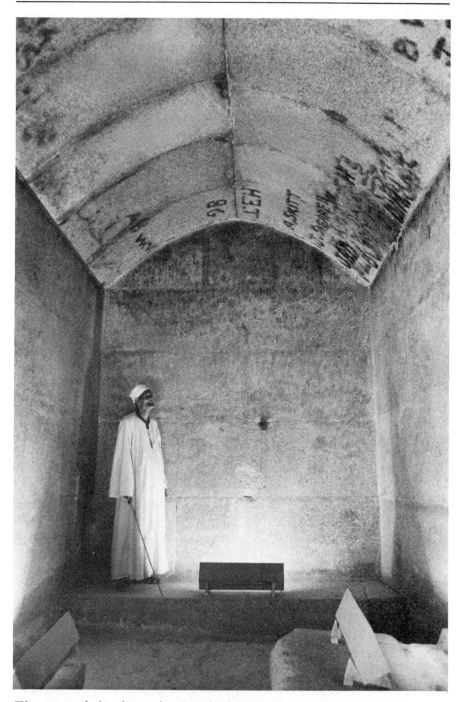

The principal chamber under the Third Pyramid.

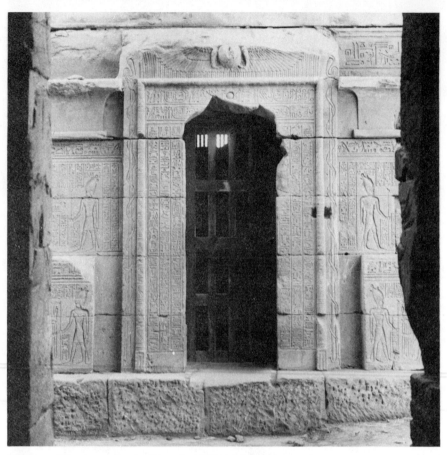

Decorated doorway in the Temple of Karnak.

Gizeh monuments and the rest of Egyptian pyramids and temples indicate that they do not fit neatly into the contended chronology for dynastic Egypt. But if they do not belong to dynastic Egypt, there is only one direction in which they can be moved – not forward but back, further into the past. In accounting for these differences there is much to support the position that the major Gizeh monuments are the products of an advanced initiatory culture of 10,500 B.C. Even the layout of the Gizeh complex suggests that the Great Pyramid was not an integrated unit in a giant preplanned cemetery, but was there before the tombs and other pyramids and was built around in later times.[30]

After the building of the Pyramid the general historical pattern is one of decline in knowledge and engineering ability.

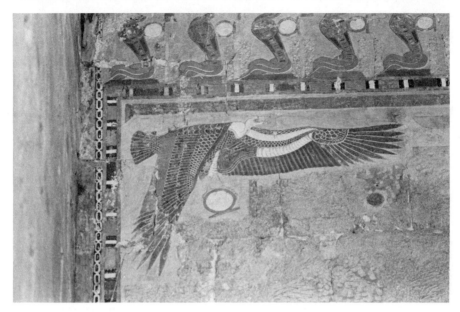

Intricate mosaic on the wall of Hatchepsut's Temple.

In religion the gods multiplied and superstition gradually replaced enlightenment. In art and architecture, the pure simplicity of the Great Pyramid and the Valley Temple gave way to a profusion of symbols, inscriptions and sculptures which embellished later temples and tombs.

In practically everything that remains to us from the oldest Egyptian eras, there is this same indication of a high culture before the dawn of history. The Egyptians possessed not only elaborate hieroglyphs but also true alphabetic signs at least 3500 years before their use by any other race.[31] Few of the Egyptian arts and crafts ever surpassed the quality of those attributed to the Old Kingdom.[32]

There is another indication of very early activity elsewhere in Egypt. All over the earth, one of the most persistent patterns archaeology has discovered is the reconsecration and reuse of ancient sacred sites. Christian churches and cathedrals in England and Europe were often built directly over the remains of older shrines and temples. Many of the pyramids in Mesoamerica were built on top of earlier smaller pyramids and platforms. In Egypt, at the Luxor Temple a mile or so from Karnak, the same pattern can be seen today. There a modern Muslim mosque has been built inside the walls of an ancient

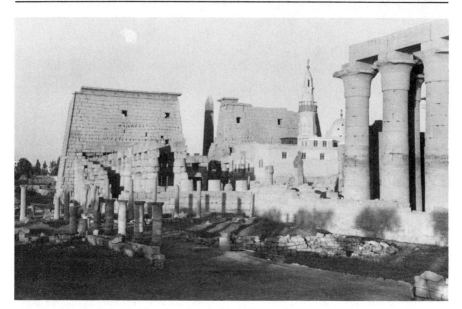

The Luxor Temple with a contemporary mosque inside its walls.

Axis of the Karnak Temple, looking east.

Egyptian temple. The present temple at Karnak, which dates from the New Kingdom (1567-1085 B.C.), may likewise have been built over a much earlier ground-plan. Surveys of the orientation of the axis of the Karnak Temple suggest that it may have been laid out around 11,000 B.C. (See Part IV of the Appendix.)

These explorations into Cayce's psychic descriptions amount to significant verification of a few key details in the Egyptian transcripts. Further support is provided by inconclusive but suggestively parallel details gleaned from the wide literature of Egyptology. The incredible thing is that an impartial observer could well conclude that, slight as the evidence is, there is as much or more to support Cayce's descriptions of the building of the Pyramid as there is to recommend Egyptological theories. As a result, some may rush to accept Cayce's account wholesale, but this, after all, is only one more perspective and it should not be assumed that his is a complete description. It is now clear, however, that there is a significant possibility that the Egyptian transcripts are generally accurate and, like any other hypothesis, should be tested with whatever evidence may be uncovered in the future.

Of course, there will also be resistance to the fact that some fellow could go into a trance and come up with answers that have long eluded the world's leading scholars. But despite the sophistication of our modern world, we understand too little about the prehistoric period, or for that matter the fundamental processes of nature and the mind of man. The greatest mystery on the planet is still the appearance and mission of man himself, and no other ancient monument raises so many questions about our past as the Great Pyramid. On this basis alone it is intriguing to follow up on Cayce's wider descriptions of prehistory to see where they lead, especially since we really know so little about the Pyramid.

ATLANTIS
AND THE
CYCLES OF TIME

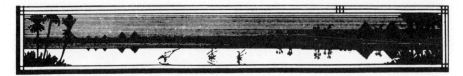

12

On the Road to Atlantis

The history of man may be far longer and stranger than we think. The Great Pyramid may indeed not fit in with what we believe about the past and the nature of the world. Thousands of years ago someone measured the earth with remarkable accuracy and recorded this information in the dimensions of the largest and possibly the oldest stone building on our planet. Our journey in search of the meaning of this extraordinary fact has revealed that there is good reason to date the Pyramid at 10,500 years before Christ – long before our history books speak of any advanced civilization.

What happened to the high civilization with the science and technology required to measure the planet and build the Pyramid? Is it possible that a civilization with certain abilities far in advance of our own completely perished from the earth? Dozens of ancient traditions answer in the affirmative. In very ancient times there appears to have been a universal cosmology describing all history and prehistory as divided into great ages which were terminated by enormous disasters. These disasters were predictable and had in some way to be overcome if man was to maintain the continuity and consciousness of his race. The Great Pyramid was built before the last of these disasters and was designed to withstand the anticipated destruction.

As if to ensure their message would not be lost, the builders of Gizeh may have left us something else in addition to the Pyramid – something they intentionally planned to be found near the end of the following age, over 12,000 years later.

The Guardian.

Cayce's transcripts tells us that around 10,500 B.C. some Atlanteans and Caucasians were aware of these large cycles and knew that the remainder of Atlantis would soon be destroyed. The final destruction amounted to the end of the third world age, occurring about 9600 B.C. They also foresaw the fourth great age as lasting until A.D. 1998-2001, and that this would be an age of increasing intellectual darkness until near its end. Only in the last few decades of the twentieth century would the nature of Gizeh and the prehistoric world be rediscovered.[1] Cayce gave repeated, detailed descriptions of Atlantean records in hidden passages and chambers and even in a small buried pyramid near the Sphinx.[2] One transcript states that the remains of an Atlantean called Exli may be found in an unexcavated mound in front of the Sphinx.[3] There is, in fact, a low but definite mound about 200 yards (183 meters) in front of the Sphinx which is only now being excavated. There are supposed to be passages leading from the right paw of the Sphinx to some of these Atlantean remains.

The most important records are said to have been brought by the Atlantean Keeper of the Records, Hept Supht, from Poseidia (the last remaining major island of Atlantis) in order to

The Sphinx and vicinity. The unexcavated mound is immediately to the south of the village in the open area at the upper left.

preserve the history of Atlantis and of the Law of One, an extremely ancient cosmology and religion stretching back 200,000 years. Here is the description in the transcripts of what is buried in a "Hall" or "Pyramid of Records" somewhere in front of the Sphinx.

> **Q.** Give in detail what the sealed room [at Gizeh] contains.
> **A.** A record of Atlantis from the beginnings of those periods when the spirit took form or began the encasements in that land, and the developments of the peoples throughout their sojourn, with the record of the first destruction and the changes that took place in the land, with the record of the sojournings of the peoples to the varied activities in other lands, and a record of the meetings of all the nations ... for the activities ... that became necessary with the final destruction of Atlantis and the building of the Pyramid of Initiation [the Great Pyramid], with who, what, where would come the opening of the records that are as copies from ... sunken Atlantis; for with the change [coming in the earth] it must rise again.
> This [sealed room] in position lies, as the sun rises from the

waters, the line of shadow falls between the paws of the Sphinx, that was later set as the sentinel or guard, and which may not be entered from the connecting chambers from the Sphinx's [right] paw until the time has been fulfilled when the changes must be active in this sphere of man's experience. [It is] between ... the Sphinx and the river.[4]

In other words, these records supposedly contain information indicating when and by whom they will be opened in the future!

Is all of this fantasy? As in a great many other respects, the transcripts are not unique in describing buried archaeological treasure at Gizeh. According to some reports, the fourth century philosopher Iamblichus (? – A.D. 330) said the Sphinx served as an entrance to sacred corridors in which were inscriptions and records that were the foundation of all knowledge. Ammianaius Marcellinus, quoted earlier, gave a similar account. Many modern scholars have come to parallel conclusions, a corridor from the Sphinx connecting with secret rooms in the Great Pyramid being an especially popular idea.

The Temple of the Sphinx.

Contemporary archaeology is testing these traditions by applying modern sensing techniques which can detect underground chambers from the surface. Early in 1977 Stanford Research Institute conducted electrical resistivity and acoustic surveys that gave preliminary indications of a number of such chambers at Gizeh. These include what may be a room more than 60 feet (18 meters) under the Second Pyramid, another possible room under the King's Chamber in the Great Pyramid, and the suggestion of at least four shafts and tunnels around the Sphinx, one of them under the right paw.[5] The investigations continue.

Cayce further describes the records near the Sphinx as written partially in "old" early Egyptian characters and partially in "newer" Atlantean forms. A remarkable feature of these records which seems designed to ensure their attribution as Atlantean is that identical records are reportedly stored in three separate places. One set was sealed in the lost Temple of Iltar in or near the Yucatan, another in sunken Poseidia (part of which is supposed to rise again), and the third in the as yet undiscovered Pyramid of Records at Gizeh.

However, even if the transcripts are correct and even if

Unexcavated mound approximately 200 yards in front of the Sphinx.

future excavations around the Sphinx disclose exotic remains, it is highly likely that they will be subject to many different interpretations, just as has everything else at Gizeh. The problem is that no one knows what genuine Atlantean artifacts and remains are supposed to look like because we have no verified examples. Unfortunately, Cayce's hints as to the location of the Atlantean records in the western hemisphere are extremely vague, and it seems unlikely that these will be found in the near future, if ever.

Furthermore, excavating under and around the Sphinx itself may not be a simple operation of removing stone and sand. Test drillings in the vicinity have hit ground water at a depth of only a few feet. In the late 1930s a descending shaft behind the Sphinx was opened and explored by archaeologist Selim Hassan. After a yard or two it filled with ground water. Any Atlantean remains in the area are not only buried but possibly under water. In the transcripts, finding these records also seems tied to certain major geophysical changes and alterations in consciousness which must take place around the same time.[6] These many uncertainties make swift solutions unlikely. But whether further verification of Cayce's descriptions comes easily or at all, there are now many indications of a high prehistoric civilization. Recent findings provide a sufficient basis for us to continue our travels through patterns of information down the road to Atlantis without undue speculation.

If there is any archaeological subject of greater controversy than the Great Pyramid, it is Atlantis. In the last 150 years over 5000 books, articles and pamphlets about Atlantis have appeared with an amazing array of theories, disclaimers and items of proposed evidence. Various proponents of Atlantis have claimed it was in the Atlantic, the Mediterranean, the North Sea, the Indian Ocean, the Caspian, or that it never sank at all and was an ancient civilization in what is now Antarctica, Greenland, Ireland, France, Venezuela, North Africa, Spain, Portugal, England, Sweden, or a number of other places.[7] Like the Great Pyramid, Atlantis is an emotive subject and for a similar reason. If there was a great Atlantic island kingdom of high attainments, vast wealth and imperial power as described by Plato, and if this civilization vanished in a catastrophe, it conflicts strongly with modern theories of geological stability, historical continuity and indefinite progress.

The Atlantis connection in the Cayce transcripts is not dependent upon a few chance references. There are hundreds of descriptions of Atlantis itself and these inject a new and startling dimension into the controversy, and one which has a direct bearing on what has previously been described. According to the transcripts, Atlantis had the highest scientific and technological culture the earth has ever seen, a technology and science which in some respects has not yet been equaled by North America and Western Europe in the fourth quarter of the twentieth century.

In addition to all the accomplishments the transcripts credit to the international society in Egypt when the Pyramid was built, the Atlanteans are supposed to have had television and audio recordings, electricity and photography ("photographing from a distance ... reading inscriptions through walls, even at distances"[8]), highly developed music and psychology, ships or planes that not only traveled in the air but on and under the seas, international communications systems, a knowledge of levitation, a death ray, and above and beyond everything else they had the crystal, a device called "terrible" and "mighty",[9] which harnessed the energy of the sun, married it to internal influences in the earth, and provided the basis for a far flung energy system.[10]

The history of Atlantis seems to have been as fantastic as its civilization, extending back 200 millennia, cyclically rising and falling, reaching sublime heights and plummeting – literally – to profound depths. Originally a great continent stretching from the eastern Atlantic near southern Spain across to the Great Bahama Bank, the southeastern edge of the United States and the Sargasso Sea, Atlantis underwent three great catastrophes. These occurred around 50,000 B.C., 28,000 B.C. and 9600 B.C. During the first two destructions much of the continent broke up and sank until all that was left prior to 9600 B.C. was a major island in the vicinity of the Bahama Bank called Poseidia which, however, still commanded power and influence on an imperial scale.

The principal cause of these disasters was the Atlanteans themselves. They lost control of themselves and the things which they had made. On two occasions the great crystals were "tuned too high", and huge fluxes of energy went into the earth causing volcanic upheavals. In each of these destructions, it was not just Atlantis that was involved. Another ancient continent in the Pacific called Mu or Lemuria experienced a parallel history, while elsewhere land masses rose or sank and at least once the earth's axis pivoted, producing different polar and equatorial regions.

The transcripts say many Atlanteans knew in advance of the eventual demise of their continent and scattered over the earth. They emigrated especially to the Yucatan, Peru and Egypt, carrying with them the seeds of the high prehistoric civilizations which flourished in those places. Some who went to Egypt did so with the specific intention of leaving a message which they knew would have to endure 12,500 years – until the end of the following age.

From this perspective, the Great Pyramid suddenly appears to be the chief landmark on the road to Atlantis. As might be expected, the greatest difficulty we face in pursuing Atlantis is sifting reliable information about the prehistoric era from the oceans of material available. Yet this task has its rewards. With an "information explosion" taking place in archaeology as in many other fields, we can now determine better than ever before whether this vision of the past is mere imagination – or something that approximates part of the lost history of man.

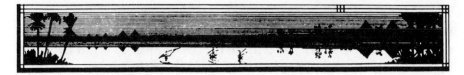

13

A Few Wild Reports

Evidence for Atlantis has been interpreted from classic texts, legends, myths and findings in the sciences of linguistics, archaeology, biology, anthropology, geology, botany and seismology. Only a small fraction of this vast literature is relevant here. What we are looking for is evidence of a high scientific civilization in deep antiquity in addition to the evidence of the Pyramid itself. Even very positive indications of an island civilization on the floor of the Atlantic that merely reached the level of Greece, Carthage or Rome would not measure up to our requirements. Of course, many students of the subject doubt that there is enough evidence to posit the existence of an Atlantis on the level of Greece or Rome. But it is not necessarily improbable that we could find traces of a much higher civilization, whose remains would be more enduring, more pervasive and on a greater scale than that of a lower civilization.

The last fifteen years have produced accumulating evidence of high technical and scientific accomplishment in the prehistoric era attributed, for the most part, simply to unknown civilizations. Although these remains may not be directly attributable to Atlantis, and some do not even pertain to areas said to have been colonized by Atlantis, they may still be relevant to the Atlantis question. If Atlantis had a civilization of world-wide impact and involvement, much as Europe and North America have now, remains of high technical and scientific accomplishments should be found around the earth, just as American and European technology has invaded practically every nation on the planet.

The remains we shall examine and the civilizations that produced them may be conventionally dated from thousands of years B.C. to the beginning of the Christian era. But this wide temporal range does not diminish the likelihood that the knowledge and abilities of these civilizations came from earlier sources which can ultimately be traced back to a single source, or possibly a few major centers. Indeed, virtually no ancient civilization claimed it developed independently. Almost every ancient culture attributed its attainments in the beginning to civilizing and colonizing figures referred to as "gods", "demi-gods", or "heroes". In fact, the home of these heroes is often described as sunken lands in the Atlantic or Pacific.[1]

That much is straightforward enough. But as with the Great Pyramid, the difficulty with literature about ancient science and technology is that writers often make greater claims than they have evidence to support. As we struggle through the darkness and ignorance that surrounds prehistory, we stumble across many wild reports which divert attention and give false impressions. For a traveler following the implications of the Great Pyramid, such reports are truly "sirens' songs", seductive and fanciful. For example, there is a report that ancient gold-plated copper articles have been found at Chan Chan in the Chimu district of Peru. They are extremely finely crafted and fashioned so expertly that the archaeologist A.H. Verrill has said that their high quality makes them indistinguishable from articles produced by the modern electroplating process.[2] Verrill himself said it was "beyond belief" that the Chimus possessed any knowledge of electricity, but some writers, keen to put forward the case for ancient technology, have made it sound as if these articles actually were electroplated.[3] This would imply, of course, that the ancient Peruvians did know electricity.

The trouble with granting ancient Peruvians electricity on account of these articles is that they can be perfectly explained otherwise, in terms of known metallurgical techniques. By using an alloy of roughly 80 percent copper and 20 percent gold, the Indians produced gold-covered copper articles through a process they called *tumbaga*. Modern metallurgists call the same process "depletion gilding".

The alloy is first formed and then heated, oxidizing the copper on the surface. The gold does not oxidize. The oxidized copper can be removed by a mild abrasive, or with an acidic solution, such as urine or certain plant juices.[4] The remaining thin layer of pure gold is then burnished and made smooth. The result – when produced by a mastercraftsman – is an expertly gold covered object all but indistinguishable from modern electroplated work.[5] In some cases, this technique was used with an alloy of copper, silver and gold. These articles, then, are not actually evidence that the Peruvians knew electricity, although it is naturally a favorable comment on their technical abilities that they could produce gold or silver covered objects as well as we can with electricity.

Another misleading report is that articles made of platinum have been found in Ecuador. Pro-Atlantis types point out that platinum has a melting point of 1773°C. or 3223°F. and that this must mean pre-Columbian peoples could generate very high temperatures.[6] What they don't mention is that the platinum in pre-Columbian jewelry and art has not been melted. Using a technique called sintering, platinum dust and gold dust are heated to the melting point of gold. The platinum flecks are then held in a mortar of gold. After beating and burnishing, the platinum in these objects has the smooth appearance of having been melted and cast when in fact it was not.[7]

In the 1950s, reports began to circulate about huge sculptures of exotic animals on the remote Marcahuasi plateau of Peru. A typical account runs: "Large sections of mountain rock have been carved and modified to be alligators, hippopotamuses and also something resembling a prehistoric stegosaurus."[8] Another claims that lions, cows, elephants and camels as well as Caucasian, Negro and Semitic faces are represented.[9] Curiously, these carvings are supposed to be recognizable only at certain times, when light striking them from exactly the right angle brings out their features.

Intrigued by several such reports I, in my ignorance, thought there must be something of great importance on the Marcahuasi plateau, especially since most of these animals became extinct in the western hemisphere many thousands of years ago. One writer declares that it "cannot be doubted" that the sculptors coexisted with exotic animals and estimates that the sculptures are at least 10,000 years old.[10] However, when I saw photographs of these lumps of rock I was extremely disappointed. All I can say is that I once had a dog that from a certain angle in a certain light at a certain distance looked a little like a horse, but there are precious few people who would have bought that dog as a horse!

Some of the most extreme claims made for ancient civilizations involve astronomy and remains with astronomic significance. In the thirties and forties artist and writer K.E. Maltwood claimed a discovery which she called the Glastonbury Zodiac. Influenced by Arthurian legend and a study of place names, she was bent on proving that King Arthur's

The Vale of Avalon with Glastonbury Tor at its center is the focus of many legends and theories.

Round Table was actually a description of the constellations of the Zodiac and that giant effigies recording the symbols of the constellations were carved into the landscape around the town of Glastonbury in Somerset, England. On maps of the area, using lines demarcating hills, roads, canals, rivers and field boundaries such as hedges, she colored in crude zodiacal figures such as the Lion (Leo) and the Bull (Taurus). Maltwood was convinced that these figures were traces of a giant prehistoric landscaping project ten miles (16 km) in diameter that dated from around 2700 B.C. Even as drawings, the figures are too amorphous to be convincing and there is no documentation that most of her arbitrary boundary lines result from prehistoric human activity.

Subsequently, this fanciful work was popularized by a younger generation of English antiquarians. Many have leaped to the conclusion that the Glastonbury Zodiac is actually formed by ancient earthworks. Aerial photographs and the evidence of one's eyes do not support this hypothesis, but this has not prevented enthusiasts from attributing great significance to this "zodiac", describing it as a bona fide archaeological discovery, dating it anywhere from 2700 to 15,000 B.C., and searching for others on modern maps. If one only reads brief secondary reports, the "zodiac" may sound convincing. In *Mysteries From Forgotten Worlds* Charles Berlitz soberly describes the Glastonbury Zodiac in the same terms as the physical remains at Stonehenge.[11]

Other claims made in the name of ancient astronomy are even more fantastic. It is an established fact that the Mayan system of astronomy did record sophisticated and exact information. Their calendar dated back to about 3113 or 3420 B.C.[12] and they are credited with inventing the world's most remarkable numerical system.[13] Some researchers claim that the Maya determined the length of the year more precisely than the figure on which the contemporary Gregorian calendar is based. The Mayan lunar calendar is supposed to have been accurate to within one day over a period of 300 years[14] – an amazing exactitude and far beyond what one might expect of "primitive" peoples.

It is also recognized that the Maya calculated time using a brilliant system of interlocking cycles based on two values for the solar year, lunations, the synodic revolutions of the planets and a sacred cycle of 260 days. Their awareness of synodic periods and the synthesis of these with their system of cycles is but one example of Mayan sophistication and technical skill. The synodic return of a planet is the time it takes the planet to reappear at a particular place in the sky as seen from the earth. Venus revolves around the sun in 224.7 days, but because the earth is also revolving, the synodic period of Venus is 583.92 days. The Maya knew the synodic revolutions of Mercury, Venus, Mars, Jupiter and Saturn with great precision. Although the Maya are credited with knowing the exact synodic period of Venus, it is also believed that they took it as 584 days, because 584 x 5 equals 8 x 365. The synodic period of

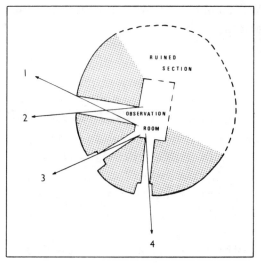

Floor plan of the Caracol,
Mayan observatory, Chichen Itza,
Mexico, showing astronomic sight
lines.

1. *Extreme declination of the winter moon; +29°*
2. *Equinox sunset; 0°*
3. *Extreme declination of the summer moon; -29°*
4. *North-south meridian line.*

Mars is 780 days, which is just 3 x 260. In *La Piedra del Sol*, Raul Noriega states that almost all the visible eclipses of the sun and moon in Mesoamerica between 1204 B.C. and A.D. 2250 are also related by a number of days whose factor is 260.

It can then be concluded that the Maya did know the length of the year with extreme precision, that they were aware – at least within a certain range – of the interlocking cycles of time, and that they had a sophisticated system of calculation which could handle a wide range of numbers. The length of time required to establish this knowledge seems to be far greater than the presently known historical range of the Maya.

While their calendar goes back to the fourth millennium B.C., the farthest back they can be traced by the dating of archaeological remains is about 1200 B.C., and even that date was arrived at as recently as 1976. What happened to the missing 2000 years? Only an estimated ten percent of the Mayan remains have been excavated, leaving us to wonder what will be revealed by future research. It is possible that the Maya could have inherited their mathematical and astronomic accomplishments from another civilization, such as the largely unknown Olmecs, and that either or both of these peoples were descended from Atlantean refugees.

The Maya were indeed fantastic astronomers. The respected Mayanist J. Eric Thompson reports that they calculated a date over 500,000,000 years in the past without an error. Faced with such astonishing calculations, it is sometimes difficult to know where fact ends and fantasy begins. In *Mysteries of the Mexican Pyramids,* Peter Tompkins presents the conclusions of Maurice Chatelain, a NASA technician who studied the Mayan calendar system. Chatelain claims that a figure for 147,420 million days (147,420,000,000) occurs in the Mayan glyphs. This is supposed to represent 78,170 cycles of 260 Saturn-Jupiter conjunctions, one conjunction happening every 20 years. Chatelain presented many other equally astounding calculations.

Chatelain keyed the significance of his calculations to the existence of the number 195,955,200,000,000, which was reportedly found on a cuneiform tablet in Babylon. This figure represents the number of seconds in 240 precessions of the equinoxes, each precession lasting 25,890 years. Tompkins calls this number "the Nineveh constant". 147,420 million days is just 65 times this constant, and another Mayan number interpreted by Chatelain, 34,020 million days, is just 15 times the same figure. Hugh Harleston, another Tompkins source, tells us that the builders of the huge ceremonial complex at Teotihuacan, Mexico, were acquainted with the twelfth root of two – a contemporary esoteric concept employed only in the most abstract mathematics.

However, O. Neugebauer, the leading expert on Babylonian mathematics, rejects the Nineveh constant as a phantom. The figure 195,955,200,000,000 does not occur on any tablet found in Babylon or anywhere else. Neugebauer explains that the Nineveh constant was perpetrated upon the scientific community by Hilprecht in 1906, who misinterpreted simple multiplication tables and through "some wild artifices" transformed symbols reading either 70 or 1-1/6 into 195,955,200,000,000 – possibly one of the grandest cases of inflation on record.[15]

Since the Nineveh constant is one of the key concepts upon which Chatelain and Tompkins build their image of ancient astronomy, the integrity of similar information they report is also suspect. One wonders about Chatelain's "interpretations" of the enormous numbers he derived from the Mayan glyphs -- and about the twelfth root of two.

Of course, it is possible to bounce sophisticated modern mathematical concepts off pyramids and other ancient remains and come up with one kind of correspondence or another, but beyond geometry, arithmetic and simple algebra, there is no indication that the ancients used the same concepts we use today. This raises the question of utility. The practical implications of the high geographic science incorporated in the Great Pyramid are obvious. A global concept of geography would have enabled the builders to travel the world at will with great commercial benefits. But what are the practical benefits of the twelfth root of two? If mathematical interpretations of ancient sites are to carry much weight, they have to be extremely simple and straightforward.

Another confusing situation developed in the late 1960s and early 1970s with a flurry of reports of archaeological finds in the vicinity of the Bimini Islands. Interest in the area was originally sparked by a prediction Edgar Cayce had made in 1940:

> Poseidia will be among the first portions of Atlantis to rise again. Expect it in '68 and '69; not so far away.[16]

Cayce had also said that Bimini was itself a small fragment of Poseidia – the last remnant of Atlantis – and indicated that remains of Atlantis could also be found in the Straits of Florida.

In late 1968 it was reported that the remains of what could have been an Atlantean temple had been photographed in shallow water on the Great Bahama Bank. Even more tantalizing was the statement that this temple appeared to have the same ground plan as the Temple of Turtles at Uxmal, Yucatan.[17] Similar reports described the submerged remains of columns and other buildings in the Bimini area. Because of the Cayce prediction, many jumped to the conclusion that Poseidia had at last been discovered. However, a closer look revealed that the Atlantean temple was nothing but a 1930s sponge corral and there are good reasons to question the rest of the supposedly ancient remains around Bimini. The most noteworthy of these is the so called Bimini Wall or Road, a linear formation of giant stones, some 15 by 20 feet (4.5 by 6 meters), stretching about 1800 feet (548 meters) along the sea floor. One end of the formation curves back on itself, forming a giant "J". Some investigators contend this is a natural formation of beach rock, while others, equally qualified, say it is an artificial, man-made formation.[18]

Naturally, if one learns that what was at first presented as an 11,000 year old Atlantean temple is nothing but a 40 year old sponge corral, he is apt to dismiss all reports from the same area as equally inflated. But despite some preliminary appearances, it is more than likely that the Bimini Road is man-made.

Perhaps the most persistent investigator of the Bimini site has been Dr. David Zink, who has been studying the area for years. Zink is convinced the "road" is man-made. In *The Stones of Atlantis,* he documents impressive evidence for this with detailed maps of the formation and curiosities such as a tongue-and-groove pavement slab he found on the sea floor. Recent neutron activation analyses of cores Zink took from the "road" blocks and the underlying sea bed have provided preliminary indications that they are of different origins. This also tends to support an archaeological interpretation of the site. Even if future research produces overwhelming evidence one way or the other, that still will not end the controversy, because opinions for and against Atlantis are held with such strong conviction.

It is another of those "curious coincidences" though that the

The Bimini Road.

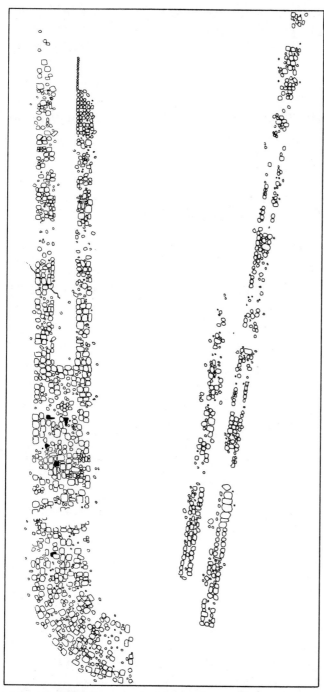

First detailed map of the Bimini Road, compiled by David Zink from aerial photographs and on-site surveys. Estimated accuracy 80 percent. Drawn by John Parks.

initial discoveries were made at exactly the time and place Cayce specified for the reappearance of part of Atlantis. Some Cayce believers are even convinced that the sea floor did rise around Bimini bringing the "road" into view, but this is apparently conjecture. There has been no report that the sea bed rose even a few inches off North Bimini Island in 1968-1969. The "road" appeared not because of an upheaval, but because the powerful Gulf Stream current running through the Florida Straits is continually moving sand around on the ocean floor. The "road" has apparently been covered and uncovered many times, and it happened to be exposed when people aware of Cayce's Poseidia prediction were looking for remains of Atlantis. Can it be that Cayce's prediction referred to an archaeological, not a geological event?

Whether the issue is the Bimini Road, the nature of Mayan astronomy, or countless other archaeological controversies, even a consensus among authorities is no guarantee that they are describing reality. Authoritative opinion once held that the earth was flat and at the center of the universe. But if the authorities are often suspect, so is everyone else. By simply relying on the reports of others we can not only invent entire dynasties from a few controversial cartouches, we can also give electricity to pre-Columbian Peruvians if we don't understand metallurgy as well as they did; create a 17,000 year old landscaped zodiac ten miles in diameter because an imaginative artist colored in some maps; expand the consciousness of Babylonian and Mayan astronomers to infinite dimensions through faulty translations; transform a 40 year old sponge corral into an 11,000 year old Atlantean temple via premature assessment; and raise the floor of the sea to suit our convenience – if one insists on believing that his favorite psychic was never wrong.

It should also be pointed out that the sources of these wild reports do contain some valuable and interesting information. Berlitz and Valentine have produced a much needed updating of the Atlantis mystery and few writers match Tompkins's range of research.

There is much indeed that is strange on earth, but it is necessary to balance imagination with scepticism and to look at things from more than one perspective.

14

Back Home in Poseidia

Out of the mists of illusion and back onto a vast sea separating us from a lost world, the next thing we notice is a lot of curious debris. Some of the things that have come floating by lead anyone to wonder if the prehistoric era wasn't far different from what has been long imagined.

All over the planet there are strange artifacts and remains, some of which have been known for decades. Interpretations of the Great Pyramid as an expression of scientific geography were attempted as early as 1798. Around 1900 the British astronomer, Sir Norman Lockyer, suggested that ancient temples and other prehistoric sites may have been laid out with respect to astronomic criteria. But these ideas, as valuable as they are, were largely submerged by the dominant scientific conservatism of the day, until they surfaced again in the 1960s.

In terms of broadly disseminated ideas, the first notable attempt in modern times to account for the mysteries of prehistory came in 1882 with Ignatius Donnelly's *Atlantis: The Antediluvian World*. With massive research and forceful prose, Donnelly presented the existence of Atlantis as an inescapable conclusion. His work is still worth study.

In 1919 *The Book of the Damned* was published in which Charles Fort wrote entertainingly upon the expanded theme of every crazy event and object that had ever embarrassed scientists. He cites instances of inscribed coins and stones bearing unknown characters found under "Indian mounds" and by well-diggers in the United States. Fort was disgusted that scientists would dismiss such objects as "frauds" (without evidence of fraud) or simply ignore them entirely when they could not be assimilated by current theories – a general pattern of behavior that persists today. With much humor Fort revenged himself and his readers upon science's provincialism by dragging out every wild report he could find that does not fit into the "official" version of the world. The more outrageous the report, the more Fort liked it. He documents black rains, white frogs, dead fish and showers of blood that have fallen from the sky. Fort's interest was not primarily in prehistory, but his works still stand as islands of open-minded questioning.

As this century progressed, more and more research was focused upon the prehistoric horizon. In 1950 Immanuel Velikovsky startled the scientific community with *Worlds in Collision,* an interpretation of ancient times in which the earth is nearly struck by a giant comet on a wild trajectory. While many question the chronology and causal agents Velikovsky suggests, he has probably done more than any other writer to convince people that there have been huge and destructive events on this planet since man has been on the earth. Velikovsky shows that ancient records describe giant meteor swarms hitting the earth, tremendous volcanic eruptions, tidal waves, hurricanes and fires of continental proportions, global earthquakes, and shiftings of the axis.

Then in the sixties, with space probes and moon landings in the news, writers and researchers on all fronts began interpreting prehistoric remains in terms of scientific concepts. Astronomer G.S. Hawkins "decoded" Stonehenge as an eclipse predictor.[1] Charles Hapgood found an unglaciated Antarctica on an ancient map.[2] E.E. Cayce described his father's vision of Atlantis as a superior civilization with parallels to our own.[3] John Michell disclosed "the view over Atlantis" from the perspective of a forgotten science called "geomancy" which was practiced in ancient Britain,[4] Maria Reiche showed us a mystery on the desert in Peru,[5] and Erich von Däniken told everyone it was a set of airfields for extraterrestrial visitors in the distant past.[6] Whatever else he may have done, von Däniken convinced millions of people that many ancient remains on this planet do not look as if they were made by primitive savages.

Since then dozens of writers have interpreted ancient remains in terms of scientific concepts. The results vary from the careful quantitative work of Hapgood and Alexander Thom to the wildest whimsies. Conservative historians have good reason to dismiss much of this literature as an unwarranted projection of contemporary space-age fantasies onto the prehistoric scene. But while it is true that popular literature on prehistory contains many misleading or inaccurate reports, it is also true that scientists themselves are less than infallible.

Much prehistoric evidence has been dismissed or ignored because investigators did not know what they were looking at. Simply because an object is excavated by an archaeologist and turned over to a museum is no guarantee whatever that it will be adequately studied or preserved. In *The Exact Sciences in Antiquity*, Neugebauer tells a typical story about numerous stacks of cuneiform tablets in the basement of the British Museum. The tablets had been excavated in Nineveh in the 1920s and by the 1950s their location when excavated could only be approximated by checking the dates of the newspapers in which they were wrapped against the dates of the different excavations. The great majority of the tablets and records from Nineveh have never been examined for the lack of qualified people to study them.

If this happens to Nineveh tablets in the British Museum, what happens to more peculiar objects in the hundreds of smaller museums around the world? Often the only option a museum or scientist has is to forget about them. No one knows their real significance and it might take centuries to find out. When a scientist is forced to say something about a find, even if he'd rather not, he will often say the least controversial thing possible and attempt to explain remains in terms of known practices and peoples. To a certain extent this is healthy and natural, but the explanations that come about in this way are not always convincing.

What reports can we trust? Probably not very many. But there are instances when even an uncorroborated report may still be worth bearing in mind, if only because many similar reports are all now equally difficult to verify and there is every chance some of them may be accurate. Here are a few examples.

There are many reports now difficult to trace of metal objects of artificial origin that were found in geologically "impossible" places. A gold chain of intricate workmanship was reportedly discovered in a lump of coal in Morrisonville, Illinois in 1891. Nails with complete heads have supposedly been found inside blocks of stone and quartz. Reports of these prehistoric nails come from Peru, northern Britain and California.[7]

In *We Are Not The First* Andrew Tomas adds another curious item to such reports. Because of the difficulty of the manufacturing process, aluminum is thought to be strictly a modern metal, first obtained in recent times in 1825. Yet according to Tomas, the Chinese general Chow Chu (A.D. 265-316) was buried with a metal girdle, analyzed by a spectroscope to be 5 percent manganese, 10 percent copper and 85 percent aluminum. It is unfortunate Tomas does not cite a source for this report.[8]

Tomas has also cited uncorroborated evidence suggesting the existence of prehistoric firearms. In the Museum of Natural History in London, according to Tomas, is a human skull estimated to date from 38,000 B.C. It was found in Rhodesia and has a perfectly round small hole in the left side of the cranium. The right side of the skull is shattered.[9] Cold weapons or arrows could not have produced this effect, which, Tomas says, is practically identical to the remains of contemporary soldiers' skulls struck by rifle bullets. In the Palaeontological Museum of the Soviet Union there is a skull of an auroch - a long-horned wild ox that supposedly lived many thousands of years ago. It too has a small round hole like that made by a rifle bullet.[10]

The Dogons are a people of west Africa located in what is now the Republic of Mali. They are well known for their involved system of metaphysics and cosmology. There is a report that the traditions of the Dogons speak of "the dark companion of Sirius".[11] Sirius, or the Dog Star, is the brightest star in the heavens and is part of a binary system. It has a faint companion star that cannot be seen without the aid of a telescope - a body that indeed qualifies as "a dark companion".

In 1933, Dr. D.F. Weidenreich excavated a number of skulls and skeletons at Chou-kou-tien near Peking. One was reportedly identified as an elderly European male, another as a

Melanesian girl, and a third as an Eskimo woman. The burial was dated at about 28,000 B.C.[12]

If true, these last two reports imply ancient peoples had telescopes and that international travel took place in prehistoric times. Similarly, the others suggest that a much higher level of technology existed in earlier eras than has commonly been assumed. It would not be difficult to gather a library of literally thousands of undocumented but intriguing reports such as these. Entire books are filled with them. Of course, many may be misconstrued information. But some may be accurate descriptions whose wider implications have been largely forgotten or ignored. If only a few are true, it pushes the date for sophisticated technology back tens of thousands of years.

Even without these thought-provoking but frustrating items, there is much documented evidence suggesting that we are not the first scientific civilization on this planet. Reports of advanced metallurgy cover the remotest prehistoric eras down to historic times. Numerous writers have pointed to a 24 foot (7 meter) tall iron column in India called the Kutb Minar pillar. It is reportedly incorruptible, having withstood monsoons and tropical sunshine for sixteen centuries. An inscription on the column is said to still be legible. Few old iron artifacts exist because under most conditions iron and steel oxidize and turn completely to rust in less than 2000 years. The preservation of this pillar was partly explained by J.C. Hudson in *Nature* in 1953. His research shows that the corrosive conditions in the Delhi area are very mild and that it is damp enough to rust iron only about one month per year.[13] (Humidity of 70 percent is required, according to Hudson, to effect significant rusting. Little or no rusting occurs below 20 percent humidity.) Nevertheless, 1600 years is a long time for an iron object to endure so successfully, and it seems open to question whether the low humidity of Delhi's present climate is the entire explanation.

In 1885 a block of coal was broken in an Austrian foundry and a small steel cube 2.6 inches by 1.8 inches (67 mm by 47 mm) fell out. It was encircled by a precisely turned groove and its edges were rounded on two faces. It is very difficult to explain this object as other than man-made. The original cube has been lost but a cast of it is still in the Linz Museum.[14]

There is a report from a reliable archaeologist that fragments of extremely finely woven textiles have been found in Peru. As of the 1920s, not even modern machinery could equal this work. According to A.H. Verrill: "No other race ever has yet woven – by hand or machine – textiles to equal those produced by the ancient Peruvians."[15]

Maybe someone in antiquity *did* have electricity. In 1938-1939, a German archaeologist named Wilhelm König unearthed what looked like pottery jars at a 2000 year old site near Baghdad. The jars had inner cylinders of copper lined on the inside with asphalt. The upper ends of the cylinders were also plugged with asphalt, in the center of which was a solid piece of iron, reminding König of electric batteries. König described his find in *9 Jahre Irak* in Austria in 1940. After World War II Willard Grey of the General Electric Company built a duplicate and filled it with an electrolyte. The jar reportedly functioned perfectly as a battery. The originals may still be seen in the Baghdad Museum.[16]

In the Cairo Museum is a model found in a tomb of what was at first thought to be a bird, having the head of a hawk. This was later recognized by Dr. Khalil Messiha to be a model of a glider plane incorporating such necessary aerodynamic principles for a heavier-than-air machine as a vertical tail, a feature never seen in birds.[17] The model is still capable of flight. Once its nature was perceived, other potential planes or gliders were also identified. In 1972 the Cairo Museum presented an exhibition of fourteen such models. Other dramatic indications of prehistoric flight are found in the Sanskrit classics the *Mahabharata*, the *Samarangana Sutradhara* and the *Ramayana* in which detailed descriptions are given of sophisticated flying machines called *vimanas*. Some of the *vimanas* could navigate on and under the water as well as in the air – exactly like the Atlantean aircraft described by Cayce.[18] The *Mahabharata* is thought to have been recorded in its present form between 1500 and 200 B.C. but describes events many thousands of years before those dates.

As interesting as such objects and references are, remains implying advanced geographic or astronomic knowledge are far more significant. A sophisticated sense of global geography and the companion knowledge of astronomy would have been a necessity for an Atlantis with a scientific civilization and international trading patterns. As world travelers necessarily carried this knowledge with them, traces of these sciences would be most likely to survive – even if Atlantis itself were completely destroyed.

Geography and astronomy are closely related because measurements of one are often made in terms of the other. In order to find our latitude, we must look at the stars. In order for a navigator crossing an ocean to know where he is, he must have a chronometer and check the sun's position. In a certain sense, astronomy is simply the geography of the sky. Not only would these sciences be most likely to survive because of their global scope, but information pertaining to them is also relatively easy to verify. Even though the stars slowly change positions, the angle of the ecliptic is gradually diminishing, and land forms are continuously transformed, prehistoric man saw much the same sky and earth as we do today. It is not surprising then that the most important researches of recent years increasingly point to sophisticated geographic and astronomic knowledge in deep antiquity.

In the British Isles there are 600 archaeological sites called "stone circles". At these sites, rough, often large stones are embedded in the earth marking out circular patterns. No one knows how old these circles are. They are usually estimated to have a minimum age of 3500 years. Since the early 1960s they have been intensively investigated by astronomers and engineers. It has recently been established that these deceptively simple stone circles are actually prehistoric observatories and function as scientific instruments.

The most complex and best known of these stone circles is Stonehenge, situated on the Salisbury Plain in south central England. Stonehenge is remarkable in several respects. It has a much more accomplished appearance than the rest, and as with many other ancient structures, some of the stones in it are gigantic. The largest of these, the trilithon uprights, rise 22 feet (6.7 meters) from the surface and weigh about 50 tons. They extend 7.5 feet (2.3 meters) into the ground. They are thought to have been brought from the Marlborough Downs, about 20 miles (32 km) to the north. There are other smaller stones of a different type incorporated into Stonehenge called

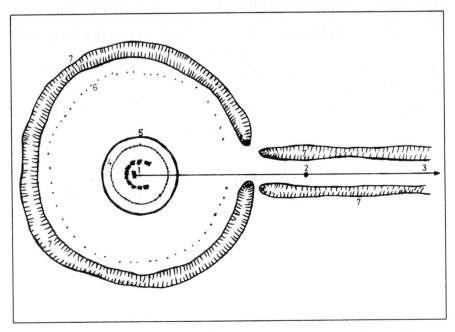

Simplified sketch of the original appearance of Stonehenge as seen from above.

1. *Inner semicircle of Sarsen stones and the "altar stone".*
2. *The heel stone.*
3. *Direction of the midsummer sunrise.*
4. *Circle of bluestones.*
5. *Outer circle of Sarsen stones.*
6. *Aubrey holes.*
7. *Ditches.*

"bluestones". These average 4.5 tons and are believed to have been brought from the Prescelly Mountains in Wales, 150 miles (241 km) distant, where the nearest deposit of this stone is found. Assuming primitive labor techniques were used, the astronomer Hawkins estimated it would take 1,500,000 man-days to construct Stonehenge.

Various elements of the structure produce alignments that indicate extreme positions of the sun and moon as they rise and set on the horizon. Lunar and solar eclipses occur in definite patterns and intervals with respect to these extreme rising and setting positions. Hawkins pointed out that Stonehenge is laid out in such a way, and indicates these key positions so precisely, that coming eclipses can be predicted. There is some disagreement among experts as to the precise method the builders of Stonehenge used to predict these events (since more than one technique was possible) but astronomers other than Hawkins who have studied the site in detail, such as Fred Hoyle, affirm that with the use of this giant instrument it was possible to predict all (or almost all) lunar and solar eclipses, even those which were not visible from the site.[19]

Another important feature of Stonehenge is its latitude. As Hawkins has explained, from the standpoint of astronomic measurement Stonehenge could not have been built further north than Oxford or further south than Bournemouth, cities approximately 70 miles (112 km) apart. Within this narrow band the extreme rising positions of the sun and moon along the horizon form right angles to each other. Stonehenge's circular structure incorporates an earlier rectangle that marks these extreme positions. Further north or south, these right angles, hence the rectangle, would not exist. It seems the site was deliberately chosen for its peculiar latitude – another indication of geographic science in antiquity.

Stonehenge.

The astronomic function of Stonehenge has been further supported by the work of Alexander Thom, professor emeritus of engineering at Oxford, who has conducted careful surveys of 300 of the remaining 600 stone circles.[20] He has concluded that these lesser circles, too, provide extremely accurate means for studying the movements of the sun, moon and stars. He has discovered the unit of measure with which they were built, the megalithic yard of 2.73 feet (.83 meters), and has determined that there was an exact knowledge of the length of the year in Britain about 2000 B.C. Thom has also shown that the stone circles are not actually true circles, but a variety of geometrically sophisticated shapes, including ellipses, flattened circles and egg-shaped rings. Analyses of these revealed that their builders knew the 3:4:5, 5:12:13, 8:15:17 and 12:35:37 Pythagorean right angle triangles. As with the Great Pyramid, it is evident that these special triangles were known thousands of years before the Greeks.

No less remarkable, Thom has found that the builders of the stone circles were acquainted with a slight oscillation in the

Vertical aerial view of Stonehenge. The "heel stone" is on the left.

A great trilithon at Stonehenge. The largest stones are estimated to weigh over 50 tons.

motion of the moon across the sky that amounts to only nine minutes of arc (.15°) deviation from its larger cyclical patterns. Part of its significance is that the period of this oscillation, 173.3 days, defines half an "eclipse year". Eclipses happen only when this slight variation approaches an extreme position. This minute movement was first recorded in historic times by the Danish astronomer Tycho Brahe (1546-1601). However, some of the prehistoric circles are so accurate that, according to Thom, it is possible with their help alone to determine the magnitude of this lunar eccentricity.

Castle Rigg stone circle near Keswick in Cumberland. This is one of the most beautifully situated ancient sites in the British Isles.

Castle Rigg. Alignments of stones across the circle, and/or the directions marked by stones sighted from the center of the circle, indicate astronomically significant points on the horizon.

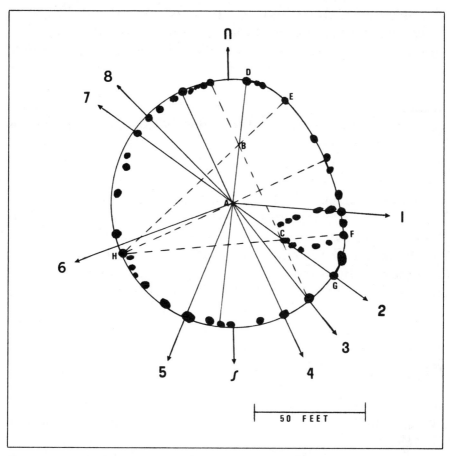

Castle Rigg, Cumberland.

Sketch of Thom's survey with geometric construction superimposed. Arc DE is struck from B; Arc EF from H; Arc FG from C; Arc GHD from A. Note outline of right triangles. Thom refers to this construction as a "flattened circle, type A."

The major declinations indicated are:
1. *Equinox sun*
2. *Candlemas rising sun*
3. *Midwinter rising sun*
4. *Most southerly rising moon*
5. *To notch on the horizon and most southerly setting moon*
6. *To outlying stone (296 feet, 90 meters)*
7. *Midsummer setting sun*
8. *Most northerly setting moon*

The use of such circles may have been widespread. There are indications that in earlier times the American Indians or their predecessors carried on a parallel tradition of astronomic observation. Hawkins has described the remains of a circular pattern of post holes at a prehistoric temple complex near Kahokia, Illinois, which produces astronomically significant alignments. Recent research has shown there are a number of astronomic stone circles on the Great Plains in the United States and Canada similar in style and function to those in Britain.[21]

Did ancient peoples have telescopes? It is not impossible. Archimedes, the inventor scientist of Sicily, was credited by Plutarch as having optical instruments "to manifest to the eye the largeness of the sun". True optical lenses have been found in Nineveh and Carthage with magnification powers between five and eight.[22] A recognized authority attests that the Babylonians recorded observations of the four large moons of Jupiter and the seven satellites of Saturn, none of which can be seen without a telescope.[23] An ancient "stone telescope" 8 inches long and 1.33 inches in diameter (20 cm x 3.4 cm) was found in North Dakota. Its design is said to show "Mayan influences".[24] No doubt this could also be called a "peace pipe", a "ceremonial object of unknown use", or any number of other things.

It is often difficult or impossible to tell what use an ancient artifact had. On the other hand, traces of an advanced science of geography are more dramatic and sometimes more tangible. It is well known that in the third century B.C. Eratosthenes calculated the circumference of the earth using a 7.2° angle of shadow in Alexandria when the sun was directly over Syene. As 7.2° is 1/50th of a circle, the distance between Alexandria and Syene was 1/50th of the earth's circumference. Using an accurate measurement of the distance between these two cities, this method gives a circumference of 26,000 miles (41,843 km), which is about 1100 miles (1770 km) greater than the actual circumference of the earth, 24,901.5 miles (40,075 km).[25]

It is much less widely appreciated that the ancient Hebrews may have known the earth's circumference far more precisely than Eratosthenes. In the nineteenth century a gentleman

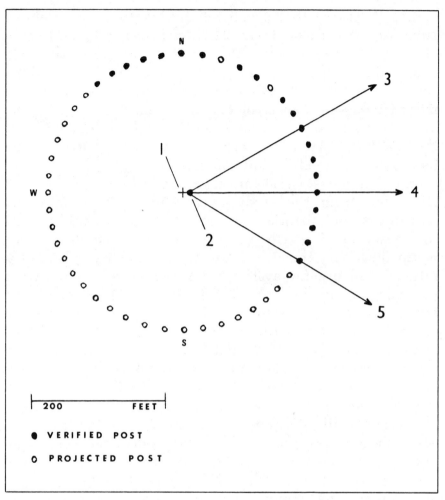

Plan of a prehistoric temple complex, Kahokia, Illinois. (Sketch after Hawkins.)

1. *Geometric center of the circle.*
2. *Siting post displaced five feet to the east.*
3. *Line to point on horizon marked by midsummer sunrise (summer solstice).*
4. *Line to point on horizon marked by vernal and autumnal equinoxes (due east).*
5. *Line to point on horizon marked by midwinter sunrise (winter solstice).*

named Wackerbarth determined the length of the Hebrew cubit (or ell) at 1.82405 feet (21.8886 inches or 55.59715 cm). He concluded there were 12,000 of these cubits in a parasang, and cited the *Talmud's* statement that the circumference of the earth was 6000 parasangs. This gives a circumference of 24,873 miles (40,029 km), an error of only 28 miles (46 km).[26] The *Talmud* is variously dated between the sixth century B.C. and the fourth century A.D. There is now no way of knowing how its writers obtained this information.

One of the most significant traces of prehistoric geography has come from the study of ancient units of measure. Metrologist and historian L.C. Stecchini has declared that all the measures of length, volume and weight of the ancient world (including those of India and China) were part of a rational and organic system.[27] Measures of weight were derived from measures of volume, which in turn were derived from measures of length, such as feet and cubits. Feet and cubits, in turn, were defined as fractions of degrees, minutes or seconds of latitude or longitude. This concept is very similar to the more recent attempt to define the meter (as was originally done) as a fraction (1/10,000,000th) of the distance between the pole and equator.

In other words, it can now be demonstrated that there was something like a universal metric system in very deep antiquity. Ancient units of measure are of varying size, because they were calculated as different fractions of a larger base unit, and diminishing communication among ancient peoples gradually reinforced these differences. However, many ancient units of length can still be shown to be even fractions of one another, implying that they derive from an earlier, simpler and more universal system. (See Part III of Appendix.) Stecchini concludes that the concern for precision in measurement and the understanding of geography upon which the system was originally based were greater the further back we look into the past.

Of all the indications of an advanced civilization before the dawn of history, some of the most dramatic have come from the study of Renaissance maps. There are several old maps from the early 1500s depicting Antarctica nearly 300 years before the continent was "discovered" in 1818. Even more unusual is the fact that some of these maps show Antarctica in an unglaciated condition. Analyses indicate the maps were copied, probably from copies of copies, based on originals whose origin is lost in another age of the earth.

The definitive study of the subject is *Maps of the Ancient Sea Kings* by Charles Hapgood. Hapgood demonstrates that even old maps that do not show Antarctica reveal surprising details. There is a map of the Mediterranean world attributed to Ibn Ben Zara and dated 1487. Hapgood believes this map to be far more accurate in depicting the longitude of certain places than was possible with the instruments available at the time. Although the determination of latitude (distance from the equator) is fairly simple, the determination of longitude (distance east or west of a base line) is much more difficult and requires more highly developed instruments. Hapgood has concluded that the accuracy of longitude on the Ibn Ben Zara

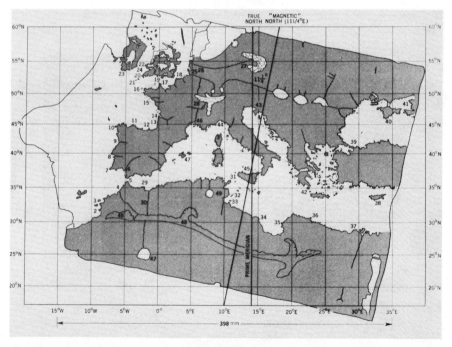

Construction of the Ibn Ben Zara map of 1487 on a square grid.

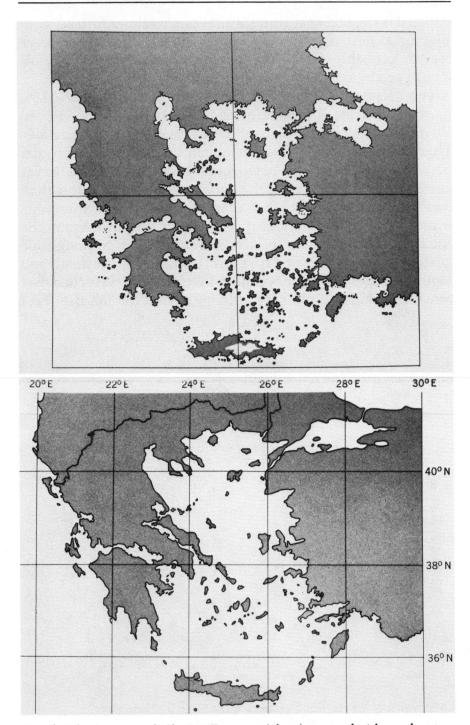

Detail of the Aegean on the Ibn Ben Zara map (above) compared with a modern map of the Aegean. The Ibn Ben Zara map shows many small islands no longer visible.

map could only have been possible with a chronometer invented about 1780, nearly 300 years after the map was drawn.

The extreme age of the source map from which the Ibn Ben Zara map was copied may be indicated by the water level shown in the Aegean; in some places it seems to be much lower than at present. The map shows many small islands no longer visible, and other islands significantly larger than their present size. The accuracy of its other features suggests that these are not simple errors. This map also shows minute indentations on coast lines representing the mouths of rivers. It shows a large bay at the mouth of the Guadalquiver River in southern Spain that has since become a delta about 30 miles (48 km) wide and 50 miles (80 km) long. Hapgood suggests it would have taken a small river like the Guadalquiver thousands of years to form such a large delta.

The famous Piri Reis map of 1513 shows many features of the western Atlantic and South America that, at that date, had not been discovered or explored, much less mapped. This map even shows a portion of the Antarctic coastline. However, Antarctica is not as clear or as extensive on the Piri Reis map as it is on other maps of the same era which for some reason have not received the same publicity. The Oronteus Finaeus world map of 1531 clearly shows a representation of the entire continent of Antarctica in an unglaciated condition.

Many Renaissance geographers were convinced of the existence of a southern continent around the pole, but their assumption, although correct, does not account for the level of accuracy of a map like the Oronteus Finaeus. The overall contours of the Antarctic coastline are surprisingly accurate and the map also shows mountain ranges and rivers which are now under ice more than a mile thick in places. Some of the features the map records were found only in 1957-1958 during the International Geophysical Year when sonic profiles were used to chart the subglacial topography of the polar continent. Hapgood says the chances of anyone accidentally getting as many features correct as those he has studied on the Finaeus map are less than one in a hundred million.

The greatest error in this map is that the continent is shown as too large, the sort of error, Hapgood says, that would result

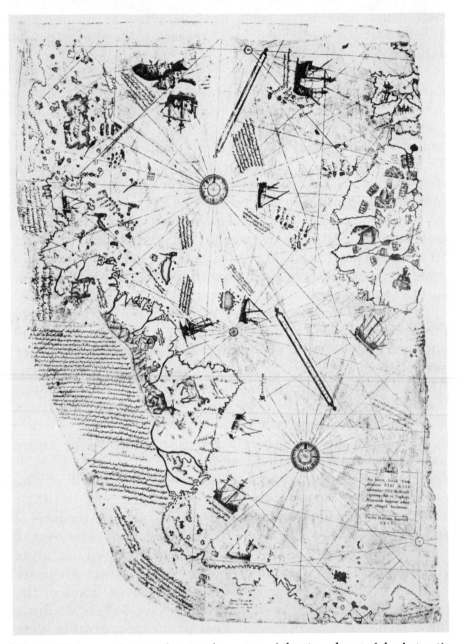

The Piri Reis map of 1513 showing the western Atlantic and part of the Antarctic coastline.

The Oronteus Finaeus map of 1531.

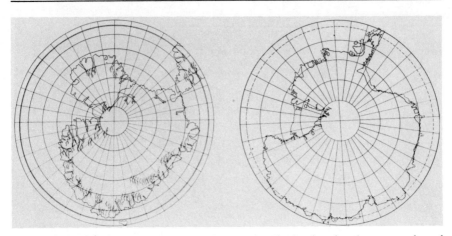

Antarctica on the Oronteus Finaeus map of 1531 (left) reduced to the same scale and grid as a modern map of Antarctica.

from a copyist mistaking the 80th parallel for the Antarctic Circle (66°33'). Another Renaissance map showing Antarctica is the 1538 world map of Gerardus Mercator. Mercator published a second world map in 1569 which was much less accurate than his earlier one. Hapgood suggests that Mercator relied more on the inaccurate reports of sixteenth century navigators in 1569 than on the source maps on which he based his 1538 production.

How long ago was Antarctica unglaciated and when were the original source maps produced? Some geologists believe the continent has been covered with ice for hundreds of thousands of years, but deep sea cores from the Ross Sea indicate it may have been ice free as little as 6000 years ago.

The cartographic matters Hapgood has brought to light do not rest upon one map or the work of one man. All of the maps are well authenticated. In 1961 Captain Burroughs, Chief of the United States Air Force Cartographic Section declared:

> It is our opinion that the accuracy of the cartographic features shown in the Oronteus Finaeus map suggests, beyond a doubt, that it also was compiled from accurate source maps of Antarctica.[28]

Reverend Daniel Lineham, who is a former director of the Weston Observatory of Boston College, a seismologist and cartographer with the U.S. Navy and who has participated in explorations in Antarctica, also studied these maps. So have

Richard Strachan, I.I. Walters, a cartographer with the U.S. Hydrographic Office, and A.H. Mallery, an authority on ancient maps. In 1956 a radio discussion of these maps took place in which the participants were Lineham, Walters and Mallery. A statement was made to the effect that it would seem impossible that the originals upon which the Piri Reis copies were based could have been produced without the aid of aerial surveys. If this is a serious possibility, it is certainly compounded in that these surveys must have taken place before the southern continent was covered by glaciers.

The implications of these maps can hardly be overestimated. Hapgood has concluded:

> The evidence presented by the ancient maps appears to suggest the existence in remote times, before the rise of any known cultures, of a true civilization of a comparatively advanced sort, which either was localized in one area but had a world-wide commerce, or was, in a real sense, a world-wide culture.

Hapgood has found that most of these maps are centered on Egypt and that cartographic science had been in decline over thousands of years until its revival several hundred years ago. Of course, a prehistoric world-wide civilization that made its last great input into Egypt is precisely what we have been in search of. As Hapgood modestly puts it, the prehistoric depiction of an unglaciated Antarctica on an old map "is no slight matter". It is almost like finding a map of Atlantis.

Three key geodetic measurements incorporated in the Great Pyramid, the reconstruction of ancient geography by Tompkins and Stecchini, and the maps of the ancient sea kings studied by Hapgood all complement and reinforce each other and point to the same conclusion – an international prehistoric civilization with a high geographic science.

There is also somewhat more circumstantial evidence pointing toward the same thing. In 1900 pieces of bronze and wood which had been fused together by the action of the sea were found on an ancient wreck off the Greek island of Antikythera. About sixty years later this fragile relic was cleaned, revealing a geared mechanism with inscriptions and directional indications. It took the work of several archaeologists to unravel its function. It turned out to be a mechanical model of the solar system, built like an ingenious and elaborate clock which was used to compute the motions of the sun, moon and planets. Its purpose and function have been authenticated by Dean Merritt, Professor Stais, George Stamires and Derek de Solla Price, and it has been dated at about 65 B.C. Nothing as sophisticated as this instrument was thought to exist at that time. It is not comparable to anything known from any literary or scientific text. On one occasion, Price said: "Finding a thing like this is like finding a jet plane in the tomb of King Tut."[29]

It is extremely unlikely that the Antikythera computer was one of a kind. This and similar instruments would also have had value as navigational aids in determining a ship's position at sea. There were large navies in the ancient world and there are many indications that much long distance travel took place. In the siege of Syracuse, 415-413 B.C., Athens sent 42,000 men on 134 triremes and 73 war galleys against the Sicilian port. In 480 B.C. over 1000 ships accompanied Xerxes' army in its attack on Greece. One wonders if hundreds of large ships with thousands of men simply went blundering around on the sea without navigational aids.

Inscriptions in Celtic Ogham and in Phoenician, Minoan and other ancient Mediterranean languages in the New World imply prehistoric transatlantic travel which was likely made possible with large ships, maps, instruments and a knowledge of distances. There are hundreds, perhaps thousands, of ancient inscriptions in Brazil, Venezuela, Colombia and the United States which have been identified with these languages. For example, Inscription Rock near Albuquerque, New Mexico has the Ten Commandments on it in Phoenician and has been known for decades.[30] Since the 1870s archaeologists have steadfastly maintained the theory that no European explorers crossed the Atlantic before Columbus. Until recently, all such inscriptions were dismissed as frauds – a position as convenient as it was sweeping since most American archaeologists did not have sufficient knowledge of the languages involved to know what they were looking at.

In 1885 an engraved stone was excavated from an "Indian mound" where Bat Creek joins the Little Tennessee River in Loudon County, Tennessee. It was uncovered by Cyrus Thomas excavating for the Smithsonian Institution and the engraving on the stone was published in a Smithsonian report in 1890. Thomas declared that the characters were "beyond question" letters of the Cherokee alphabet said to have been invented by George Guess about 1821.[31] Around 1964 writer and researcher Dr. Henriette Mertz pointed out that when publishing this stone, the Smithsonian had unknowingly inverted the inscription – leaving one to wonder if Thomas also saw it upside down. When read right side up, the inscription, according to Dr. Cyrus Gordon of Brandeis University, turns out to be Canaanite (a language closely related to Phoenician), reading: "for Jehu".[32]

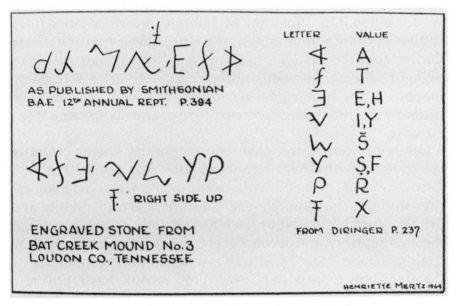

Ancient inscription reading "for Jehu" discovered at Bat Creek.

Through the work of researchers like Mertz, Gordon and Harvard professor H.B. Fell, the entire nature of prehistoric America is now open to radical reinterpretation. In 1976 Fell's *America B.C.* was published in which he convincingly documents Old World inscriptions, languages and alphabets in the Americas. Fell's range of evidence and considerable scholarship eliminate fraud as an explanation. He has deciphered inscriptions indicating Phoenicians, Celtic Iberians and Libyans had early and numerous contacts with the western hemisphere.

There is now sound archaeological evidence indicating not only substantial prehistoric transatlantic travel, but good reason to raise on yet another front the possibility of an earlier connecting culture between the hemispheres – such as Atlantis. In any case, it is well documented that the Phoenicians and their colonies enjoyed an enduring naval dominance in Mediterranean and Atlantic waters and long maintained secret trading routes. The range of their travels and the duration of their supremacy both suggest that Phoenician navigators must have known where they were going with considerable reliability.

Another suggestion of long range prehistoric travel surfaced in 1952 when B.E. Gilbey and M. Lubran performed blood tests on tissues of Inca mummies in the British Museum. The tests showed that the tissues came from men who did not appear to belong to the native population of South America,[33] possibly supporting the Inca legend attributing the high civilization of ancient Peru to bearded white culture bearers who came from the east.

Ominous indications that contemporary science is only rediscovering what was known in past ages comes from the discovery of patches of vitrified sand and rock at archaeological sites in Peru, the Gobi Desert, California, Iraq, Palestine and Britain. Vitrification occurs when sand and rock are heated to the melting point and become glass, as has happened at nuclear testing sites in New Mexico, Nevada and northern China. A skeleton with radioactivity fifty times normal has reportedly been exhumed in India.[34] Sanskrit texts describe a weapon whose power and destructive effects sound much like those of a thermonuclear device:

> A single projectile charged with all the power of the universe. An incandescent column of smoke and flame, as bright as ten thousand suns, rose in all its splendor ... It was an unknown weapon, an iron thunderbolt, a gigantic messenger of death which reduced to ashes the entire race of the Vrishnis and Andhakas ... The corpses were so burned as to be unrecognizable. Their hair and nails fell out; pottery broke without any apparent cause, and the birds turned white. After a few hours, all foodstuffs were infected.
> ... To escape from this fire the soldiers threw themselves in streams to wash themselves and all their equipment ... [35]

The most revolutionary theory of history is also the oldest: there is nothing new under the sun. Men with knowledge and technical abilities equal to or surpassing ours have been on the earth for countless thousands of years. Surveying these discoveries and reports, it is not difficult to imagine ourselves back home in Poseidia – a Poseidia inhabited by people disconcertingly like ourselves.

The Great Decline

Beauty, it is said, is in the eye of the beholder. So is evidence for Atlantis. For some, the reports we have seen will be enough to establish the Atlantis hypothesis as a serious probability. For others, there will never be enough evidence. For many, the idea of a high prehistoric civilization that vanished in a catastrophe is too upsetting because it implies that science and technology are not in themselves enough to preserve our own civilization, any more than they were of old. With the example of Atlantis before us, life in our own rapidly changing times seems to become even more uncertain.

Ever since Darwinism took hold, the standard teaching has been that man progressed from barbarism to civilization during the last eight to ten thousand years. There is, of course, ample evidence that many peoples all over the world lived in primitive conditions for long periods of time. But not everyone did. For those who wish to follow it, there is a great broad path leading to the prehistoric horizon marked by giant and enduring remains whose significance is not dependent upon clever academic theories, but only upon the evidence of our eyes. The strangest thing about this path is that as it approaches the present from the past, it is not a long climb upward but a great and troublesome decline.

The simplest and grandest testimonies of ancient abilities are the giant stone structures and sculptures scattered around the earth – many of which western man cannot match today. One of the most impressive of these is the great fortress or wall of

Sacsayhuaman near Cuzco, Peru. Many of the stones in this wall weigh 100 to 300 tons. They fit together so perfectly that a razor blade cannot be inserted between them, yet the blocks are capriciously cut with as many as twelve butting faces, each of which fits its neighbor precisely. This wall is of unknown age, attributed only to pre-Inca peoples. Professional masons declare they cannot now match the work in this wall, even with modern equipment.

The achievement of the ancient builders can also be measured by the endurance of their structures. Within the city of Cuzco are somewhat smaller pre-Inca walls, now forming the foundations for many modern buildings and homes. In 1950 a major earthquake in Cuzco destroyed or damaged 90 percent of the modern structures. None of the ancient walls in the vicinity was even cracked. Possibly they were designed to be earthquake-proof because of past experience.

Peru has an abundance of cyclopean masonry. Other major remains showing the same technical expertise are found at Ollantaytambo, where 150 to 200 ton blocks perch on top of a 1500 foot (457 meter) cliff. At Machu Picchu, a "lost city" until 1911, facilities for an entire community cover a mountain top

The great wall of Sacsayhuaman near Cuzco, Peru.

Four hundred and forty ton cut stone, Sacsayhuaman, Peru.

amid remote and inaccessible terrain. In Bolivia, at Tiahuanaco near Lake Titicaca, 100 to 200 ton blocks are found in a huge prehistoric complex at an altitude of over 13,000 feet (3960 meters). Originally, the walls of this complex were held together with silver tenons which were removed by the Spaniards, causing the walls to collapse in subsequent earthquakes. As Charles Berlitz has noted, 13,000 feet "is too high for corn to grow, for cats to live, for white women to give birth, and certainly too high for a population large enough to have built and carved the enormous stones that comprise the city."[1] At least it is too high for them to have done this through any means we can document today. A strong possibility suggested by many writers is that the entire area of Lake Titicaca has been upheaved many thousands of feet since the city was built.

Traces of the same extraordinary ability to handle huge blocks of stone are found far and wide. The Black Pagoda in India is 228 feet (69 meters) high, capped with a single massive slab of stone reportedly 25 feet (7.6 meters) thick and estimated to weigh over 1000 tons. At Baalbek in eastern Lebanon the platform of the Temple of Jupiter contains three massive blocks

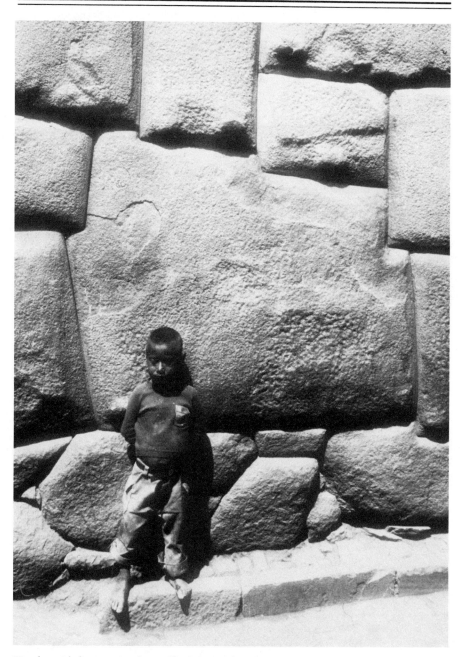

Twelve sided stone in the wall of Sacsayhuaman.

65 x 12 x 15 feet (19.8 x 3.6 x 4.5 meters) that weigh 750 tons
each. It is likely that the present temple was built over an older
site that included these blocks. Another block, perfectly cut,
but still resting in a nearby quarry, is estimated to weigh 2000
tons.

Remains of cyclopean masonry are found around the
Mediterranean basin, some of which, such as the massive

*Prehistoric "earthquake walls" in Cuzco, on top of which contemporary buildings
have been built.*

*Giant stones at Ollantaytambo, Peru. Note the reclining figure on the right for
scale.*

Machu Picchu, high in the Peruvian Andes. Note terracing on top of the central peak.

Stonework at Machu Picchu.

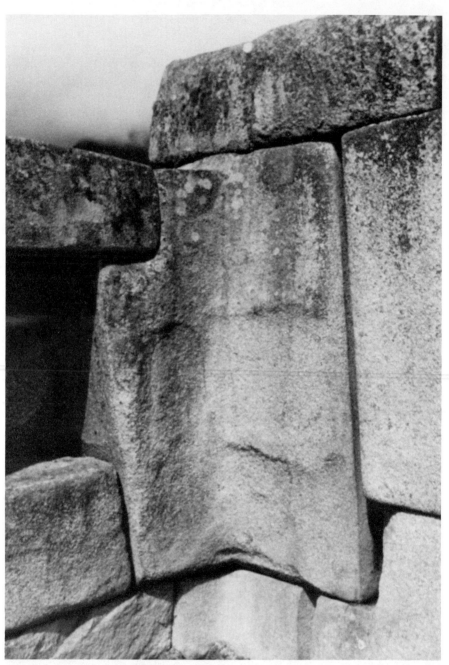

Interior corner of a temple, Machu Picchu, Peru.

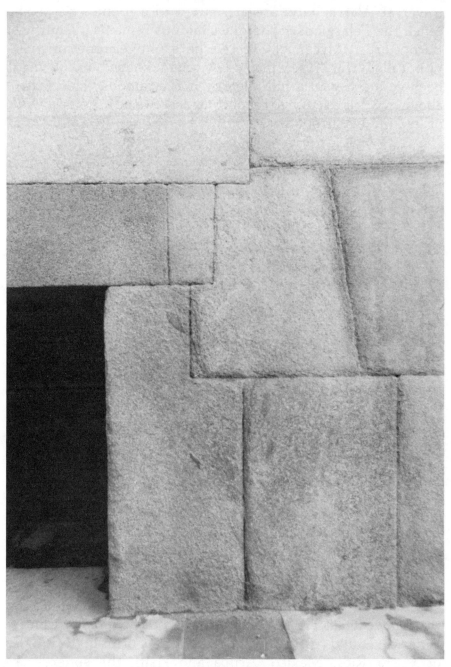

Masonry in the Valley Temple at Gizeh, showing a style similar to that found at Machu Picchu, Cuzco, other sites in Peru, and Easter Island.

tower at Alatri, Italy, are attributed to a prehistoric people called the Pelasgians.[2] The most famous remains in southern Europe are at Mycenae, Greece where a huge stone construction called the "Treasury of Atreus", shaped like a giant beehive, nestles in a hill. Nearby is the famous "Lion Gate", above which is a sculpted relief considered to be the oldest work of its kind in Europe.

Treasury of Atreus, Mycenae, Greece.

At La Venta, Tres Zapotes, and other sites in Mexico are giant stone heads attributed to the Olmecs, thought to be the oldest culture in the area. Carved from black basalt, the heads are 4.5 to 10 feet (1.4 to 3 meters) high and 5 to 40 tons in weight. The nearest basalt quarries are 30 to 60 miles (48 to 96 km) away through swamps and jungles. Somewhat similar to the Olmec heads are the mysterious stone spheres of Central America. Found resting on small stone platforms in the jungles of Costa Rica, Mexico, Aruba and Haiti, the spheres are perfectly formed and vary in size from a few inches up to 7 feet (2.1 meters) in diameter. They weigh as much as 16 tons. No one knows how old they are, who sculpted them, or what purpose they served.

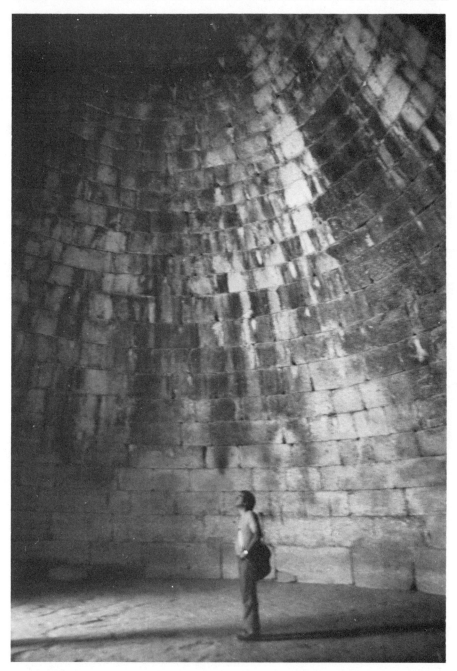

"Beehive construction" inside Treasury of Atreus, Mycenae, Greece.

Lion Gate, Mycenae, Greece.

Giant Olmec head, Villa Hermosa, Mexico.

The Caracol, a Mayan observatory, Chichen Itza, Mexico.

Stepped pyramid, Chichen Itza, Mexico.

All over the earth the pattern is the same. The oldest stone remains are generally the largest and the most perfectly executed, and this pattern is repeated in the case of prehistoric earthworks. In many countries giant prehistoric landscaping projects were carried out on a scale and executed with an elegance belying the notion that these were the works of primitive man. It is little known that a surprising number of these earthworks are found in North America. Despite the hundreds of institutions of higher learning in the United States and Canada, it is a curious fact that North American archaeology is a much neglected field, possibly because of a lingering embarrassment over the treatment of the Indians and a consequent reluctance to probe more deeply into their origins.

Great numbers of artificial mounds and earth-walled enclosures in the United States were destroyed by plunderers or by not-so-scientific nineteenth century excavators hunting buried artifacts. Countless others were obliterated by the plow and by land development. Often the best records we have of what they looked like are illustrations produced in the last century. The most famous remaining earthwork in America is

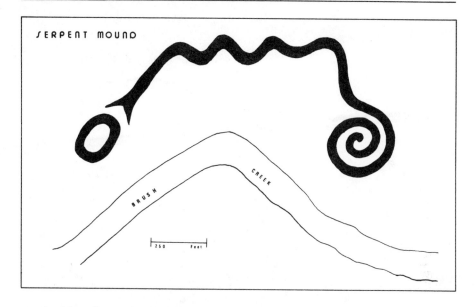

SERPENT MOUND

BRUSH CREEK

250 Feet

probably the great Serpent Mound, 1348 feet (410 meters) long, near Brush Creek, Ohio. In Ross and Licking counties in Ohio are huge complexes of squares, circles, octagons and parallel walls covering many square miles. The circles are 20, 30 and 40 acres in area with diameters up to 1720 feet (524 meters). There are parallel "roadways" 2.5 miles (4 km) long.[3] Tens of thousands of smaller mounds related to the same culture cover hundreds of square miles in the Ohio and Mississippi Valleys. At Poverty Point on the banks of the Arkansas River are the remains of six geometrically perfect concentric octagons, three quarters of a mile (1.2 km) in diameter. The octagons are formed by embankments presently 4 to 6 feet (1.2 to 1.8 meters) high and 80 feet (24 meters) wide. The construction of these embankments required moving 500,000 cubic yards of earth. Over the centuries, part of these octagons has been lost to river erosion.

These carefully conceived, large scale geometric forms imply mathematical and engineering abilities considerably beyond those of the Indians of three or four hundred years ago. Excavation has sometimes produced evidence showing that the builders were racially identical to the Indians, but when questioned by early settlers, even the oldest chiefs time and again denied any knowledge of the builders. Many of the "Indian mounds" were once thought to date from A.D. 500 to

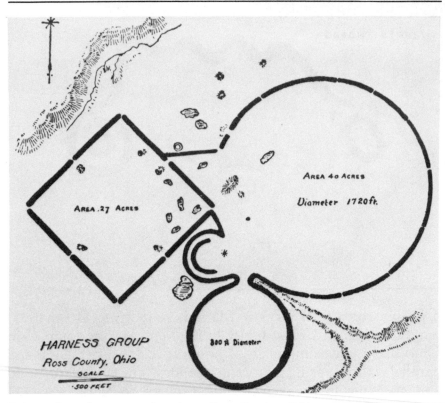

Large scale prehistoric earthworks in Ross County, Ohio.

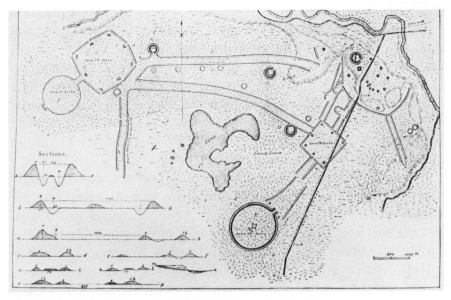

Complex of prehistoric earthworks near Newark, Ohio.

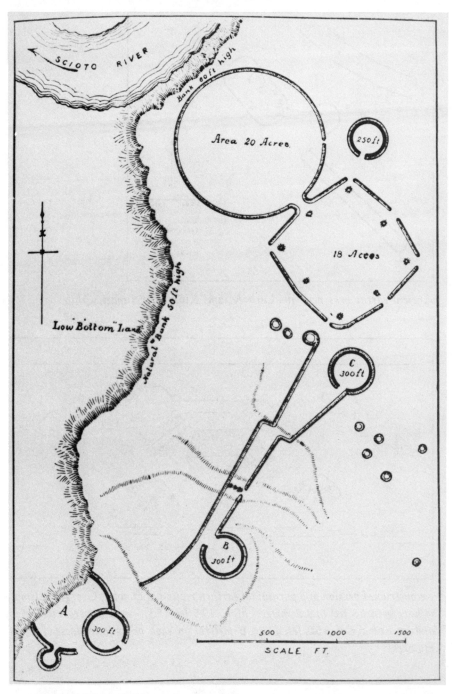

Prehistoric earthworks, Ross County, Ohio.

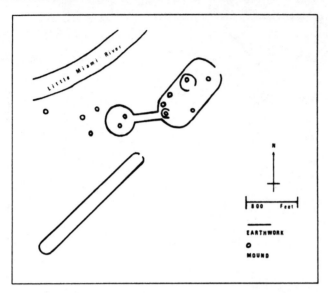

Ancient earthworks near the Little Miami River, Cincinnati, Ohio.

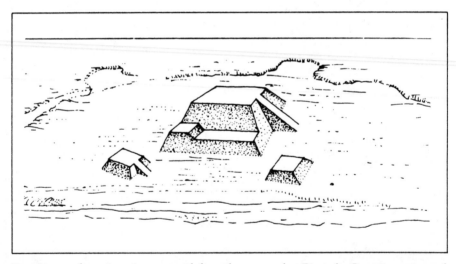

Reconstructed version of a pyramidal earthen mound at Etowah, Georgia, estimated to have been 63 feet (19.2 meters) high, 175 feet (53.3 meters) across its flat top, and an average of 350 feet (106.6 meters) on each of its four sides. (Jacquetta Hawkes)

1500, but while there may have been occupation of some of the sites during that period, carbon dating has pushed the age of others back to 2000 to 7300 B.C.[4] We are left with the possibilities that the earthworks were built by men racially identical to but culturally different from the Indians, or that the cultural peak the earthworks represent took place so far in the past that – even if they were built by ancestors of the Indians – thousands of years and gradually deteriorating circumstances caused them to lose all record of those events.

England also has a large number of prehistoric earthworks. Some are called "rings"; these are large concentric moats and banks somewhat similar to the Ohio Valley earthworks, but without a precise geometric design. The largest of these rings is called Maiden Castle; it encloses 120 acres. A smaller site, but one which has been called "the largest prehistoric temple in Europe", is located about 18 miles (28 km) north of Stonehenge, in Avebury. Here there is a circular earthwork 1400 feet (426 meters) in diameter marked by a moat and bank 55 feet (16 meters) from top to bottom. Inside the moat and bank, a circle of huge stones marked the inner edge of the area. Nearby, a mile or two to the southeast, is Silbury Hill. It is the largest

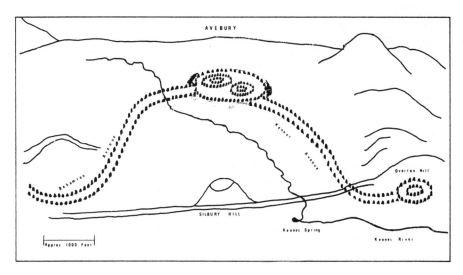

Sketch of the original configuration of the Avebury complex in England, showing its similarity to the Serpent Mound in Ohio. Most of the large monolithic stones that formed the pattern were broken up and used for building material in the eighteenth century.

Giant prehistoric earthwork known as "Maiden Castle" southwest of Dorchester. Hatch marks indicate the course of Roman roads in the area.

Avebury, with Silbury Hill in the distance.

Silbury Hill, the largest artificial mound in Europe.

A small artificial mound known as Bryn Celli Ddu, in Anglesey, northwest Wales.

Old Sarum earthworks, southeast of Stonehenge.

artificial mound in Europe, measuring 130 feet (40 meters) high and covering 5.25 acres. Maiden Castle, Avebury and Silbury Hill are the largest of thousands of earthworks in the British Isles. Dates around 1500 to 2000 B.C. have been suggested for most of these remains, but there is little conclusive evidence to determine their true age and purpose, or who built them.

In addition to their number, size and the mystery surrounding them, the most remarkable fact about many ancient British sites is that they are aligned with each other over many miles and in some cases were intentionally located at even intervals from each other. As impressive as many of these remains are individually, their greater significance is that they are part of a larger system which once again could not have been conceived

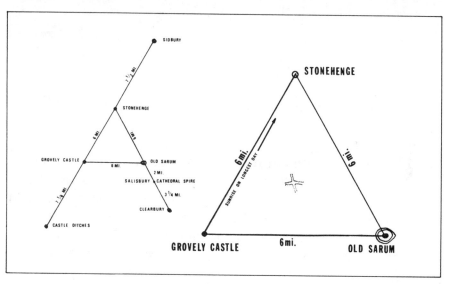

The relationship of major ancient sites in the vicinity of Stonehenge. The figure showing the Stonehenge – Grovely Castle – Old Sarum triangle in detail also shows that the oldest crossroads on the Salisbury Plain occupy the center of the triangle and that the orientation between Grovely Castle and Stonehenge is the same as the axis of Stonehenge. (After Lockyer.)

Alignment of ancient mounds at Winterbourne Crossroads, near Stonehenge.

and executed without considerable geographic, astronomic and engineering abilities.[5]

The prehistoric often lurks beneath the veneer of the historic. Many of the pyramids in Mexico and the Yucatan are actually a series of larger pyramids built directly around and entirely enclosing smaller, older pyramids beneath them. In some cases the last, largest and most recent layer has been estimated to be one to two thousand years old, but we have little idea of the age of the first small structures that set the pattern.

Similarly, there are indications that a prehistoric road system exists beneath the layer of Roman roads in Britain. The Romans developed a very extensive road system throughout England and the standard account of this is that it was purely a Roman product. However, we know the Romans came to Britain in A.D. 43 and ancient dated travel itineraries imply that the major elements of the network were in place by A.D. 47 to 50[6] – an almost impossible rate of road building, considering the size of the system. The relation of some supposedly Roman roads to much older earthworks creates the distinct possibility that the Romans inherited a vast pre-existing network which they merely resurfaced. For example, just south of Steep Hill in Lincoln, Lincolnshire, excavation of a Roman road revealed four distinct layers of material:[7]

15 inches of broken surface stone,
15 inches of rough stony soil,
 8 inches of concrete,
18 inches of additional embankment material.

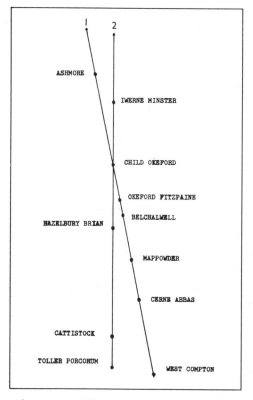

Alignments of Dorsetshire churches. Old parish churches were frequently placed on sites sacred to the preceding order. It is approximately 25 miles (40 km) from Ashmore to West Compton. (After Michell.)

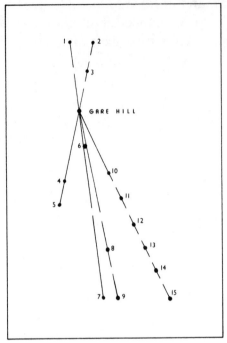

Alignments of ancient sites in Britain.
Convergence of alignments on Gare Hill, Wiltshire. (After Michell.)

Many churches and cathedrals in England were built directly over prehistoric sites, thus preserving ancient alignment patterns. A line connecting Glastonbury Abbey and Stonehenge passes through Gare Hill, which is itself marked by a church dedicated to St. Michael. Lines connecting Woodhenge and Wells Cathedral also pass through or terminate here. The enumerated elements are as follows:

1. *Glastonbury Abbey*
2. *Wells Cathedral*
3. *Witham Friary*
4. *Artificial mound*
5. *Roman temple on pre-Roman earthwork*
6. *Old priory*
7. *Stonehenge*
8. *The Cursus, a linear earthwork*
9. *Woodhenge*
10. *Horningsham Church*
11. *Crocketon Church*
12. *Bishopstrow Church*
13. *The center of Scratchbury Hill Fort, an ancient earthwork*
14. *Artificial mound*
15. *Tilshead Church*

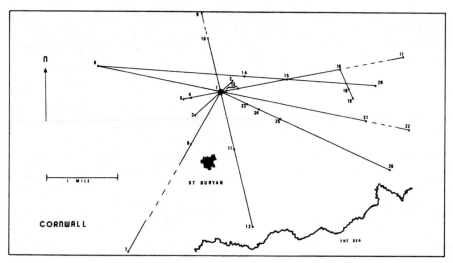

Radiating pattern of alignments formed by megalithic remains near St. Buryan, Cornwall.

1. "Boscawen-un" stone circle
2. Large standing stone
3. Minor stone
4. Standing stone
5. Standing stone
6. Standing stone at Trevorgans
7. Stone cross
8. Large standing stone
9. Artificial mound
10. Stone cross
11. Stone cross
12. Stone cross
13. Stretch of old road
14. Standing stone
15. Stone cross
16. Tresvannack Pillar (11'6" or 3.5 meter standing stone)
17. St. Piran Church, Perranuthnoe
18. Standing stone
19. Standing stone
20. Standing stone
21. Standing stone
22. St. Clements Isle
23. Standing stone on high ground
24. Prominent standing stone
25. Large erected boulder
26. Standing stone with "cup marks"

Ancient radiating pattern in the landscape near Radley, Berkshire, similar to the alignment patterns elsewhere in England. Research has shown the roads, hedgerows, public footpaths and crop marks in England often indicate prehistoric patterns that have endured for centuries.

The eight inches of concrete and the embankment appear to be a pre-Roman causeway. Nearby, the layer of concrete is 10 to 14 inches (25.4 to 35.5 cm) thick, and is described as "very hard". It is well established that the oldest elements in the ancient English road system are also those showing the greatest engineering ability. The earliest parts of the network are high raised embankments, once paved, which run dead straight for miles. Excavation has shown that the narrower, simpler, meandering parts of the system were added later. Aside from the possibility that the roads may have first been built by the ancient Celts, who were reputedly excellent charioteers and would have required good roads, there is again little to suggest how old the roads are or who built them.

As extensive as the old road system in England was, neither the Celts, nor the Britons nor the Romans ever equaled the great Inca road. Stretching some 3250 miles (5230 km) from Quito, Ecuador to Chile, this road is one of the great feats of prehistoric engineering. In the words of A.H. Verrill:

> The highest ranges of the mighty Andes, the deepest, most impassable canyons, the most fearful precipices, the widest deserts, the snow-capped peaks and the foaming torrents were treated as though non-existent. Vast abysses were spanned by suspension bridges, their immense cables of fiber and hair ropes fastened in holes cut through solid rock. Gorges were filled with masonry to form immense causeways. Mountains and cliffs were pierced by tunnels which are still in use. The loftiest ranges were surmounted by the most perfectly computed gradients and hairpin curves, and throughout much of its length the roadway was paved and surfaced with asphalt, and to this day some portions of it are still used as a motor highway.[8]

The scale of the work sounds almost like the accomplishment of the Atlanteans described by Plato, and as more and more signs of great abilities emerge from Peru, one cannot help but think of Cayce's statement that Peru, along with Egypt and the Yucatan, was one of the principal areas of Atlantean immigration.

Another extraordinary feat of prehistoric engineering was discovered in Peru in recent times. Aerial photographs led to the uncovering of a gigantic network of lines and figures cut

The megalithic builders of the British Isles also left large stone constructions called "dolmens" which served unknown purposes. This dolmen is in Wales.

One of the largest dolmens in Europe, now partially collapsed, at Browne's Hill, County Carlow, Ireland. The capstone is estimated to weigh 100 tons.

The course of an ancient road from Badbury Rings to Dorchester reflected in the landscape.

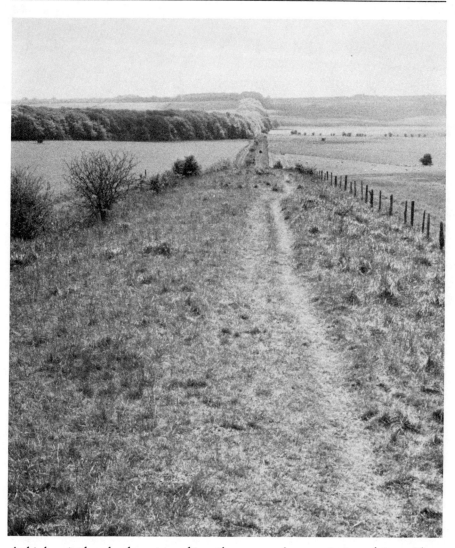

A high raised embankment marking the course of an ancient road in southern England.

The course of an ancient road north of Stamford, Rutland, indicated by a crop mark.

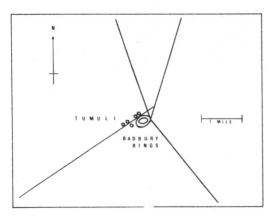

The course of ancient roadways convergent upon Badbury Rings. The relationship of supposedly Roman roads to earthworks many centuries older suggests the roads themselves may have existed in pre-Roman times and were only resurfaced by the Romans.

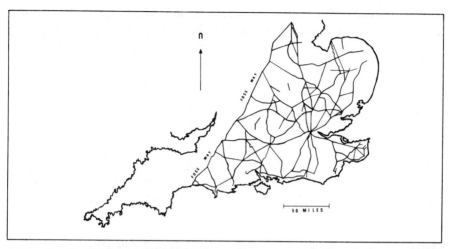

Major Roman roads in southeast Britain. *(After Margary.)*
Roman travel itineraries indicate the main features of this extensive network were
already in place by A.D. 47-50. The Romans entered Britain in A.D. 43.

High altitude photograph of Badbury Rings earthwork. The courses of ancient
roads, long thought to be Roman, are indicated by hatch marks as they converge on
the site.

into the surface of the desert near Nazca. This huge, integrated system of ground drawings covers about 100 square miles (258 square km). The exploration and documentation of this enormous site was accomplished mostly by a lone woman, mathematician and geographer Maria Reiche, who worked for nearly three decades in the Peruvian desert uncovering, photographing and mapping the complex. She has described the site in *Mystery on the Desert* and *Peruvian Ground Drawings*.

Reiche has tentatively dated the site at about A.D. 525 but this is derived from carbon dating a single wooden post found on the location. As with the dating of many other ancient sites,

Prehistoric markings on the Peruvian desert near Nazca. The area shown is roughly 3000 feet (910 meters) from left to right.

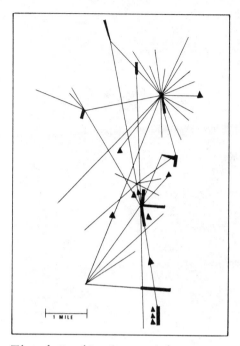

The relationship of some of the geometric forms, lines and radiating centers in a minor portion of the Peruvian desert complex. The triangles represent animal figures or giant spirals. The actual patterns are more dense and complex than this illustration indicates and cannot easily be represented on this scale. (After Reiche.)

The width and depth of the lines on the desert.

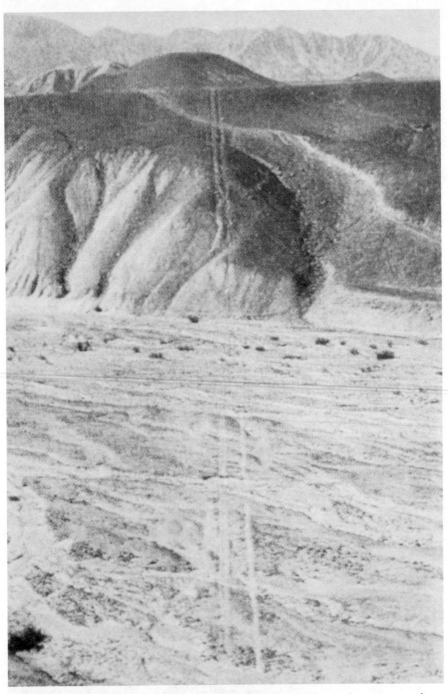

Remarkable ancient lines on the Peruvian desert, running straight up a steep slope.

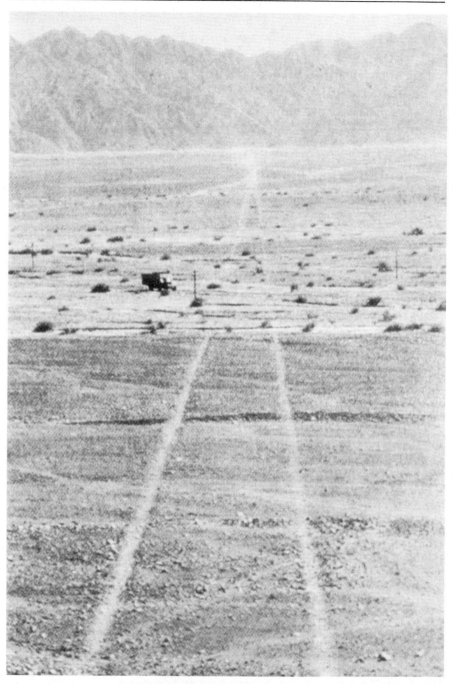

Ancient parallel lines crossing the Pan American highway in the Peruvian desert. They are about 1.5 miles (2.4 km) long and begin at a small hill. Fifty other lines begin at the same hill, radiating in different directions, each ending at another line, a delineated surface, a figure, or another radiating center.

the problem is that we have no way of knowing whether the dated object, in this case one post in a 100 square mile area, was part of the original construction or later imported to the site, possibly thousands of years after it was designed.

Clues to the purpose of the site are no clearer. Some of the lines in the network point to solstice positions of the sun, for example, to where it sets on the twenty-first of December. This suggests a connection with astronomy and calendar science, but it is a far from comprehensive explanation since only a few of the thousands of lines indicate astronomically significant points on the horizon. Aside from these questionable indications, it is the same old refrain – we don't know its age, who built it or why.

Much of the interest in Reiche's work was preempted by Erich von Däniken's sensational exploitation of some Nazca photographs; he claimed that they showed landing strips used by extraterrestrial visitors who colonized the earth. On aerial photographs, elements of the network do indeed look like landing strips, but the ground is too soft to have served that purpose and some of these "landing strips" are on uneven terrain. Now that the dust has settled, this huge network is as much of a mystery as ever.

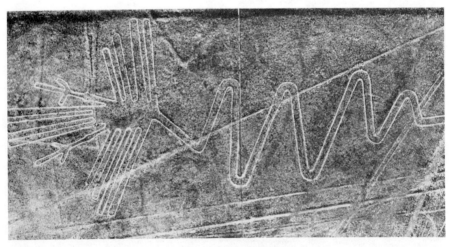

This part of a birdlike figure is over 400 feet (120 meters) long. The head lies to the right of the long snakelike neck. The bird's bill, not shown here, is longer than the rest of the body and points in a solstice direction. The diagonal line crosses another bird figure 1.5 miles (2.4 km) distant.

Some of the lines in the network go straight up mountain sides; others run dead straight over a distance of 5 miles (8 km). Intermingled in this network are huge rectangles, (the so-called landing fields), triangles and spirals as well as giant drawings of birds, spiders, monkeys and lizards. The animal forms are executed with a single continuous line that never crosses itself, strangely like a neon light circuit in a huge sign.

It had long been known that there were some sort of prehistoric remains in the area. They were thought to be Inca highways or traces of an irrigation system. It was not until the 1930s when the area was first flown over, that part of the network was recognized as something else. Practically everyone commenting on it has wondered what could have motivated people to produce figures and patterns that can be seen only from the air unless they themselves could fly. It is also a legitimate question whether this vast site could have been planned and constructed without that ability. Reiche has come to the conclusion that the builders must have had instruments and techniques of which we are ignorant. It seems clear that the Incas of the sixteenth century were also ignorant of these instruments and techniques.

Occasionally the decline of a people may be traced more closely. In the 1950s early Eskimo settlements and burials were excavated near Point Barrow in Alaska. At the time, it was thought that these were the earliest Eskimo remains to have been discovered. According to T.C. Lethbridge in *The Legend of the Sons of God*, these arctic hunters were without peer in making beautiful flint implements. Yet Lethbridge suggests that their carvings in ivory clearly showed that they had once been well acquainted with the use of metal. Lethbridge describes carved chains of interlocking rings and other designs that, according to him, were obviously copied from metalwork. At the same site, a few tiny tools were also found, one of which still had a minute metal blade. Lethbridge concluded that this people had been forced to take up flint after they had in some way been cut off from the basis of their metal culture.

In terms of higher cultural attainments, the aboriginal peoples of Africa, Australia and the Americas were in relatively primitive conditions when they were intercepted by European expansion 100 to 500 years ago. Yet even according to their

A spider 150 feet (46 meters) long, executed with a single continuous line.

own traditions, they were long degenerate and had fallen into a low condition. Almost invariably, they were conscious of powers and abilities they had lost. It is a strong argument against conventional notions of evolution that nowhere have we seen such peoples rise by their own efforts toward higher civilization. Instead, we find the opposite. When they first came into contact with European influence, their condition was not as advanced as that of their predecessors who, thousands of years earlier, had produced great works which are still visible today.

There is a worldwide prehistoric pattern directly contradicting the idea that man evolved from semi-barbarism in the last 8000 years. It shows instead that scientific, artistic and engineering accomplishments are often greater, the further back in time we go. Two great questions then arise. What was the source of these civilizations? What caused their decline?

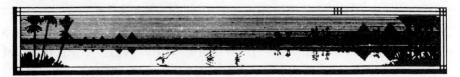

16

Teaching of the Old Priest

The legends of humanity the world over are remarkably consistent in describing the oldest peoples and nations as having what seemed godlike powers. Consistently we hear of vanished nations and gods who could travel and build at will, who lived in another age of the earth terminated by disaster, and who set cultural patterns that endured for thousands of years. Long considered by western anthropologists as the fantasies of children, the substance of the ancient legends has been increasingly supported by discoveries in many fields.

Still the most famous and valuable account in the western tradition is the information provided by Plato (427-347 B.C.) in the dialogues *Critias* and *Timaeus.* He described Atlantis as an exotic, large, powerful and extremely wealthy island kingdom in the Atlantic. Plato derived his report from his ancestor Solon, the Greek lawgiver, who was several generations older. Solon, in turn, received his information from the priests of Sais in Egypt, who claimed to have very ancient records.

The founder of the Atlantean kingdom was said to be Poseidon, who had five sets of male twins by a maid named Cleito. Beginning with his eldest son, Atlas, Poseidon divided the island into ten regions, giving a region to each son. The successors of these ten are said to have ruled Atlantis for many generations and to have been men of virtue. Plato goes on to describe giant landscape projects carried out on Atlantis, creating alternate zones of sea and land around a sacred hill which became the center of the kingdom. He tells of a great temple "having a strange and barbaric appearance", over 600 feet (182 meters) long and 300 feet (91 meters) wide, entirely covered with silver and gold.

The Atlanteans were renowned for countless years as men who valued virtue more than gold, but as the divine element in them gradually grew weaker, they degenerated, eventually engaging in aggressive military adventures against the ancient Athenians and other Mediterranean peoples. The Athenians, according to Plato, successfully resisted the great empire, which shortly thereafter disappeared into the sea in enormous earthquakes which produced huge floods of water and mud. It is said the sea there became impassable due to the mud created by the subsidence – a reputation similar to that of the Sargasso Sea until recent times. Plato dated the subsidence of Atlantis 9000 years before Solon.

Plato's description of massive engineering feats by the Atlanteans is consistent with the claims made for Atlantean civilization in the Cayce transcripts and suggests a cultural pattern that merges organically with the phenomenon that the biggest and most finely executed prehistoric remains are generally also the oldest. A further correspondence is that Plato's name for the founding king, Poseidon, is reflected in the transcripts' name for the last remaining major island – Poseidia.

Plato was not the only writer of classical times to describe Atlantis. In that era, the belief in the former existence of Atlantis was widely accepted, and it was often referred to as Poseidonis after Poseidon, the founding king. The writings of Krantor (fourth century B.C.), Marcelinus (A.D. 330-395), Proclus (A.D. 410-485), Timagenes (first century B.C.), Diodorus Siculus (first century B.C.), Tertullian (A.D. 160-240), Philo Judaeus (20 B.C.-A.D. 40) and Arnobius Afer (third century A.D.), all contain references to the great land that had sunk in the Atlantic.[1]

Proclus mentioned a Greek historian, Marcellus (Aethiopiaka), whose report of Atlantis was older than Plato's and thus an independent confirmation. Marcellus wrote:

> The inhabitants of this island [probably one of the Canary Islands] had preserved the memory handed down to them of Atlantis, the largest of the islands situated here, which, in the

course of many centuries, dominated over all of the Outer Sea and also was dedicated to Poseidon.[2]

Physical evidence for a sunken continent in the Atlantic and the Caribbean is mounting. Lava particles taken from the ocean floor near the Azores at a depth of two miles (3.2 km) have the appearance of lava that formed in the open air. These particles have a vitreous structure, whereas lava that has solidified under water has a crystalline structure. Since lava decomposes considerably in 15,000 years, the area from which these particles were taken must have been above water within that period of time. French geologist Pierre Termier surmised from the condition of the lava that it had been submerged soon after cooling. Termier believed that "the entire region north of the Azores and perhaps the very region of the Azores ... was very recently submerged, probably during the epoch which the geologists call the present."[3]

A report made to the USSR Academy of Science by Dr. M. Klionova in 1963 confirms that possibility. Rocks taken 60 miles (96 km) north of the Azores from a depth of 6600 feet (2011 meters) showed evidence of having been exposed to the atmosphere in approximately 15,000 B.C. Similarly, sedimentary material culled by oceanographers from the mid-Atlantic ridge showed the "exclusive presence" of remains of fresh water plants, indicating that part of the ridge had once been above sea level.

Further evidence of the submergence of the mid-Atlantic ridge is seen in the presence of beach sand on underwater shelves in the area of the Azores. These shelves are sometimes thousands of feet deep, whereas beach sand is formed only in shallow water along coastlines and is not normally found at great depths.[4]

Evidence of massive seismic subsidence has also been found in the Caribbean and the Gulf of Mexico. In 1969 a Duke University research team took granite from 50 sites along the Aves Ridge north of Venezuela. This granite was a light granitic or acid igneous rock, a type indigenous to continents. The crust of the earth beneath the sea is composed of heavier, dark-colored basaltic rock. Dr. Bruce Heezen of the Lamont Geological Observatory commented: "The occurrence of light-colored granitic rocks may support an old theory that a continent formerly existed in the region of the eastern Caribbean and that these rocks may represent the core of a subsided, lost continent." To the north, hydrographic surveys by the U.S. Geological Survey off the Florida Keys revealed 400 foot (121 meter) depressions in a shelf 500 feet (152 meters) under water. These are "presumed to have been fresh water lakes in areas which subsided."[5]

Near Andros Island, the largest in the Bahamas, underwater explorer Jacques Cousteau found a huge submerged grotto 165 feet (50 meters) beneath the surface. In the grotto are stalactites and stalagmites, which can be formed only in the open air. Marine sediments on the walls of the grotto enabled scientists to estimate that it was submerged around 10,000 B.C.[6]

Further to the west, Cousteau explored the famous "Blue Hole" off the coast of Belize. He found a series of underwater caves which also contained stalactites and stalagmites, but

Pillars on the floor of the ocean at a depth of 6000 feet (1828 meters) 55 miles (88 km) off the coast of Peru. The arrow points to archaic writing.

these were slanted from vertical, indicating the area had been profoundly displaced by earthquakes. An estimate as to when these caves were last above water again produced a date around 10,000 B.C.[7] These dates coincide with Plato's submergence date of 9600 B.C.

On the Lemurian side of the question, the oceanographic vessel *Anton Brunn* photographed upright pillars protruding from the mud on the floor of the Pacific Ocean at a depth of 6000 feet (1828 meters) while searching for specimens of a small sea mollusk 55 miles (88 km) off the coast of Peru. The pillars are estimated to be over 2 feet (60 cm) in diameter and to extend 5 feet (1.5 meters) out of the floor. Other nearby pillars were recumbent. A photograph shows that one of these upright pillars has a glyph on it – an archaic form of writing.

In the *Timaeus* Plato also recorded a conversation between Solon and a priest of Sais "of very great age". Solon had been describing the antiquity of his lineage, when the old priest told him that he and the rest of the Hellenes were but children when it came to understanding antiquity. "There have been, and there will be again, many destructions of mankind arising out of many causes," the old priest said. The Greeks remembered one deluge only, "whereas there were many of them." And the priest described how the earth had been destroyed by fire due to "a declination of the bodies moving around the earth and in the heavens," and also by floods. But Egypt, he declared, had been largely spared from these disasters due to its location, "for which reason the things preserved here are said to be the oldest."

Undoubtedly, if this old priest were confronted with conventional twentieth century beliefs about antiquity, he would conclude that we know even less than the Greeks. Plato did not invent Atlantis nor the idea of recurrent disasters. Atlantis was a shared memory of peoples living on both sides of the Atlantic. Such legends are found not only in Greece and Egypt, but also in Morocco, Portugal, Spain, France, Wales, Ireland, on islands in the Atlantic and among Indian tribes in Central and South America, Mexico and the United States.[8] Legendary accounts among widely separated peoples refer to sunken lands in both the Atlantic and Pacific from which the founders of tribes, nations and peoples had emigrated. The widespread belief in these submergences and migrations amounts to a common cosmology generally consistent with the words of the old priest.

All over the earth the oral and written histories of ancient and primitive peoples describe what we call prehistory as a succession of four or more great ages. The first of these ages, sometimes called the Golden Age, was said to be the best; the second, the Silver Age, the next best; and so on through Bronze to Iron. The present Iron Age – the last, hardest, and most contracted – is in some ways supposedly the worst of all. Certain branches of Christianity,[9] the Cayce transcripts,[10] the epistles and quatrains of Nostradamus,[11] the prophecies of the Maya,[12] the Hopi Indians,[13] and of Cheiro (Count Louis de Hamon)[14] all declare that the fourth age is now about to end and a new cycle, the fifth age, is about to begin.

Mayan record of a catastrophe. A frieze photographed at an unknown location in the Yucatan by Teobert Maler (1842-1917) shows a pyramid collapsing as the land sinks and a volcano erupts.

Piecing together information from various sources, a possible breakdown of these ages is as follows:

The Golden Age	200,000 B.C. to 50,000 B.C.
The Silver Age	50,000 B.C. to 28,000 B.C.
The Bronze Age	28,000 B.C. to 9600 B.C.
The Iron Age	9,600 B.C. to A.D. 2001?
The Millennium	A.D. 2001 to ?

Ancient cosmologies are virtually unanimous in describing these ages as terminated by great disasters – volcanic eruptions, giant winds, massive earthquakes, land sinkings and upheavals, great floods, tiltings of the earth's axis and avalanches of glaciers. Not all of the disasters were global, so not all of the traditions refer to the same disasters or to the same number of ages, but most peoples recorded at least four ages, and aside from these variations the uniformity of the pattern is overwhelming. For instance, the legend of the great flood as told in *Genesis* has been found throughout the Middle East, Egypt, India, China, the Mediterranean, western and northern Europe, and in the Arctic. Among the American Indians over 130 separate peoples had a parallel tradition.[15] Virtually all ancient peoples and nations had the same story and virtually all had the same basic cosmology of history as a succession of ages ended by recurrent disasters.

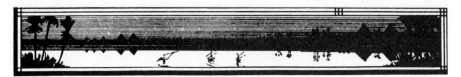

17

Through the Looking-Glass

Making sense of the Great Pyramid and the information encoded in it requires a fundamental re-visioning of history and the nature of man.

Contemporary scholars and educators are virtually unanimous in defining history as an ascending line of progress from stone-age barbarism to modern man and his institutions as the culmination of the race – an idea which developed during the expansion of Europe and the industrial revolution.

Yet many able scholars, content to present only the results of their immediate investigations without commenting on the controversial implications, have found reflections of the former world order where least expected. William Thompson points out in *At The Edge of History* that myth is not an early level of human development. The most "primitive" peoples investigated, Thompson says, are not the beginning of something, but the end of something else. In *Hamlet's Mill*, professors von Dechend and de Santillana remark that the literature of even the earliest peoples on record is concerned with terms and traditions that even for them were already "tottering with age". They demonstrate that much of ancient myth is actually a record of the basic events of an archaic science of astronomy. Von Dechend and de Santillana declare: "Those first predecessors of ours, instead of indulging their whims with childlike freedom, behave like worried and doubting commentators: they always try an exegesis of a dimly understood tradition."[1]

The more we look into our origins, the more it seems that

everything is the reverse of what we thought it was. The ancient myths and legends are not fantasies; they are the remains of a history of cycles. And the lineal progressive history we thought we had is, as Voltaire once said, "the lie commonly agreed upon". What we have been hiding from ourselves with that lie are the teachings of the old priest of Sais.

Those who believe in lineal history may assume that the facts are all on their side. The conflict, however, is not between those who have the facts and those who do not, but between *interpretations* of the facts. Atlantis may be a fantasy to the orthodox, but if history is neither lineal nor progressive, *their* world view becomes a fantasy – and in view of the discoveries at the Great Pyramid, the foundations for lineal history have crumbled.

The irony of it is that orthodox Egyptologists, archaeologists, anthropologists and historians have been largely (but not entirely) responsible for the spade work that has undermined the concept of progress. It is now well established that man in one form or another has been on this earth for millions of years and has been using fire for 750,000 years. And even orthodox anthropology now dates the appearance of *homo sapiens* at 100,000 years ago.[2] The remains of Cro-Magnon man, a tall, erect predecessor with a cranial capacity *greater* than modern man, testify that well formed, highly intelligent humans have been here for tens of thousands of years.

Undeciphered scripts and symbols which may be a form of writing have now been dated as 15,000 to 30,000 years old.[3] In *Ancestral Voices*, James Norman reports that bones marked with notations which record the phases of the moon and other seasonal variations in nature have been carbon dated to 135,000 years ago. If the theories are correct which hold that the alphabetic symbols were originally derived from the zodiac and phases of the moon, and that these symbols functioned as numbers before they were used as letters, it may be that writing is the child of mathematics. Man may have been numbering, calculating and measuring for tens of thousands of years before written language evolved.

In re-visioning history, it is helpful to keep in mind that our own culture has leaped from Columbus' tiny ships to moon rockets in less than 500 years. Rather than viewing the

100,000-year range of *homo sapiens* as largely a period of technological stagnation at the stone-age level, it is, given the nature of man, far more realistic to allow for many high civilizations to rise and fall within that great period of time.

The legend that the Great Pyramid was built to preserve the knowledge of another age of the earth from a great disaster and to carry that knowledge across the next cycle of history until it could again be perceived and understood is indeed the only explanation of the Pyramid that ultimately makes sense, if we assume its builders were at least as intelligent as ourselves. The simple fact of the matter is that it is neither necessary nor intelligent to move six million tons of stone and to finish 21 acres of it to within 1/100 of an inch of mathematical perfection in order to build a tomb, a temple of initiation, a sundial, an observatory, a water pump, a Bible in stone, a public works project, to incorporate geodetic measurements, or to accomplish any other purpose ever attributed to it. The only reason for building a structure to those incredible specifications is that it was designed to last through something like 12,500 years of earthquakes, floods and vandalism.

If history is indeed a succession of ages, it becomes less than fantastic to hypothesize that the priests and leaders of Atlantis and predynastic Egypt could have foreseen the general contours and duration of the age to follow. Even without "a science of phophecy", which they may well have had, they could have predicted that the fall of Atlantis and its culture would result in a general deterioration in the international political situation, a gradual lessening of contacts among peoples, and a long term decline in science and understanding throughout the world.

They might have foreseen that this general deterioration would amount to an age of intellectual darkness which would have a very long way to go before it reversed itself, and that by the time this reversal finally took hold, knowledge of the preceding ages would be largely lost. To enlightened leaders of humanity, it would have been apparent that some sign would be required to indicate the existence and nature of previous human attainments to that distant future time when science and understanding would again begin to be recovered.

They built a six million ton, virtually indestructible

monument, the mere existence of which would testify to their engineering abilities. They located it and designed it, utilizing measures and proportions that would testify to their scientific understanding. By recording in enduring form the range of their awareness on the material level, they have effected a continuity of consciousness from one age to another.

This may be the only intelligent reason for having built the Great Pyramid to its incredible specifications and to have placed it in the center of the earth's land mass, but it still leaves another question unanswered. Why should they bother? What difference would it make to them what people understood or did 12,000 years later? As enlightened as they may have been, it is very difficult to imagine anyone moving six million tons of stone unless they themselves had a direct and compelling interest in the results of the project. Maybe they had. To understand how this is possible, it is necessary to go "through the looking-glass" into another perspective of the ancient cosmology as it was 12,000 years ago – and as it is today.

The essential ingredient in this cosmology is reincarnation, the widely held concept in both ancient and modern times that the spirit and soul of each human being are eternal, and that individuals return to the earth again and again over great expanses of time to witness and work with the consequences of their previous actions. In deep antiquity it was understood that a time would come again in which there would be problems and opportunities similar to those which existed before the fall of Atlantis. The ancients believed that those beings who were incarnate then would, in the future, return *en masse* to face what they had faced before.

From this perspective, there is much to suggest that huge waves of those who had dwelt in the science wonderland of Atlantis began reentering the earth around the turn of the century, and that a new and continuing wave began shortly before World War II. In terms of the ancient cosmology, the explosion of science and technology in this century – without parallel over thousands of years – is the result of the return of Atlantean energies expressed through individuals who had dwelt in Atlantis.

With reincarnation, the past, present and future magically blend into each other. Time collapses into an "eternal now" –

and we face the strange proposition that *we* are the Atlanteans and predynastic Egyptians who built the Pyramid. We ourselves are those who dwelt in Atlantis. We built the Pyramid for ourselves as a reminder, after some 12,000 years, of our heritage.

The increasing interest in Atlantis and the Great Pyramid are more than temporary fads. For millions they have the intrigue of the vaguely familiar. What is the source of advances in science and technology? Where do the images come from, these descriptions of magical science, battles with great animals, mythical creatures and human giants that fill the comic books and fantasy literature? Is it all pure invention or does some of it spring from memories of the earth as it once was?

Far from being a novel idea, this concept of memory is the heart of the most important classical philosophy. Twenty-four hundred years ago Plato wrote that all knowledge is merely remembering. Education can do no more than remind us of what we have already known and experienced in former states. Plato, the Bible and the Cayce transcripts all express the same basic insight that there is no new thing under the sun. If reincarnation is a fact, this view through the looking-glass explains the fascination in current media with psychic influences, fantastic technology, science fiction, exotic violence, depravity, lost civilizations and disasters as expressions of unconscious memories from another time. And if history is cyclic, the past becomes a mirror that shows us the future.

The present cycle will come to an end as surely as preceding ages have, and it is certainly very curious that millions of people seem to be anticipating just that. Increasingly, on the broadest possible cultural front, there is the expectation of great impending change, as if the earth were moving toward some unnameable event as we near the year 2000. This expectancy finds expression in everything from economic forecasts, to themes in science fiction and popular music, to those who anticipate huge earthquakes, the invasion of extraterrestrials or the return of the Messiah. Even traditional prophecy and the century's most interesting psychic can be interpreted as suggesting that a major turning point of some kind is on the horizon.

Today there is a huge groundswell of apocalyptic Christian literature, much of which claims that we are now in "the latter days" of Biblical prophecy – the period immediately preceding the end of the age and the Second Coming of Christ. As signs of the times increasing numbers cite the resurrection of Israel, the rebirth of the Roman Empire in the form of the European Economic Community, a world-wide moral, economic and military crisis, the increasing militarization of the Middle East and the approaching final battle of Armageddon.

They also refer to Jesus' prophecy for the end of the age which included earthquakes "in diverse places". He further declared that at the end of the age "the sun will be darkened, and the moon will not give its light, and the stars will fall from heaven", an image which suggests a shifting of the earth's poles, since "the stars falling from heaven" would be a natural way to describe the appearance of the night sky during such an event. How strange it is to hear that in the cosmology of the Lapps the end of the age will be marked by the movement of the Pole Star, as a result of which "the heaven will fall",[4] and stranger still to hear that the Skidi-Pawnee of the Great Plains also tied the end of the age to the movement of the North Star, and that before this "the moon will turn red and the sun will die in the skies".[5]

Cayce says the same thing: "As has been given of old, the sun will be darkened and the earth will be broken up in diverse places."[6] He stated that around 1998 to 2001 the poles of the earth will (again) shift, terminating the present cycle of history and beginning another, with our planet transformed by global climate changes and many other alterations. Interestingly, the Mayan world age is supposed to end in earthquakes by the year 2011. As Isaiah prophesied, there will be "a new heaven and a new earth".

Cayce also made a number of famous predictions specifying other untoward events affecting well known places. It is not clear whether all these events are to precede the polar shift; most of them, presumably, could take place when and as the poles shift. Of course, it is also not certain that they will happen at all. If these predictions are no more literal on the geological level than the "rising of Poseidia" has so far proven to be, it is possible that the world might pass through them unscathed.

However, it is still possible that these predictions will be fulfilled and if they are, they may serve as signs that we are nearing the end of an era.

Within three months of the eruption of Mt. Vesuvius or "Pelee",[7] Cayce said, the southern coast of California would be hit by major earthquakes. Areas from Salt Lake City to southern Nevada would also be affected. In one transcript it sounds as if Los Angeles and San Francisco will more or less "disappear", although it is not clear over what period of time. Cayce saw also the destruction of New York City (through earthquakes or war), the submergence of parts of the Carolinas and Georgia, the submergence of most of Japan, land rising off the east coast of the United States and in the Caribbean, and an alteration in upper Europe "as in the twinkling of an eye", probably implying that the lowlands will sink.

If these submergences and upheavals suggest the end of Atlantis, there is a profound pattern in Cayce's statements that it is precisely the return of the Atlanteans with their extremist tendencies that makes these disasters more than likely. The great upheavals that broke up and destroyed Atlantis were, for the most part, due to man's upsetting the balance of nature through the tremendous energies he harnessed and misused.

It is interesting that lineal history is strangely amoral, because despite man's many shortcomings things are, by definition, "getting better and better". Cyclic history, on the contrary, is thoroughly moral, because the disasters which terminate the ages are not primarily the blind workings of nature, but in large measure result from man's ignorance and evil. The theme of human responsibility for disasters is found in Plato and in other traditions as well. "Down on the bottom of the seas," Hopi legend relates, "lie all the proud cities, the flying *patuwvotas,* and the worldly treasures corrupted with evil, and those peoples who found no time to sing praises to the Creator from the tops of their hills."[8]

Of course, if man can cause disasters, he can also prevent them. Yet man is now changing the earth on such a vast scale that these prophecies and portents seem to fit too closely not to be disquieting. We are altering the atmosphere, the waters and the land in truly tremendous ways. There are now 500,000 man-made chemicals in the planet's eco-system, and the long-term effects of underground nuclear testing and the massive extraction of off-shore oil and gas could provide some rude surprises. It is even conceivable that we could in some way, directly or indirectly, contribute to a shifting of the poles.

There is solid evidence that the poles have shifted before,[9] and compelling reason to think that man was on earth when these upheavals took place. Hopi legend tells us the second world age ended and the third began when the earth "teetered off balance, spun around crazily, then rolled over twice. Mountains plunged into the seas with a great splash; seas and lakes sloshed over the land."[10] This sounds cataclysmic, but if the ancient myths and legends of previous cycles mean anything, they show that our species has survived great catastrophes before. Man is not doomed by catastrophes; he is cleansed and transformed by them.

No doubt the specialist, used to looking at the world as a set of separate questions, will be scratching his head wondering how we ever got from the Great Pyramid to prophecies for the end of the age. But in reality, there may be no separate questions. The Great Pyramid leads us to both edges of history – into the future as well as the remotest past. And if its implications raise doubts about our immediate future, they also conjure up a more exalted image of man, his origin and his destiny than has been popular in our time.

In the old tradition, man is not a risen ape, but a fledgling god from the stars fallen into matter and time to strengthen and purify himself. Man's spirit and mind are eternal and come not from the earth, but from heaven. Man himself is an extraterrestrial. As Cayce saw it – and here again his conception is supported by echoes in dozens of ancient creation myths – when the invisible human spirits arrived on this planet, some had the ability to imagine the forms they wished to become and then to cause these forms to take on physical substance. Others took the highest physical creatures then on the earth – one of the anthropoid apes – and in a very short time radically transformed them into a suitable form for man to inhabit.[11]

This conception addresses the outstanding problem of physical anthropology – the problem of the "missing link". The development of the form that became the human form took place with an "unnatural" and otherwise unaccountable rapidity. In terms of time as measured by the evolution of other species, man appeared suddenly and at once.

The "missing link" in anthropology and in all of lineal, progressive history and modern science is simply the spiritual and eternal nature of man. For those who see history as cyclic, the need to reaffirm man's essential nature is a sign of the intellectual darkness of the modern world. But it is just this simple truth, largely forgotten in the academies, that dissolves the apparent tragedy of history.

What we gain from history is experience and increased consciousness. On one level of his being or another, man slowly learns the lessons of the earth. If history is cyclic, it also may be seen as a spiral. If man came from the stars, his destiny may be to return to them. We do not merely endlessly repeat in one age what has happened in earlier ages. There is progress and upward movement in human history, although in the shadow of the Great Pyramid it is now obvious that it is not the progress of science.

The Great Pyramid is not only a record of the attainments of a lost world; it is a portent of the future and a key to the nature of man. We have a message from the past that turns the world upside down. Viewed in its total context, this message changes the meaning of history, and suddenly, as swift as thought, the ancient vision of who and what we are flashes before us to guide us anew, even as it guided men over twelve thousand years ago.

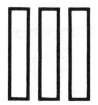

THE
RECKONING

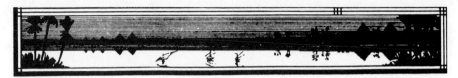

Three Drops in the Ocean

Studying the Great Pyramid, one clue leads to another and bodies of information intersect in such a way that one is staggered by the relationships and patterns that emerge. Egyptologists, geographers, engineers, surveyors, metrologists and mystics can all indulge the luxury of concentrating on their specific areas of interest. Few specialists go beyond the boundaries of their disciplines and thus overlook the web of interconnecting implications surrounding the Pyramid. But searching unrestrained for a solution to the mystery of the Great Pyramid, we find that no part of our lives or beliefs is ultimately separated from its implications.

It is very like entering the ultimate fairy tale where the past magically expands to an unlimited horizon full of exotic lands and peoples we have all but forgotten. In this fairy tale the Pyramid becomes the closest thing on the planet to the concept of the "miraculous stone", the "philosopher's stone" of alchemy. To perceive the stone and to attempt to comprehend it transforms the consciousness of the seeker. The mystery of the Pyramid leads to multitudes of possibilities, each separate and yet connected, until we face ultimate questions concerning the origin, nature and destiny of man.

It has often been remarked that we cannot know where we are or where we're going until we know where we have been. Despite the centuries-long fascination with the last remaining wonder of the ancient world, archaeological excavation has so far barely scratched the surface of Gizeh, and it is highly probable that important discoveries remain to be made. The Sphinx and the temples immediately in front of it rest upon the lowest presently visible level of the Gizeh Plateau. East of these temples the limestone formation drops off and is covered by sand and soil deposited by the Nile after the complex was constructed. By all the criteria imaginable – legends, old texts, the character of the surroundings and the geologic history of the site – the area east of the Sphinx is an archaeological "natural". Research activities in Egypt are quickening in the late seventies, and with this increasing interest it is highly likely that eventually Gizeh will yield a major – perhaps an unparalleled – find. In the near future we may have a much more detailed picture of where we've been than ever before. But even if war or other circumstances should intervene and nothing more is ever found, the lightning has already struck. What we can be certain of may seem like three drops in the ocean, but the information now exists to revolutionize the outline of history.

Where does the reality end and the fantasy begin in this story of the Pyramid? In 1971, *At The Edge of History* by William Irwin Thompson was published. In this work Thompson did his own

Riders south of the Third Gizeh Pyramid.

insightful re-visioning of history. Approaching the subject from the perspective of social history, he also deduced that Atlantis may be more than myth and that we are rapidly drawing to the close of an age. He concluded: "Bits and pieces of a new world view seem to lie scattered around us, and as suddenly as the imagination perceives them in a new form, the old world view seems all the more incredible. Still, imagination is not knowledge; we do not *know* anything yet."

Now, several years later, we do know something. We know that someone in very deep antiquity was aware of the size and shape of the earth with great precision. The three key measurements of the earth are incorporated in the dimensions of the Great Pyramid. The perimeter of the Pyramid equals a half minute of equatorial latitude. The perimeter of the sockets equals a half minute of equatorial longitude, or 1/43,200 of the earth's circumference. The height of the Pyramid, including the platform, equals 1/43,200 of the earth's polar radius. These are well founded objective data. They constitute the first conclusive evidence of a scientific civilization as high as our own in deep antiquity. Any careful survey of the Pyramid will reveal substantially the same values reported. These three basic measurements of the Pyramid, all on the same scale, match the three key geodetic values of our planet so precisely that it is simply absurd to suppose they are not the result of intentional design. These measurements mean that whoever built the Pyramid had measured the earth precisely. We do not know how they measured it, but that they did so is now an article of knowledge.

The second thing we know is that the previously unknown unit of measurement Cayce said was used in Egypt at the time the Pyramid was built does account for the dimensions and architecture of the Great Pyramid better than any other unit. If he knew how long their yardstick was, it is tempting to think he could tell an Atlantean from an Egyptian, that he knew the date – 10,490 B.C., and how the Pyramid was built – by levitation. It is also tempting to think that only a truly brilliant and scientific consciousness would have chosen the center of the earth's land mass for its purpose and that we are now witnessing the unfolding of that purpose.

The third thing that we know is that the more we study the

history and nature of man, the more it seems that what is apparently fantasy at one time becomes reality at another, and when we look into the distant past or the future it becomes increasingly difficult to separate the fantastic from what we call "real". History shows that man's conception of the earth and his place in it has changed fundamentally many times and doubtless will change again. History has not come to an end, and as enlightened as we like to think we are, there is no guarantee that we will not look as foolish to future generations as the "flat earth believers" look to us. For some, any account of man's history that includes Atlantis will be nothing but a fairy tale. But fairy tales sometimes become reality, and this Pyramid odyssey may eventually prove for even the most sceptical to be the same kind of fairy tale as the legend of Troy, or the fantastic notion that the earth is a sphere.

APPENDIX

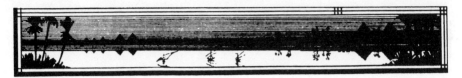

I

Geodetic Measurements and the Great Pyramid

Measurement of the Earth's Equator
There is no single, uniform and generally agreed upon figure for the earth's equator.[1] Here are a few sample figures (based on mean sea level) for the equatorial circumference.

Miles	Kilometers	Source
24,901.68	40,075.452	Clark Spheroid
24,902.39	40,076.596	International Spheroid
24,902.45	40,076.688	1964 Encyclopaedia Britannica
24,901.55	40,075.239	1977 World Almanac
24,901.5	40,075.159	1976 Encyclopaedia Americana article on "Geodesy"

Although it is the minimum figure from the list, we will take 24,901.5 miles as a basis for comparison in our calculations since it comes from a recent authoritative source.

Measurement of the Perimeter of the Great Pyramid's Sockets
When I first attempted to calculate the perimeter distance of
the Pyramid's sockets, I was unaware of any survey which had
measured this distance directly. Since Cole's 1925 survey is the
most recent and accurate, I used Cole's figure of 921.453
meters for the perimeter of the Pyramid and added to this the
distances between the outside edges of the sockets and the
corners of the Pyramid as these distances had been reported by
Cole and others.

Cole gives the distances of the socket edges (expressed in
centimeters) from the corners of the Pyramid (on the platform)
as follows:

Socket	Edge	Distance
Northeast	North	85
	East	85
Southeast	South	83
	East	85
Northwest	North	75
	West	76

Cole states that the southwest socket was too broken to give
any information. However in Tompkins's work there is an
illustration which shows values for the southwest socket and
which otherwise uses the values of Cole's survey.[2] In this
illustration the values shown for the southwest socket are:

Edge	Distance
South	51
West	51

These figures for the southwest socket, however, ignore a
basis for measurement which other surveys have taken into
account. The point where the extension of the Pyramid's
diagonal comes out of the socket is indicated by an incised line
51 cm from the corner. But according to Davidson,[3] Rutherford[4] and earlier surveys by Petrie and the Royal Engineers,[5]
the western edge of the southwest socket is some 17.5 inches
or 44 cm west of the incised line. Rutherford claims there is a
second incised line at this point.

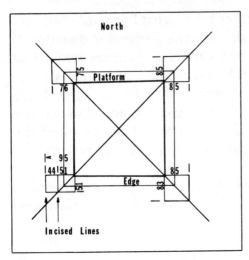

North

Platform

7|5

8|5

| 7|6

8|5 |

|◄ 9|5
|44|5|

8|5 |

Edge

15|1

8|3

Incised Lines

The ground plan of the Great Pyramid showing the distances of the socket edges from the corners of the Pyramid. The size of the sockets is greatly exaggerated.

If these figures for the distances of the socket edges from the Pyramid's corners are added together (85 cm + 85 cm + 83 cm + 85 cm + 75 cm + 76 cm + 51 cm + 51 cm + 44 cm) they total 635 cm or 6.35 meters. The perimeter of the outermost socket corners is larger than the perimeter of the Pyramid by this amount. The perimeter of the sockets is therefore 921.453 + 6.35 meters or 927.803 meters, which equals 36,527.604 inches or 3043.967 feet. An equatorial circumference of 24,901.5 miles implies a half minute of longitude of 3043.5166 feet (927.66571 meters).

In evaluating the correspondence of the figures here, it is necessary to bear in mind that the distance of 3043.967 feet (927.803 meters) is the distance between the outermost corners of the sockets. In the original condition of the Pyramid, presumably these outermost corners were not visible, but likely were covered by cornerstones and the surrounding pavement. It would have been necessary to indicate these points on the surface of the pavement in some manner, and virtually all investigators agree that the sockets originally held cornerstones – which would have met this requirement.

Examination of the masonry elsewhere in the surrounding pavement blocks and on the edge of the platform shows that the builders had a general tendency to taper many of the butting surfaces of these stones. It seems highly likely that the outside faces of the cornerstones also would have been slightly tapered instead of rising absolutely vertically from the socket edges.

If this taper amounted to only 3/8 inch (.95 cm) on an edge, this would shorten each side by 3/4 inch (1.9 cm) and the perimeter of the sockets by 3 inches (7.6 cm) overall. This would produce a socket perimeter of 36,524.6 inches or 3043.716 feet (927.726 meters).

These calculations are corroborated by another survey of the Pyramid. After I had made these calculations I discovered that Flinders Petrie had produced direct distance measurements between the outside corners of the sockets. Davidson and Aldersmith show Petrie's figures as follows:[6]

N.W. corner to N.E. corner	9129.8 inches
N.E. corner to S.E. corner	9130.8 inches
S.E. corner to S.W. corner	9141.4 inches
S.W. corner to N.W. corner	9119.2 inches
	36,521.2 inches
	(927.64 meters)

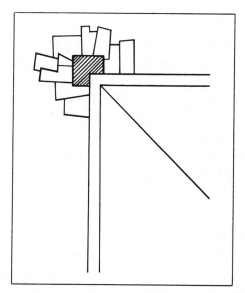

A cornerstone seen from above.

The illustration shows the corner of the Pyramid, the platform jutting out from under the Pyramid, the cornerstone (with shading) and limestone pavement blocks around the cornerstone.

This is some 6 inches short of my first raw calculation and some 3 inches short of my estimate allowing for tapered cornerstones. The edges of the sockets are now rounded and broken and the decision as to where a socket begins or ends is necessarily somewhat arbitrary. In view of this, the agreement between these figures is so close that they substantially confirm each other. If we average my first rough calculation of 36,527.6 inches and Petrie's 36,521.2 inches we get 36,524.4 inches or 3043.7 feet (927.72161 meters), a figure within a fraction of an inch of my estimate allowing for tapered cornerstones. We will use this figure of 3043.7 feet for comparison to a half minute of equatorial longitude and the earth's circumference.

	Feet	Meters
Perimeter of the sockets	3043.7	927.72161
A half minute of equatorial longitude based on 24,901.5 mile (40,075.159 km) circumference	3043.51	927.66571
Difference	.19	.0559

The difference is about 2.2 inches (5.59 cm).

The accuracy of this correlation can be tested further by comparing the earth's circumference of 24,901.5 miles (40,075.159 km) with the circumference implied by the Pyramid's socket measurement. Because the Pyramid is built on the scale of 1/43,200 of nature, all we have to do is multiply the Pyramid measurement by 43,200.

3043.7 feet x 43,200 = 131,487,840 feet = 24,903 miles
927.72161 meters x 43,200 = 40,077,573 meters = 40,077.573 km

Pyramid figure	24,903 miles	40,077.573 km
Earth's circumference	24,901.5 miles	40,075.159 km
Difference	1.5 miles	2.414 km

Considering the range of values we have seen for both the earth's equator and the sockets' perimeter, these correspondences are virtually perfect. By comparison, the French measurement upon which the metric system was originally based is off 2 kilometers on the arc of meridian (the distance from the pole to the equator) and is thus about 8 kilometers or 5 miles in error in relation to the polar circumference or total length of a meridian.

If Petrie had considered the possibility of geodetic measurements and if he had not been blinded to the significance of the sockets by his dispute with Smyth and his theories, he could have pointed out the incorporation of a half minute of longitude in the late nineteenth century, but neither he nor anyone else ever has – with a demonstration and figures to back it up.[7]

It should be understood that the 24,903 mile (40,077.573 km) figure implied by the sockets' perimeter does not necessarily mean the Pyramid builders were in error by 1.5 miles (2.4 km) in reckoning the circumference. That figure results from the convenience of taking an average value of 3043.7 feet (927.72161 meters) between the figures supplied by Petrie and Cole for the perimeter of the sockets. The small difference in their measurements creates a minor range of uncertainty as to the exact socket dimensions and the equatorial circumference implied by them. The actual circumference of the earth falls within this range of uncertainty.

Sockets' perimeter according to Petrie:
Minimum Implied Circumference

36,521.2 inches
3043.4333 feet   24,900.816 miles
927.64033 meters   40,074.062 km

Sockets' perimeter from Cole's figures:
Maximum Implied Circumference

(921.453 + 6.35 meters)
36,527.604 inches
3043.967 feet   24,905.183 miles
927.803 meters   40,081.089 km

As we have seen, values for the circumference vary between 24,901.5 and 24,902.45 miles (40,075.159 and 40,076.688 km). Looking at the figures in this light allows for the possibility that the builders knew the earth's circumference precisely.

Measurement of the Earth's Polar Radius
Like the measurement of the equatorial circumference, variations for the length of the polar radius also occur from

source to source. Instead of quoting a series of slightly differing figures for the polar radius, I have chosen the figure from the same source as I used for the equatorial circumference, namely the article "Geodesy" in the 1976 edition of the Encyclopaedia Americana (Vol. 12). This figure for the polar radius of "the best fitting ellipsoid" matching the earth is 3949.9081 miles (6356.774 km).[8]

Measurement of the Pyramid's Height

As with everything else, figures for the Pyramid's original height differ from source to source. Heights as variable as 480, 480.5, 480.7, 480.9, 481.4, 481.5, 484 and 484.9 feet are mentioned. The best figure seems to be 480.9 feet or 146.59 meters as reported in the Encyclopaedia Britannica and a number of other sources. Since the capstone (or pyramidion) and the top seven or eight layers of the Great Pyramid are now missing, no one can be absolutely certain of its original appearance or its original height. However, there is a method for estimating it which is simpler and better established than any other. This method produces figures which round off to 146.59 meters or 480.9 feet. It seems to be well established that the height of the Great Pyramid was just 7/11 of its base length.[9]

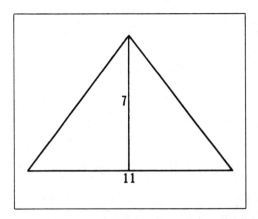

Since each side is slightly different in length, it is best to divide the total perimeter distance by 4 to establish an average length per side.

North	230.251	meters	755.41515 feet
East	230.391	meters	755.87446 feet
South	230.454	meters	756.08115 feet
West	230.357	meters	755.76291 feet
Total	921.453	meters	3023.1336 feet
Average	230.36325	meters	755.7834 feet
x 7/11 =	146.59479	meters =	480.95306 feet
			= Pyramid's height

Now if the Pyramid incorporates the dimensions of the earth
on the scale of 1:43,200, the height of the Pyramid should
indicate the distance from the earth's center to the north pole.
If we take the Pyramid's height as produced above and multiply
it by 43,200, we get a figure – although short by about 14 miles
or 23 kilometers – which is amazingly accurate if we assume it
was calculated by supposedly primitive people.

	Miles	Kilometers
Expected figure	3949.9081	6356.774
Calculated figure	3935.0704	6332.8949
Difference	14.8377	23.8791

On the other hand, if we assume a highly scientific civilization
designed the Pyramid's height to correspond to the earth's
polar radius, then this difference is somewhat more considerable. There is, however, that man-made stone platform under
the Pyramid which has always been ignored in mathematical
interpretations of the building, and if we add the thickness of
that platform to the height of the Pyramid, an extraordinary
correspondence emerges.

The Platform under the Great Pyramid
While the sockets, sides, height, angles, orientation and
proportions of the Great Pyramid have been described and
measured again and again, the platform under the Pyramid has
been almost totally ignored. In 1837-1838 Col. Howard-Vyse
burrowed down through the piles of rubble and bored through
the edge of the platform, the thickness of which he reported as
roughly 21 inches. The best (and in fact the only) current
measurement recorded in technical literature is an average
thickness of 55 cm reported by Maragioglio and Renaldi in
L'Archetettura Della Piramidi Menfite.[10]

The thickness of the platform has been largely ignored because of the common assumption that the "zero level" of the pyramid is the upper surface of this platform. It is easy to see how this arose since the top of the platform is level with a surrounding pavement of approximately the same thickness, but of course we do not really know what the builders took as the zero level, and a good case has been made that both the Great and Second Gizeh Pyramids were actually conceived as three-part structures having a capstone (or pyramidion), a main body and a platform or base. (See Part II of the Appendix.) To establish what happens if the thickness of the platform is added to the height of the Pyramid as it stands on top of it, we will work with Maragioglio and Renaldi's figure of 55 cm (21.6535 inches or 1.80445 feet).

	Feet	Meters
Pyramid's height on top of platform	480.95306	146.59479
Thickness of platform	1.80445	.55
Total height	482.75751	147.14479

Multiplying this new height by 43,200 produces a remarkable result.

482.75751 feet x 43,200 = 20,855,124 feet = 3949.834 miles

147.14479 meters x 43,200 = 6,356,654.9 meters = 6356.6549 km

	Miles	Kilometers	Feet
Expected figure	3949.9081	6356.774	20,855,515
Calculated figure	3949.834	6356.6549	20,855,124
Difference	.0741	.1191	391
			(119 meters)

Another way of appreciating the remarkable perfection of this correspondence is to calculate 1/43,200 of the polar radius and compare that with the Pyramid's total height.

	Feet	Meters
1/43,200 of 20,855,515	482.76655	
1/43,200 of 6,356,774		147.14754
Pyramid's total height	482.75751	147.14479
Difference	.00904	.00275
Or	.108 inches	2.75 millimeters

Accuracy and Implications of these Calculations

Because we are extrapolating by a factor of 43,200 even the addition of 1/10 of an inch to the height of the Pyramid adds 360 feet to the implied value for the polar radius. If the height of the Pyramid, as we have calculated it, were only about 1/9 of an inch (2.75 mm) greater it would correspond to the figure for the polar radius perfectly.

There is, then, an almost imperceptible difference between the Pyramid's value for the polar radius and that of modern geodesy. The figures for the polar radius and equatorial circumference we have been using are estimates for "the best fitting ellipsoid". This is not defined in a way to allow for mountains and valleys, but is based on "the shape of the mean sea level surface, continued under the land in a logical fashion".[11] We do not know upon what basis of definition or upon what conditions in nature the Pyramid builders have made their calculations. Their basis of definition may have been different, and/or it may be that there has been a slight alteration in the shape of the earth since the Pyramid was built. The accumulation of ice at the south pole over the last 6-12,000 years, for example, may have produced factors sufficient to slightly alter the oblateness of the earth's sphere.

Another point to keep in mind is that although we have used the best figures available, it is also possible that the platform under the Pyramid could be 2 or 3 mm thicker than 55 cm or that Cole's measurements of the sides could be inaccurate by 4 or 5 mm; either possibility would alter the implied value of the polar radius by several hundred feet. Similar small uncertainties exist in the measurements of the sockets.

Taking these minor uncertainties in the dimensions of the Pyramid and the earth into consideration, it can be said that the Pyramid's perimeter, height (including the platform), and sockets imply geodetic values for the equator and the polar radius as accurate as the best modern estimates.

These calculations indicate the Pyramid builders knew the dimensions of our planet about as precisely as we have been able to determine them in the 1970s with satellite surveys from space.

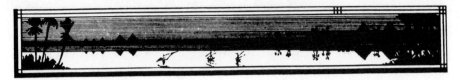

II

The Three Parts of a Pyramid

The common conception of the basic external features of the Egyptian pyramids is that they had two parts: a large body of stone built on sand or bedrock; a relatively small capstone or pyramidion a yard or two in height on top of the body. This capstone was sometimes of granite whereas the body of the pyramid was limestone. There are also indications that the capstones of some pyramids were once gilded. There are a few who believe the capstone on the Great Pyramid was entirely metal – a precious, incorruptible golden alloy.

In addition to being a handsome way to cap a pyramid, these capstones were considered separate parts of the pyramids they topped – a part that could be included or excluded from various calculations.[1] For example, the apothem (or slant height) of the Great Pyramid was the distance from the bottom of the capstone to the middle of a side at the base, and is thought by some writers to have equaled one tenth of a degree.

What only a few investigators seem to have noticed is that the Great and Second Pyramids of Gizeh (and possibly others)

were conceived and built with a third basic element in addition
to the body and capstone – a platform or base. In the two big
Gizeh Pyramids, not only were these platforms the physical
foundations of the buildings, but in the case of the Great
Pyramid the platform provided another separate element
which expresses a geodetic value related to but different from
that represented in the dimensions of the body alone. No one
has yet shown what scientific concepts (aside from the 3:4:5
triangle) may be expressed by the Second Pyramid, as it has
been studied and surveyed much less intensively. The
differential function between body and platform may not be
the same in each pyramid, but probably varies with the
architectural symbology the builders sought to represent.

The platform under the Great Pyramid is made of white
Mokkatam limestone, as are the casing blocks. It protrudes 15
to 16 inches (about 40 cm) beyond the body and is 21.6 inches
(55 cm) thick. Butted directly against this platform are blocks of
stone forming what is called the pavement. They are also of
white limestone, about the same thickness, but are usually

*The pavement and the platform on the north side of the Pyramid. The platform
(foreground) is now exposed to a much greater extent than in the Pyramid's original
state. The different styles of the stonework are easily distinguishable.*

much smaller and more irregular than the platform blocks. It is generally presumed that the pavement surrounded the Pyramid on all sides except for possibly the south. It was likely most extensive on the north side but we do not know how far it originally extended or how the outer edge was delineated. Since many pavement stones have been stolen, it is now easy to see the platform under the building. In fact, the pavement seems to have protected the platform edge. Because the cutting of the stone differs in the pavement and in the platform, the upper surface of the platform originally would have been distinguishable. But we do not know if or how the thickness of the platform (or the pavement) may have been visible originally.

In the case of the Second Pyramid the platform under it has been visible for thousands of years, but it was contemporary archaeologists Maragioglio and Renaldi who in *L'Archetettura Della Piramidi Menfite* finally drew attention to it in 1965. The base of the Second Pyramid was encircled by a single layer (or, according to some, two layers) of dark red granite which, for years, was simply regarded as the first layer of the body. The Italians pointed out that it was clearly a separate element, functioning as the foundation of the building.

> The foundation of the granite blocks is not uniform, but varied according to the height of the blocks in order that their upper horizontal faces should be at the same level.[2]

> The true zero level of the Chephren pyramid does not seem to have been that on which the first course rests, the height of which varies according to the thickness of the blocks which compose the course itself, but the upper surfaces of this which, as we have seen, is leveled with the utmost exactness.[3]

What all of this amounts to is that all measurements of the Second Pyramid have always included the platform, while the reverse was true of the Great Pyramid. It is hardly a radical suggestion that analyses of these structures proceed from the recognition that these platforms are distinct yet integral parts to be included in some calculations and excluded from others.

There is also hieroglyphic evidence to support the idea that the Egyptians themselves thought of these two pyramids as having three parts. The name of the Great Pyramid as found on the walls of mastabas at Gizeh is:[4]

The last element of this name is the determinative of the word for a geometrically true pyramid. Most Egyptologists interpret the lowest part of this symbol to be a wall surrounding the pyramid. It seems well established that the major pyramids were once enclosed by walls called "temenos walls". However, these were sometimes a considerable distance from the structure. In the case of the Great Pyramid this wall was 77.4 feet (23.6 meters) from the base on the northern and western sides, and 60.7 feet (18.5 meters) from the base on the south.[5] No traces of a wall have been found to the east.[6]

It could also be argued that the lowest element in this symbol for a pyramid is not a wall but the base or platform. At one point in *The Pyramids of Egypt*, I.E.S. Edwards is of the opinion that it represents a wall.

> The Egyptians, when depicting an object, always gave a full view, either from the front or from the side. The technique of drawing a three-quarter view was unknown to them. Thus the determinative for the word for a true pyramid ... is always written:

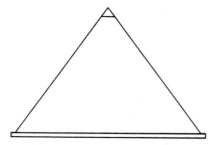

> which represents the front view of a true pyramid and of one side of the surrounding wall.[7]

But in another reference in the same book he makes an important observation which cuts across that interpretation.

Commenting on the possibility that the exteriors of the Second and Great Pyramids were painted or plastered, he wrote:

> A valuable piece of evidence which seems to have been overlooked is that the pyramid, when employed as a hieroglyphic sign on the painted walls of Old Kingdom mastabas is usually represented white with a band of brownish red stippled with black at the base and sometimes a blue or yellow capstone. The stippled band is clearly intended to indicate pink granite, as exemplified in the two lowest courses of the casing stones of the Pyramid of Chephren [the Second Pyramid],[8] the blue represents grey granite and the yellow must represent the gold overlay which was sometimes placed on the capstone.[9]

In a front-on view the band at the base of the Second Pyramid could not be seen as the temenos wall would have been in the way. Since the symbol is the determinative for a pyramid, the lowest element of this symbol is probably the platform of a pyramid and not some other structure.

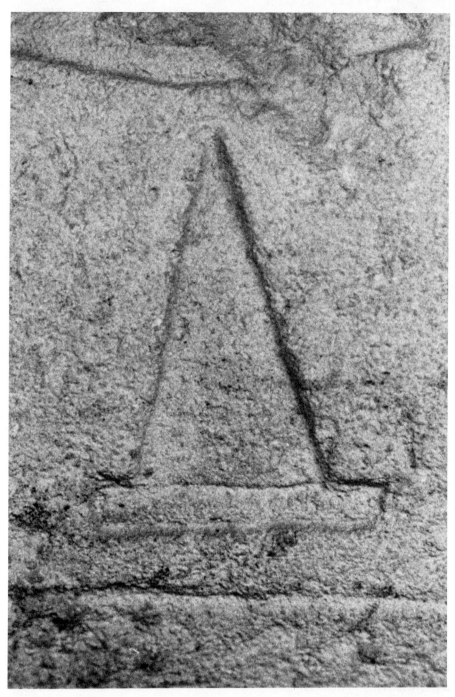

Symbol for a pyramid on a Gizeh tomb, showing what appears to be a platform on which the structure rests.

III

The Mir Cubit and a Comparison of Measures

This is an excerpt from Edgar Cayce's Egyptian transcripts describing a structure called the Temple Beautiful and a unit of measure called the mir cubit.

> ... globe within, the pyramid without, was four forty and four cubits. Twenty-seven and one half inches was a cubit then, or a mir then. The height was four and twenty and forty and four mir, making then that in the form of the ova ...[1]

Interpreting the length of the building as 444 mir of 27.5 inches yields a side of 1017.5 feet (310.13 meters). The description of the height is peculiar and, it occurred to me, can be interpreted as indicating that the interior height of the structure was advanced in stages of 4 - 20 - 40 and 4 for a cumulative height of 68 mir. Its exterior height may not have been more than 72 mir or about 165 feet (50.29 meters). Since the shape of the building is referred to as a pyramid enclosing a globe or ova, it is possible to interpret these dimensions along the following lines:

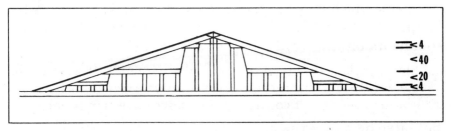

Cross section of the Temple Beautiful. The interior height of the temple was advanced in stages of 4, 20, 40 and 4 mir cubits.

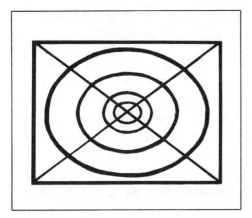

Ground plan of the Temple Beautiful showing the oval floor plan under a rectangular pyramid 444 mir cubits in length.

Although this would have been a very major structure and greater in length than the Great Pyramid, it would not have involved nearly the volume of material required for the Pyramid nor, obviously, would it have been as lasting.

Of more importance here is the signification of a unit of measure of 27.5 inches called the mir cubit. The Cayce transcripts do not directly state that the Great Pyramid was constructed with the mir cubit but imply that this was a standard unit of length of the people who built it. This clue provides the only basis for a simple quantitative test of the information in the Egyptian transcripts.

The word mir is not otherwise unknown.[2] Stecchini says

that the word mir used to refer to the pyramids and more specifically to the meridian triangle of a pyramid. He also says the Egyptians referred to their land as "the land of the mr", or To-mera, which may be related to the present Arabic name for Egypt, *al Misri.*[3] I.E.S. Edwards, in *The Pyramids of Egypt,* also comments on the word mir. He says in part:

> In Egyptian, this type of tomb [the pyramid], at least in the geometrically true form, was called m(e)r, a name which has not been suspected of concealing any descriptive significance.[4]

But later he also writes:

> M(e)r, a pyramid, would belong to the same class of [descriptive] name, if it could be established that it was a compound consisting of the prefix *m* found in Egyptian to convey the meaning "instrument" or "place"; and the verb *r*, "to ascend" ... m(e)r would then mean the "place of ascension".[5]

In the light of the association of the word mir with the pyramids and of the statement in the transcripts, it is natural to wonder if the mir cubit was the unit used in building the major structures at Gizeh. The standard process to determine if a unit of measure fits the Great Pyramid is to divide the length of the Pyramid's side by the length of the unit and see if it fits evenly. For example, Tompkins attempts to demonstrate that a wide variety of ancient units of measurement fit the side of the Pyramid evenly.[6]

Unit	Number in Side
Egyptian foot of .300 meters	770
Greek or geographic foot of .308 meters	750
Remen of .3696 meters	625
Geographic cubit of .462 meters	500
Royal cubit of .525 meters	440
Pyk belady of .5775 meters	400
Megalithic yard of .84 meters	275
Brasse or fathom of 1.848 meters	125

Unfortunately, this list is based on inaccurate information. One of the things Tompkins and Stecchini have pointed out is that there was a wide variety of earth commensurable units of length in antiquity – that is, it can be shown that a number of ancient units were figured as fractions of degrees of latitude at various points on the earth's surface. Degrees of latitude are shortest at the equator and become slightly longer as they approach the north or south pole. For example, the brasse or fathom varied between 1.843 meters (72.5 inches) and 1.862 meters (73.3 inches) becoming longer as it is found closer to the pole.[7] We have seen that the perimeter of the Great Pyramid equals a half minute of latitude at the equator, where a degree of latitude is shortest. The values of all the units as given in Tompkins's list are not equatorial values but are calculated instead on the length of a degree of latitude in the Middle East at about 32° or 33° north where the value of a degree is 110,880 meters (363,778.8 feet). (110,880 divided by 60 equals 1848 meters in one minute. 1848 divided by 1.848 equals 1000 brasses or fathoms in one minute of latitude.)

The units in Tompkins's list appear to fit the Pyramid only by assuming that it measured 231 meters on a side – a rounded-off figure Tompkins told me he chose because he made the calculations in the days before electronic calculators became common and wished to avoid the tedious business of working with five or six decimal places. But the average side of the Great Pyramid is *not* 231 meters. The average length of a side calculated from Cole's survey is 230.36325 meters. The difference is significant as it represents .63675 meters or 25.06 inches on a side. This amounts to an error of over 8 feet (2.54 meters) on the total perimeter and is certainly not exact enough to be a definitive analysis. Tompkins's work is valuable, however, because he does provide us with a list of all the other units of measure possibly used in constructing the Great Pyramid (except the so called sacred cubit); thus, we have a convenient list with which to compare the mir cubit.

The first step is to divide the average side of the Pyramid by the value of the mir cubit, 27.5 inches = .6985013 meters. (27.5 divided by 39.37 = .6985013).

230.36325 divided by .6985013 = 329.79645.

This is obviously not an even number, but it is very close to 330. Reversing the process, how long would a unit have to be to fit the average side exactly 330 times?

230.36325 divided by 330 = .6980704 meters or 27.483031 inches.

This is about .017 inch short of 27.5 inches and while obviously not exact, it fits the Pyramid at least as well as the units Tompkins proposes and is close enough to invite further analysis.

Before we examine how well each unit fits the true dimensions of the Pyramid, there are two other general tests to which the units can be subjected. The unit used to build the Great Pyramid should be expected not only to fit the side of the base evenly, but the apothem and height of the Pyramid as well.

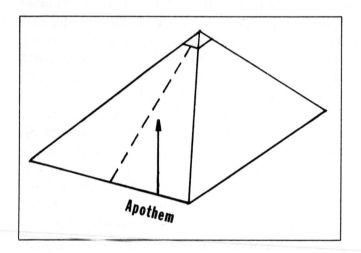

Whereas the perimeter of the Pyramid equals a half minute of equatorial latitude, many scholars have pointed out the apothem should equal 1/10 of a minute. The apothem is therefore merely 8/10 of a side. Since the height of the Pyramid stands in the ratio of 7:11 to the base, the number of times a unit goes into the side should be multiplied by 7/11 to determine if it fits the height evenly.

Unit in Meters	No. in Base	No. in Apothem	No. in Height
Egyptian foot .300	770	616	490
Greek or geographic foot .308	750	600	477.2727
Remen .3696	625	500	397.7272
Geographic cubit .462	500	400	318.1818
Royal cubit .525	440	352	280
Pyk belady .5775	400	320	254.5454
Mir cubit .6985013	330	264	210
Megalithic yard .84	275	220	175
Brasse or fathom 1.848	125	100	79.4545

As we can see, only the Egyptian foot, the royal cubit, the mir cubit and the megalithic yard fit the side of the base, the apothem and the height evenly, assuming they were all calculated on a degree of latitude at the equator.

Before we analyze these four units further, it is worth considering another possibly ancient unit some have suggested was used in the construction of the Great Pyramid – the so called sacred cubit. The sacred cubit was apparently first hatched out of the calculations of Isaac Newton when he analyzed Josephus' descriptions of the pillars of Jachin and Boaz in the Temple of Solomon. Newton concluded the pillars had been measured with a unit between 24.8 (.6299 meters) and 25.02 inches (.6355 meters) in length. Sometime later Piazzi Smyth came to believe the Pyramid was built using this cubit in the length of 25.025 inches (.6356362 meters), each cubit being 25 "Pyramid inches" long. (1 Pyramid inch = 1.001 British inches.) To validate the existence of this unit Smyth pointed out that an hereditary cubit of about 25 inches was used in the measurement of cloth in many places.[8]

Although many writers have followed the general contours of Smyth's interpretation of the Pyramid, a unit of 25.025 inches (.6356362 meters) does not fit the building very well using Cole's figures. Even allowing for variations in its length (as other ancient units also varied) and supposing it was once about 24.984576 inches (.6346095 meters) it would then fit the Pyramid 363 times at the base, 231 times on the height, but would produce an uneven apothem of 290.4.

The four units which in general terms fit the Pyramid's base, apothem and height evenly are:

	Meters		Inches	
	Stated	Required	Stated	Required
Egyptian foot	.300	.299173	11.811	11.778441
Royal cubit	.5241483	.5235528	20.635718	20.612273
	.525	.5235528	20.66925	20.612273
	.5263231	.5235528	20.72134	20.612273
Mir cubit	.6985013	.6980704	27.5	27.483031
Megalithic yard	.84	.8376845	33.0708	32.979638

This list shows the units in their stated values and in the values required to fit the Pyramid's average side perfectly using Cole's survey as the standard. We have added two additional values for the royal cubit since, according to Stecchini, it is established that the royal cubit is found in three slightly differing lengths. If the stated values are multiplied by the number of times the respective units might fit the Pyramid and the length of the average side is subtracted from that, these units all produce lengths longer than the side by these amounts:

Unit	Error	
	Meters	Inches
Egyptian foot		
.300 x 770	.63675	25.068
Royal cubit		
.5241483 x 440	.262	10.314
.525 x 440	.63675	25.068
.5263231 x 440	1.21891	47.988
Mir cubit		
.6985013 x 330	.14217	5.597
Megalithic yard		
.84 x 275	.63675	25.068

It could be objected that I have chosen Middle Eastern values for the Egyptian foot and the megalithic yard instead of slightly shorter more southerly values. However, it would take an equatorial value for any unit to fit the Pyramid perfectly and as far as I am aware there are no historical equatorial values for these units. Tompkins and Stecchini suggest that the brasse or fathom varied over a range sufficient to include an equatorial value, but we have already seen that the unit does not fit the height organically.[9]

Obviously, the two units which fit the Pyramid best are the "short" royal cubit and the mir cubit and therefore we shall limit comparison to these two measures. However other units may have varied, Egyptologists are virtually unanimous in believing that the "short" royal cubit was the unit used to build the Pyramid. Indeed, some declare that it fits the Pyramid perfectly, despite the fact that it does not.

The mir cubit's margin of error is only about half that of the royal cubit when applied to the side or perimeter of the building. In addition, there are two further significant indications that favor the mir cubit. First, it seems highly likely that there were originally 210 layers of stone in the Pyramid,

including the capstone; the height reckoned in mir cubits is also
210. There are now 201, 202 or 203 layers of stone, depending
on whose report one reads. Smyth estimated that there were
209, 210 or 211 original layers and later settled on 210 as the
most probable number. If the mir cubit were employed in the
construction, it may also explain why the word mir refers to
the height and the meridian triangle of a pyramid. No other
unit of measure fits the Pyramid's height once for each layer of
stone.

The second important test favoring the mir cubit involves
the dimensions of the King's Chamber, which are:[10]

Length	412.54 inches	10.478 meters	34.378 feet
Breadth	206.27 inches	5.239 meters	17.189 feet
Height	230.62 inches	5.857 meters	19.218 feet

It was Isaac Newton who pointed out that a royal cubit of
approximately 20.63 inches produced a room of 10 x 20 cubits.
At first glance this seems a very tight correlation, but using
Stecchini's exact value of 524.1483 millimeters (20.635718
inches) for the "short" royal cubit, this cubit is actually a bit too
long.

Length	*Inches*		*Meters*
20 x 20.635718 =	412.71436	20 x .5241483 =	10.482966
Required value	412.54	Required value	10.478536
Excessive by	.17436	Excessive by	.00443

Breadth			
10 x 20.635718 =	206.35718	10 x .5241483 =	5.241483
Required value	206.27	Required value	5.2392684
Excessive by	.08718	Excessive by	.0022146

By comparison, the mir cubit also fits the room in even
integers or fractions, making a room of 15 by 7.5 units.

Length	*Inches*		*Meters*
Required value	412.54	Required value	10.478536
15 x 27.5 =	412.5	15 x .6985013 =	10.477519
Deficient by	.04	Deficient by	.001017

Breadth			
Required value	206.27	Required value	5.2392684
7.5 x 27.5 =	206.25	7.5 x .6985013 =	5.2387597
Deficient by	.02	Deficient by	.0005087

Here the fit is nearly perfect. The mir cubit of 27.5 inches fits the King's Chamber over four times more precisely than the royal cubit. These calculations are confirmed by Petrie's remarks about the King's Chamber. He calculated that in this chamber the builders must have used a .523 meter cubit,[11] even though there is no historical example of such a cubit. In addition he observed that the King's Chamber has been badly shaken by an earthquake, causing the whole room to slightly expand.[12] Accordingly, a unit which is now slightly excessive would have been more so in the room's original condition, whereas a unit now slightly deficient may then have fitted the room perfectly.

In view of this, the mir cubit in the value of 27.5 inches (.6985013 meters) fits the room so perfectly that it may fit it too well. It seems as likely the King's Chamber was actually built using the mir cubit in the same value in which it fits the Pyramid's average side perfectly – 27.483031 inches (.6980704 meters). This value is slightly lower and allows a bit more room for the chamber to have expanded. It could be that the Pyramid was built with a unit of this length and that, as suggested, Cayce rounded off the .017 inch difference to 27.5.

Whichever value is used, there are three strong reasons for concluding the mir cubit fits the Pyramid better than the royal cubit – or any other unit ever suggested: it fits the side better; it corresponds to the probable number of layers of stone; it fits the King's Chamber better.[13] (Those interested in pursuing the subject will also find that the mir cubit fits the dimensions of "the pit" under the Great Pyramid better than the royal cubit; that it corresponds to the internal width of the sarcophagus in the King's Chamber and the internal depth of the sarcophagus in the Second Pyramid; and that it also seems to fit the external dimensions of the Second Pyramid better than the royal cubit.)

One final point about the mir cubit and other ancient units of measure is that many of these units are even fractions, or nearly even fractions, of one another. For instance, the four units which loosely seemed as if they could fit the Great Pyramid evenly are:

Unit	Number in Height	Divided by 35
Egyptian foot	490	14
Royal cubit	280	8
Mir cubit	210	6
Megalithic yard	175	5

The number of times each unit fits the height is commonly divisible by 35, and performing this division shows their basic proportional relationships to one another. In other words, if these units were all calculated on the same degree of latitude, the mir cubit would be:

> 7/3 of the Egyptian foot
> 4/3 of the royal cubit
> 5/6 of the megalithic yard

The royal cubit would be:

> 7/4 of the Egyptian foot
> 3/4 of the mir cubit
> 5/8 of the megalithic yard, etc.

In larger terms, almost all ancient units of measure appear to have an even proportional relationship to one or more other ancient units – assuming they were all calculated on the same degree of latitude. The extent to which I have been able to reconstruct those proportions for the units I have studied is shown in the following chart.

Proportions of Ancient Measures	Egyptian Foot	Geographic Foot	Remen	Geographic Cubit	Royal Cubit	Pyk Belady	Sacred Cubit	Palestinian Cubit	Mir Cubit	Megalithic Yard	Brasse or Fathom
Egyptian Foot					4/7				3/7		
Geographic Foot			5/6	2/3		8/15		12/25		11/30	1/6
Remen		6/5		4/5		16/25				11/25	1/5
Geographic Cubit		3/2	5/4		22/25	4/5		18/25		11/20	1/4
Royal Cubit	7/4			25/22		10/11		9/11	3/4	5/8	
Pyk Belady		15/8	25/16	5/4	11/10			9/10		11/16	5/16
Sacred Cubit									10/11		
Palestinian Cubit		25/12		25/18	11/9	10/9			11/12		
Mir Cubit	7/3				4/3		11/10	12/11		5/6	
Megalithic Yard		30/11	25/11	20/11	8/5	16/11			6/5		5/11
Brasse or Fathom		6	5	4		16/5				11/5	

These relationships clearly indicate that ancient units of measure were not arrived at arbitrarily as the length of a king's arm or foot, as is so often imagined. Many of them were defined on a scientific basis as a fraction of a minute or second of latitude.

Unit	No. in 1 Minute	No. in 1 Second
Egyptian foot	6160	
Greek or geographic foot	6000	100
Remen	5000	
Geographic cubit	4000	
Royal cubit	3520	
Pyk belady	3200	
Palestinian cubit	2880	48
Mir cubit	2640	44
Megalithic yard	2200	
Brasse or fathom	1000	

The fact that the mir cubit fits organically into these patterns and relationships is further evidence of its existence.

There are then a number of bases on which to test the unit used to build the Great Pyramid, and the best quantitative tests we can apply at this time conclusively show that the mir cubit fits the Pyramid better than any other unit ever advanced. This is a new development in the study of the Great Pyramid and because of its simple, empirical, quantitative basis it may have an unsettling effect upon Old Kingdom Egyptology for some years to come.

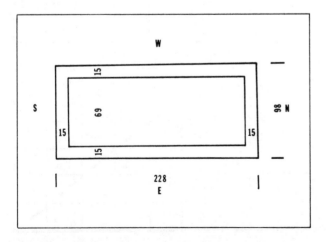

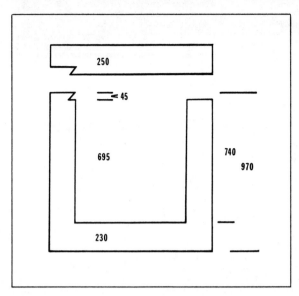

The mir cubit reflected in the dimensions of the sarcophagi of the Great and Second Pyramids. Opposite: The internal width of the Great Pyramid's sarcophagus is 69 cm. Above: The internal depth of the Second Pyramid's sarcophagus is 695 mm. Both dimensions nearly match the mir cubit of .698 meters.

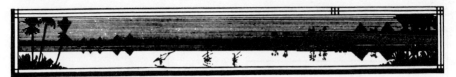

IV

The Axis of the Temple
at Karnak

Around the turn of this century the British astronomer, Sir Norman Lockyer, suggested that the axis of the great temple at Karnak in upper Egypt was laid out to indicate the position of the setting sun at the time of the summer solstice in about 4000 B.C. The obliquity of the ecliptic, or the angle of tilt of the earth's orbital plane to the celestial equator, has been changing very slowly over thousands of years. Today it is about 23°27′ while one source estimates it was about 24°6′ in 4000 B.C.[1] What this means in general terms is that viewed from most places in the northern hemisphere, on the summer solstice in 4000 B.C. the sun set on the horizon a bit north from where it sets today.

In 1921 F.S. Richards published a paper entitled *Note On The Age Of The Great Temple of Ammon At Karnak As Determined By The Orientation Of Its Axis.* This paper is a description of a survey to find the precise orientation of the long temple axis and to thus test Lockyer's theory. Richards found that in order for the temple axis to correspond with the setting sun at the time of the summer solstice the obliquity of the ecliptic would have to have been 25°9'55". Either Richards could not believe the angle of the ecliptic was ever so extreme, or this angle implied such a remote date for the foundation of the temple, that he dismissed the possibility that the temple axis was laid down to have any relation to the setting sun at the summer solstice.[2]

Richards did not give a date to which an ecliptic angle of 25°9'55" might correspond. The calculation of such a date involves many factors and uncertainties and a non-uniform rate of change. Estimates for the rate of change vary from one authority to another. Although sophisticated formulas have been developed to estimate this rate (as by the nineteenth century astronomer Simon Newcomb), even at the present time astronomers are not able to say precisely and definitely what the declination of the sun was more than several centuries ago.

Despite all these reservations, however, it is interesting to attempt an estimate of a date to which an ecliptic angle of 25°9'55" might have corresponded. A recent, representative estimate of the rate of change in the ecliptic is that it is decreasing by .75' per century.[3] This implies that it takes about 133 years to change by one minute. There is a difference of roughly 1°43' or 103 minutes between 25°9'55" and 23°27'. 103 x 133 = 13,699 years. Thus the date implied by this calculation is roughly 11,700 B.C.

There are nevertheless many reservations to be had about this figure as produced. Strictly on astronomic grounds the range of uncertainty is probably plus or minus 3000 years. In addition, further uncertainties are raised by the actual situation of the temple.

Among the unknown quantities that affect this calculation is the elevation of the temple at the time the axis was originally laid down. The illustration shows that the path of the setting sun in 4000 B.C. crossed the celestial horizon in the center of the temple axis. Apparently, this is the correlation that Lockyer noticed. However, it is the setting of the sun on the visual horizon that determines the point of reference. If the ground on which the temple stands were originally higher, and/or if

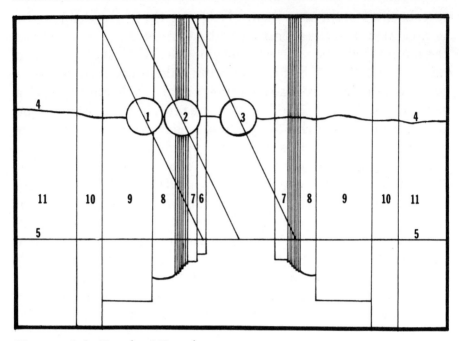

The axis of the Temple of Karnak.

Looking west-northwest down the axis of the temple, the sketch shows the position of the setting sun at the summer solstice. (Adapted from F.S. Richards.)

1. Path of the sun and its position on the horizon at present.
2. Path of the sun and its position on the horizon in 4000 B.C.
3. Path of the sun and its position on the horizon about 11,700 B.C.?
4. The visual horizon.
5. The celestial horizon.
6. Pylon I.
7. Pylon II.
8. Lotus columns.
9. Pylon IV.
10. Pylon VI.
11. The sanctuary of the temple.

Sun positions "1" and "2" cannot be seen from the sanctuary because they are hidden by the pylons.

the height of the hills on the other side of the Nile were lower, this would lower the visual horizon and bring the implied data forward. The same considerations would apply if the observation of the setting sun had been made high up in the temple rather than at ground level. None of these possibilities are considered in Richards's paper.

It is obvious that as it appears today the Karnak Temple is largely or entirely a product of the New Kingdom (1567-1085 B.C.) and I am not suggesting that anything presently visible at Karnak dates from 11,700 B.C. But it is well established that the same sacred sites were used again and again all over the ancient world and all that may be preserved from a much earlier era at Karnak is the orientation of the axis. It may also be noted that the orientation of sacred structures with respect to astronomic criteria was a widespread practice in both ancient and later times. The Great Pyramid, other Egyptian pyramids and temples, Stonehenge, Mayan structures in the Yucatan, the pre-Columbian complex at Teotihuacan, Mexico, the ground drawings near Nazca, Peru, and many temples and churches in pre-modern Europe all exhibit this same characteristic. The axis of the Karnak Temple is generally so close to the position of the setting summer solstice sun that it seems at least as likely that the axis once corresponded to that position as that it had no astronomic significance at all. It is also interesting that 11,700 B.C. ties in well with dates supplied by Herodotus, Manetho, Cayce, and indirectly by Plato, for the commencement of Egyptian monarchy.

We can conclude that there are increasing indications suggesting that the sources of Egyptian civilization began much earlier than has been thought and that – if there is any validity to dating this site by astronomic orientation – the axis of the Karnak Temple points to a much earlier date for its original establishment than the historical range of the New Kingdom.

Notes

NOTES
Chapter 2
The Wonder of the World

1. Cole, *The Determination of the Exact Size and Orientation of the Great Pyramid*.
2. 921.453 ÷ 4 = 230.36325 meters.
3. The height of the Pyramid was 7/11 of its base. 230.36325 × 7/11 = 146.59479 meters.
4. Tompkins, *Secrets of the Great Pyramid*, p. XIV.
5. See Smyth, *Our Inheritance in the Great Pyramid*, Plate II; also see pp. 85-90. Smyth credits William Petrie, father of the archaeologist William M. Flinders Petrie, as the first to notice that there is "more earth and less sea" in the Pyramid's meridian of longitude than any other. (Fourth Edition, 1880.)
6. *Ibid.*
7. See Hapgood, *Maps of the Ancient Sea Kings*, regarding the development of instruments for defining longitude.
8. A half minute of equatorial latitude is 921.45 meters. Cole's survey showed the Pyramid's perimeter was 921.453 meters. The difference is about 3 mm or 1/9 of an inch.
9. Tompkins, *Secrets of the Great Pyramid*, p. 1.
10. *Ibid.*
11. Fakhry, *The Pyramids*, p. 117.
12. Tompkins, *Secrets of the Great Pyramid*, p. 49.
13. Rutherford, *Pyramidology*. Third Edition, Vol. I, p. 27.
14. Maragioglio and Renaldi, *L'Archetettura Della Piramidi Menfite*, Part IV, p. 12.
15. Petrie as quoted by Smyth, *Our Inheritance in the Great Pyramid*, 1890 Edition, p. 20.
16. Tompkins, *Secrets of the Great Pyramid*, p. 101.
17. *Ibid.*, pp. 101-103.
18. Petrie's figures for this sarcophagus, as given by Stecchini in *Secrets of the Great Pyramid*, p. 324, are:

	Inches	Feet	Millimeters
Length	89.62	7.46	2276.35
Width	38.50	3.20	977.90
Height	41.31	3.44	1049.27

19. Tompkins, *Secrets of the Great Pyramid*, p. 103.

NOTES
Chapter 3
Recent Discoveries

1. See Stecchini, "Notes on the Relation of Ancient Measures to the Great Pyramid", an appendix in Tompkins, *Secrets of the Great Pyramid*, pp. 286-383.
2. See Stecchini, *ibid.*, for current figures and sources of earth measurements. Also see articles on "Geodesy", *Encyclopaedia Britannica* (1974) or *Encyclopaedia Americana* (1976).
3. Cole, *The Exact Size and Orientation of the Great Pyramid of Giza.*

	Feet	Meters
North Side	755.42	230.251
East Side	755.87	230.391
South Side	756.08	230.454
West Side	755.76	230.357
Total Perimeter	3023.13	921.453
1/2 Minute Equatorial Latitude	3023.12	921.45

It seems obvious that given the precision with which the Pyramid was built, the builders could have made the sides within a fraction of an inch of being equal if they had so desired. The differing lengths of the sides are likely not errors but the result of intentional design. Possibly these differences refer to subtle configurations in the shape of the earth.
4. In antiquity temples were apparently designed in measurements relating to the size of the earth because the temple was intended to represent the earth. It was the place where celestial and terrestrial influences were supposed to meet.
5. See Stecchini, "Notes on the Relation of Ancient Measures to the Great Pyramid".
6. Also see Stecchini, p. 378.

NOTES
Chapter 4
The Madness

1. Petrie, *Seventy Years in Archaeology*, pp. 36-37.
2. Maragioglio and Renaldi, *L'Archetettura Della Piramidi Menfite*, Part II, p. 7.

NOTES
Chapter 5
An Impossible Building

1. With its platform, the Pyramid was some 482 feet (147 meters) high and the hill on which it stands is about 120 feet (36 meters). The top of the Pyramid was thus approximately 600 feet (183 meters) above the level of the delta to the east.

2. Maragioglio and Renaldi, *L'Archetettura Della Piramidi Menfite*, Part IV, p. 20 and p. 108.
3. Edwards, *The Pyramids of Egypt*, p. 227.
4. Petrie, "The Building of a Pyramid", in *Ancient Egypt*, 1930, Part II, pp. 33-39; quoted by F.N. Wheeler, "Pyramids and Their Purpose in Antiquity", Vol. IX, 1935, pp. 172-174; as reported by Edwards, *The Pyramids of Egypt*, p. 226.
5. Lauer was apparently aware of this difficulty and suggested the casing blocks may have had the following shapes.

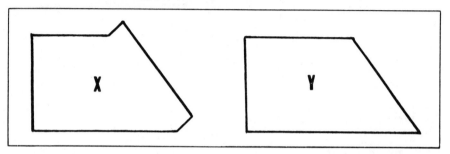

Shape "X" would certainly seem preferable to shape "Y" if the Pyramid were finished from the top down. The only intact casing stones at the base on the Pyramid's north face, however, have shape "Y" and not "X". It is still possible, of course, that shape "X" may have been employed at higher levels of the Pyramid, but there is now no way of knowing this.

NOTES
Chapter 6
Legends and the Mistress of the Pyramids

1. See *The History of Herodotus*, translated by George Rawlinson, Vol. 2, pp. 169-176.
2. *Ibid.*
3. As in Rutherford, *Pyramidology*, Vol. I, p. 35.
4. As in Sykes, *The Pyramids of Egypt*, p. 6.
    Egerton Sykes points out that Gibbon in Chapter 26 of his *Decline and Fall of the Roman Empire* pays tribute to the accuracy, fidelity and impartiality of Marcellinus.
5. Tompkins, *Secrets of the Great Pyramid*, pp. 217-218.
6. As in Sykes, *The Pyramids of Egypt*, p.6.
7. Masoudi's full name was Abd el Kadar ben Mohammed al Makrizi. The title of the work quoted, transliterated from the Arabic, is *Akbar al Zamen - Noumadj al Zemel*.
8. As in Sykes, *The Pyramids of Egypt*, p.7.
9. *Ibid.*, pp. 7-8.
10. All references from Al Makir to Al-Dimishgi from Edgar Evans Cayce, *Edgar Cayce on Atlantis*, p. 152.

11. Translated by Selim Hassan, *The Sphinx: Its History in Light of Recent Excavations*, pp. 222-224.

12. The main part of the stela contains representations of the sacred statues and emblems of the gods supposed to have been found in the temple by Khufu. Each is accompanied by an explanation of the material of which it is made, its height, and the title of the deity it represents. The stela also mentions a table and vases full of sacrificial animals which were slain and eaten in the vicinity. The final line of this part of the stela reads, "The figure of this god [the Sphinx], being cut in stone, is solid, and will exist to eternity, having always its face regarding the Orient."

NOTES
Chapter 8
Searching for Khufu

1. Adapted from Anonymous, *The Egyptian Museum, Cairo: A Description of the Principal Monuments*, and Kamil, *Luxor: A Guide to Ancient Thebes*.
2. Budge, *A History of Egypt*, p. 125.
3. *Ibid.*, p. 125.
4. *Ibid.*, pp. 113-114.
5. *Ibid.*, p. 116.
6. *Ibid.*, pp. 129-146.
7. *Ibid.*, p. 145. In neither of these versions of Manetho, nor in the more limited *Book of Sothis* or in *The Old Chronicle*, which are also derived from him, does Budge give the name "Khufu", but uses instead the name "Souphis", usually taken as a variant of the same name.
8. *Encyclopaedia Britannica Macropaedia*, 1974, Vol. 4, p. 575.
9. Africanus, as per Budge, shows the first three dynasties totaling 769 years, and that "Khufu", or "Souphis", was the second king of the Fourth Dynasty after his predecessor's reign of 29 years.
10. Dates early Egyptologists gave for the beginning of the reign of Menes are:

Champollion-Figeac	5867 B.C.
Broeckh	5702 B.C.
Lepsius	3892 B.C.
Mariette	5004 B.C.
Bunsen	3623 B.C.
Wilkinson	2320 B.C.
Brugsch	4455 or 4400 B.C.

Budge, *A History of Egypt*, p. 159.
11. Breasted, *A History of Egypt*, pp. 147-148.
12. *Ibid.*, p. 214.
13. Fakhry, *The Pyramids*, p. 102.
14. Breasted, *A History of Egypt*, p. 35.
15. Maspero, *The Dawn of Civilization*, pp. 363-364.
16. Reisner and Smith, *History of the Giza Necropolis*, Vol. 2, p. 12.

NOTES
Chapter 9
The Marks in the Hidden Chambers

1. Maspero, *The Dawn of Civilization*, p. 370.
2. Breasted, *A History of Egypt*. p. 60.
3. Petrie, *A History of Egypt*, Vol. I, pp. 42-43.
4. Maspero, *The Dawn of Civilization*, pp. 363-364.
5. Edwards, *The Pyramids of Egypt*, p. 230.
6. Petrie, *A History of Egypt*, p. 53.
7. Edwards, *The Pyramids of Egypt*, p. 241.
8. This is not to ignore the fact that there are five or six fine large statues with cartouches reading "Khafra" on them and some smaller statues with cartouches reading "Menkaura" in the Cairo Museum, nor yet that the "tomb" with the empty sarcophagus on the east side of the Great Pyramid has been attributed to Hetepheres, supposedly the mother of Khufu. No more is known about any of these figures than about Khufu. The Third Pyramid has been attributed to Menkaura only because Herodotus and Diodorus Siculus attributed it to him and because the name "Menkaura" was found written in red paint on the ceiling of a chamber in the second of the three subsidiary pyramids south of the Third Pyramid. (Edwards, *The Pyramids of Egypt*, p. 121.) No such name was found in the Third Pyramid itself. It is quite likely that the small pyramid is not contemporary with the Third Pyramid. One Egyptologist notes: "Contemporary records shed no light on the life and character of Mycerinus" (Menkaura). (Edwards, *The Pyramids of Egypt*, p. 120.) The same holds true for Khafra. There is no indication a king by that name ever existed. The Second Pyramid is attributed to Khafra by tradition and circumstantial evidence. In *A History of Egypt* (p. 47) Petrie wrote: "It [the Second Pyramid] has always been attributed to him [Khafra] by Herodotus and Diodorus and by modern writers. The only monumental evidences are the pieces of a bowl and a mace head with his name found in the temple (east) of this pyramid." Statues of Khafra have also been found in the vicinity, but Khafra – whom Petrie thought reigned from 3908-3845 B.C. – was, like Khufu and Menkaura, also worshipped in later times (Petrie, *A History of Egypt*, p. 53), and there is now no way of telling whether the artifacts and statues bearing this cartouche are products of the Pyramid Age or a later era. As for Hetepheres, George Reisner, one of the men who excavated her "tomb", wrote: "Queen Hetepheres is entirely unknown, except for the meager information supplied by the titles given upon the objects in her tomb." (Reisner and Smith, *History of the Giza Necropolis*, Vol. 2, pp. 1-12.) Again, all we have are a few names or titles. It is easy to imagine that "Menkaura", "Khafra" and other such names were put on statues of those who were considered to be material representatives or servants of the deities or cults involved. Like the small votive figurine supposedly representing Khufu, they could have been made thousands of years after the building of the pyramids now associated with those names.
9. Blanchard, *Handbook of Egyptian Gods and Mummy Amulets*, p. 6.
10. Stewart, *The Symbolism of the Gods of the Egyptians and the Light They Throw on Freemasonry*, pp. 97-98 and p. 116.
11. Blanchard, *Handbook of Egyptian Gods and Mummy Amulets*, p. 16.
12. Blavatsky, *The Secret Doctrine*, Vol. II, p. 210.

13. *Ibid.*
14. Murray, "The Book of Thoth", in *Ancient Egyptian Legends*, pp. 29-31; also see Kingsland, *The Gnosis Or Ancient Wisdom In the Christian Scriptures*, pp. 96-97 and Note 2, p. 96; also see James, *Myths and Legends of Ancient Egypt*, pp. 100-117.
15. Numbers 21:4-9.

NOTES
Chapter 10
Adventures in Wonderland

1. As explained in Part I of the Appendix, the two most authoritative figures for the sockets' perimeter derived from the surveys of Petrie and Cole are 36,521.2 inches and 36,527.604 inches. I have taken an average of these two figures, 36,524.402 inches or 3043.7 feet for my calculations.
2. See Tompkins, *Secrets of the Great Pyramid*, p. 210 ff., p. 371 ff.
3. See Tompkins, *ibid.*, for a general exposition of the history of this tradition.
4. See Sugrue, *There Is a River*, and Stearn, *Edgar Cayce – The Sleeping Prophet*, for general biographies.
5. See Edgar Evans Cayce and Hugh Lynn Cayce, *The Outer Limits of Edgar Cayce's Power*.
6. See Furst, *Edgar Cayce's Story of Jesus*.

NOTES
Chapter 11
Checking Out the Sleeping Prophet

References to and excerpts from the Cayce transcripts are identified by the index number of the transcript. Where possible, I have also shown where the transcript, or parts of it, may be found in a published source.

1. Transcript 5750-1, as in Furst, *Edgar Cayce's Story of Jesus*. p. 98; also see transcripts 341-8 and 2056-1, as in Lehner, *The Egyptian Heritage*, p. 71.
2. Transcript 2667-1, as in Lehner, *The Egyptian Heritage*, pp. 57-58.
3. Transcript 275-38, *ibid.*, pp. 49-50.
4. Transcripts 1135-1, *ibid.*, p. 58; 470-33, *ibid.*, p. 59.
5. Transcript 470-33, *ibid.*, p. 59.
6. Transcript 294-149, as in Furst, *Edgar Cayce's Story of Jesus*, pp. 88-89.
7. Transcript 900-277, as in Lehner, *The Egyptian Heritage*, p. 19.
8. Lehner, *ibid.*, referred to in many places.
9. Transcript 2329-3, *ibid.*, p. 43.
10. Transcript 470-33, *ibid.*, pp. 63-64.
11. Transcript 2533-4, *ibid.*, pp. 55-56.
12. Transcript 294-149, as in Furst, *Edgar Cayce's Story of Jesus*, pp. 88-89.

13. Transcript 281-25, as in Lehner, *The Egyptian Heritage*, p. 26.

14. *Ibid.*, also see Part III of the Appendix. Unfortunately, Cayce said that few remains of this temple would ever be found.

15. See Part III of the Appendix.

16. Transcript 281-42, as in Furst, *Edgar Cayce's Story of Jesus*, p. 79.

17. Transcript 294-150, *ibid.*, pp. 88-89.

18. Transcript 294-151, as in Lehner, *The Egyptian Heritage*, p. 86.

19. Lehner, *ibid.*, pp. 113-114.

20. *Ibid.*

21. Transcript, 900-277, *ibid.*, p. 9.

22. See Lehner for further comments on these and other palettes, *ibid.*, pp. 108-112.

23. See Herodotus, *The History of Herodotus*, Vol II, pp. 67-68.

24. See Petrie, *Religious Life in Ancient Egypt*, p. 104.

25. The Atlantis scholar, Egerton Sykes, also believes the Gizeh Pyramids date from about 10,000 B.C. See Sykes, *The Pyramids of Egypt*. In addition, we have already noted the curious coincidence that when expressed in inches, the half minute of equatorial longitude incorporated in the distances between the sockets equals the number of days in 100 years, 36,524.2. (This does not perfectly match the figure I used for calculations in the Appendix, but it is a possible value for the sockets' perimeter within the small range of uncertainty involved.) It is doubly coincidental in that this is just the length of time the transcripts state it took to build the Pyramid. If this is of significance, it is necessary to suppose that the inch and English measures in general are very ancient. Considerable research by a number of scientists indicates that this is likely. L.C. Stecchini declares that English measures can be traced back to the third millennium B.C. We have seen that the mir cubit may have been used to build the Pyramid, but this does not exclude the possibility that the builders used a multiple system of measures, just as today we have the inch, foot, yard, fathom, chain, furlong and mile, or in the metric system, millimeters, centimeters, meters and kilometers. The connection between the sockets' perimeter and the number of days in 100 years might also be seen as a confirmation of Cayce's chronology.

26. Lehner, *The Egyptian Heritage*, p. 131.

27. Reisner, *History of the Giza Necropolis*, Vol. I, pp. 3-4.

28. The only exceptions to this seem to be the Pyramid of Sekhemket at Saqqara and the Pyramid of Khaba at Zawiyet el Aryan, both of which were very poorly made and apparently never finished. See Mendelssohn, *The Riddle of the Pyramids*, pp. 42-44.

29. Edwards has noted: "It is, moreover, irrefutable that all the surviving subsidiary pyramids at Gizeh were built with internal casings, and it would be strange if the main pyramids were composed in a different way." (Edwards, *The Pyramids of Egypt*, p. 218.) However, it seems rather conclusively to be the case that the main pyramids *are* composed in a different way. The tunnel excavated into the Great Pyramid through the north face by the ninth century explorer Al Mamoon is used at the present time for access to the interior. Maragioglio and Renaldi point out (*L'Archetettura Della Piramidi Menfite*, Part IV, p. 114) that Al Mamoon's tunnel should penetrate many layer faces, but does not. They later state the structure of the King's Chamber and the relieving chamber system above this is "absolutely incompatible with a nucleus made in sloping layers". (*Ibid.*, Part IV, p. 134.)

As for the Second Pyramid, the nineteenth century archaeologist Mariette insisted he could not find any nonvertical joints in the nucleus. (Maragioglio and Renaldi, *ibid.*, Part V, p. 46.) Maragioglio and Renaldi made a similar report:

> A careful examination of the masonry of the nucleus, although it was not possible to carry it out thoroughly owing to the state of the monument, has not provided factors in favour of the theory ... according to which all pyramids were built in successive sloping layers, and has not even proved the existence of large steps in the nucleus. (*Ibid.*, Part V, p. 48.)

There is less information available for the Third Pyramid, but here again the indications are that no series of casings or sloping layers are involved. In A.D. 1215 Caliph Malek Al Aziz Othman ordered the pyramids destroyed and set to work on the Third Pyramid with a large force of men. But the size of the stones and the scale of the work were too much for this army to dismantle. All that can be seen of their work is a rather deep scar on the north face. This scar does not reveal any casings or sloping layers of construction.

30. According to Maragioglio and Renaldi, *L'Archetettura Della Piramidi Menfite*, Part IV, p. 174: "The small pyramids of the 'queens' [east of the Great Pyramid] seem to have been completely isolated from the other elements of the royal complex. No traces of a door, in fact, exist in the south wall of the ceremonial causeway ... nor of an opening in the inner enclosure wall of the Great Pyramid." The so called 'mortuary' temple in front of the Great Pyramid is also "entirely different from the mortuary temples which preceded and followed it". (Fakhry, *The Pyramids*, p. 105.) All that remains of this important temple is a floor of extremely hard, black diorite blocks. This floor, unfortunately, has been incorporated in a modern road passing over the site.

31. Breasted, *A History of Egypt*, p. 45.

32. Budge, *A History of Egypt*, pp. 98-101.

NOTES
Chapter 12
On the Road to Atlantis

1. See E.E. Cayce, *Edgar Cayce on Atlantis*; Lehner, *The Egyptian Heritage*; and Furst, *Edgar Cayce's Story of Jesus*. Each of these works contains a handful of partial, scattered transcripts describing these patterns.
2. E.E. Cayce, *ibid.*; Lehner, *ibid.*
3. Transcript 5540-5, as in Lehner, *The Egyptian Heritage*, p. 97.
4. Transcript 378-16, *ibid.*, p. 99.
5. Stanford Research Institute, *Application of Modern Sensing Techniques to Egyptology*, pp. 64-67.
6. See transcripts 2329-3, 378-1, 5748-6 as in Lehner, *The Egyptian Heritage*, p. 100; see *Earth Changes*, (anonymous), for further discussion of these transcripts. *Edgar Cayce on Atlantis* also contains some of these transcripts.
7. See Berlitz, *The Mystery of Atlantis*, pp. 177-194.
8. Transcript 519-1, as in E.E. Cayce, *Edgar Cayce on Atlantis*, p. 87.

9. *Ibid.*
10. See E.E. Cayce, *ibid.*, pp. 84-107 for a convenient collection of transcripts describing Atlantean scientific accomplishments.

NOTES
Chapter 13
A Few Wild Reports

1. Ignatius Donnelly and others have pointed out the possibility of a direct connection between Greek myths and Atlantis, saying that Greek myths are Atlantean history. Others see a similar relationship between the Flood of *Genesis* and the destruction of Atlantis. Some point out that the roots of the Hebrew word for Adam are "red earth", and that the Atlanteans are said to have been the red race.
2. Verrill, *Old Civilizations of the New World*, p. 223.
3. See Tomas, *The Home of the Gods (Atlantis from Legend to Discovery)* pp. 84-85; also see Berlitz, *Mysteries from Forgotten Worlds*, p. 24.
4. "The Golden Treasure of Palmar Sur", by Rawleigh H. Ralls, specifies three plants whose juices were used for pickling such objects in Costa Rica. These are *Oxalis L, Monsteras* and *Anthuriums.* He reports: "These juices dissolve the copper and leave a surface film of pure gold." See *Lapidary Journal*, October 1973, Vol. 27, No. 7, p. 1122.
5. See Percy Knauth, *The Metalsmiths*, pp. 138-139.
6. Tomas, *We Are Not The First*, p. 32.
7. Knauth, *The Metalsmiths*, pp. 133-137.
8. Berlitz, *Mysteries from Forgotten Worlds*, pp. 79-80.
9. Tomas, *We Are Not The First*, p. 26.
10. *Ibid.*, pp. 26-27.
11. Berlitz, *Mysteries From Forgotten Worlds*, p. 83.
12. Verrill, *Old Civilizations of the New World*, p. 96.
13. *Ibid.*, p. 49.
14. Tompkins, *Mysteries of the Mexican Pyramids*, p. 290.
15. Neugebauer, *The Exact Sciences in Antiquity.* p. 27. Neugebauer commented as follows: "The lack of a notation which determines the absolute value of a number [in ancient Babylon] made it possible to misinterpret simple tables of multiplication or reciprocals. When Hilprecht, in 1906, published a volume of 'mathematical, metrological and chronological tablets from the Temple Library of Nippur' he was convinced that these texts showed a relation to Plato's number mysticism. In Book VIII of the *Republic*, Plato gives some cabalistic rules as to how guardians of his dictatorially ruled community should arrange proper marriages. By some wild artifices, Plato's cabala was brought into relationship with the numbers found on the tablets. Thus 1,10 [Babylonian sexagesimal notation for 70 or 1-1/6 etc.] was interpreted to mean 195,955,200,000,000 and in this fashion whole tablets were transcribed and explained."
16. Transcript 958-3; June 28, 1940, as in E.E. Cayce, *Edgar Cayce on Atlantis*, p. 157.
17. Tomas, *The Home of the Gods (Atlantis From Legend to Discovery)*, pp. 120-121.

18. Mertz, *Atlantis: Dwelling Place of the Gods*, p. 29, cites the report of Pierre de Latil of the Sorbonne, *The Enigma of the Bahamas*, Paris, 1970 (trans.). According to Mertz, de Latil and his colleagues were intrigued with the conflicting reports about the Bimini Road, some of which came from the same person. John Gifford, Division of Marine Geology, University of Miami, issued two reports on the site. In the first he noted that the pattern of fragmentation in the "road" was unlike that of beach rock elsewhere in the Bahamas and that there was nothing to disprove the possibility of it being man-made. In the second, about 20 months later, he reported that no tool marks could be found on the stones, and thus doubted the archaeological nature of the site. Mertz says de Latil was open to either an archaeological or geological solution, since even if it proved to be geological in nature, this kind of formation would be "without parallel", and therefore of great interest, but he nevertheless "fully expected to confirm the geological formation at the site". After investigating, however, de Latil concluded: "We returned from the Bahamas as believers in the archaeological solution."

NOTES
Chapter 14
Back Home in Poseidia

1. Hawkins, *Stonehenge Decoded*.
2. Hapgood, *Maps of the Ancient Sea Kings*.
3. E.E. Cayce, *Edgar Cayce On Atlantis*.
4. Michell, *The View Over Atlantis*.
5. Reiche, *Mystery on the Desert, Peruvian Ground Drawings*.
6. Von Däniken, *Chariots of the Gods?* and subsequent works.
7. Tomas, *We Are Not The First*, p. 29.
8. *Ibid.*, p. 32; also see Tomas, *The Home of the Gods (Atlantis From Legend To Discovery)* p. 85.
9. In *We Are Not The First*, p. 29, Tomas says the right side of the skull is "shattered". In *The Home of the Gods (Atlantis From Legend to Discovery)* p. 65, he says this side of the skull is "missing".
10. Tomas, *We Are Not The First*, p. 28; shows a photograph of the skull in center section.
11. Tomas, *The Home of the Gods (Atlantis From Legend To Discovery)*, p. 79; also see *We Are Not The First*, p. 65, where Tomas cites M. Agrest, *Literatournaya Gazeta*, Moscow, 1963.
12. Tomas, *We Are Not The First*, p. 23.
13. See W.R. Corliss, *Strange Artifacts, A Sourcebook on Ancient Man*, Vol. 2, cites J.C. Hudson, *Nature*, 172: pp. 499-500, September 12, 1953.
14. See Tomas, *The Home of the Gods (Atlantis From Legend To Discovery)*, p. 67; also see Tomas, *We Are Not The First*, p. 29.
15. Verrill, *Old Civilizations of the New World*, p. 22, p. 322.
16. See Tomas, *We Are Not The First*, p. 93; Berlitz, *Mysteries From Forgotten Worlds*, p. 24.

17. Berlitz, *The Bermuda Triangle*, p. 156.
18. Transcript 2437-1, as in E.E. Cayce, *Edgar Cayce On Atlantis*, p. 84.
19. Hoyle, "Stonehenge – An Eclipse Predictor", *Nature*, 211: pp. 454-456; July 30, 1966.
20. See Thom, *Megalithic Sites in Britain, Megalithic Lunar Observatories*.
21. See Eddy, "Probing the Mystery of the Medicine Wheels", *National Geographic*, January 1977.
22. Corliss, *Strange Artifacts*, Vol. 2, cites *American Journal of Science*, 2:15: pp. 122-123, 1953; and *Nature*, 126: p. 445, September 13, 1930.
23. Tomas, *We Are Not The First*, p. 65, quotes George Rawlinson in *The Five Great Monarchies of the Ancient Eastern World*, Vol. 3 (New York, 1880): " There is said to be distinct evidence that they observed the four satellites of Jupiter and strong reason to believe that they were acquainted likewise with the seven satellites of Saturn."
24. Corliss, *Strange Artifacts*, Vol. 2, p. 133, cites Anon., New York *Times*, IV, 11:8, May 24, 1936.
25. National Geographic Society, *Greece and Rome, Builders of Our World*, p. 210.
26. Corliss, *Strange Artifacts*, Vol. 2, p. 106, cites A.D. Wackerbarth, Royal Astronomical Society, 33; 576-577, 1873. Wackerbarth cites the treatise *Pesachim* of the *Talmud*. fol. 94 recto.
27. Stecchini, "Notes on the Relation of Ancient Measures to the Great Pyramid", an appendix in Tompkins, *Secrets of the Great Pyramid*.
28. As quoted by Tomas, *We Are Not The First*, p. 90.
29. As quoted by Tomas, *The Home of the Gods (Atlantis from Legend To Discovery)*, p. 81, cites Sydney (Australia) *Daily Mirror*, January 9, 1959. Also see Price's comments in *Scientific American*, June 1959, and in *Natural History*, March 1962.
30. Corliss, *Strange Artifacts*, Vol. 1, pp. 64-66.
31. Mertz, *Atlantis – Dwelling Place of the Gods*, p. 107, quotes the Tomas report of 1890.
32. Mertz says the inscription reads, "The whisper of death". See Berlitz, *Mysteries From Forgotten Worlds*, p. 145, and Mertz, *Atlantis – Dwelling Place of the Gods*, pp. 105-108.
33. Tomas, *We Are Not The First*, p. 138, cites *Man*, bulletin of the Royal Anthropological Institute, London, 1952.
34. Tomas, *The Home of the Gods (Atlantis From Legend To Discovery)*, p. 40, cites Alexander Gorbovsky, *Riddles of Antiquity*.
35. *The Mahabharata* and *The Ramayana* as quoted by Berlitz, *Mysteries from Forgotten Worlds*, p. 214.

NOTES
Chapter 15
The Great Decline

1. Berlitz, *Mysteries From Forgotten Worlds*, p. 76.
2. Regarding the Alatri tower, see Corliss, *Strange Artifacts*, Vol. 2, p. 158.
3. See Mertz, *Atlantis – Dwelling Place of the Gods*, for further details on American earthworks.
4. *Ibid.*, pp. 120-121.
5. The illustrations are derived from Lockyer, "Notes on Ancient British Monuments", *Nature*, 77:56:59, November 21, 1907, as reprinted by Corliss, *Ancient Artifacts*, Vol. 2, pp. 248-250. Many of Lockyer's interpretations were revived by John Michell in *The View Over Atlantis* (1969), and since then dozens of writers have followed his lead, often claiming alignments and patterns far more questionable than those of Lockyer and Michell.
6. The standard work on the subject is *Roman Roads in Britain* by Ivan D. Margary. Margary does not accept the pre-Roman network idea, but presents much well documented evidence that can be used to support that idea.
7. See Margary, *Roman Roads in Britain*.
8. Verrill, *Old Civilizations of the New World*, p. 320.

NOTES
Chapter 16
Teaching of the Old Priest

1. See Berlitz, *The Mystery of Atlantis*, pp. 24-50, for further discussion of classical references.
2. Merejekowski, *Atlantis/Europe – The Secret of the West*, pp. 36-37.
3. As quoted in Berlitz, *The Mystery of Atlantis*, p. 69.
4. E.E. Cayce, *Edgar Cayce On Atlantis*, p. 20, cites a 1958 study by O. Mellis; also see Berlitz, *The Mystery of Atlantis*, pp. 69-70.
5. E.E. Cayce, *Edgar Cayce on Atlantis*, p. 20, quotes a 1959 report from *Military Engineer*.
6. Reported by Tomas, *The Home of the Gods (Atlantis From Legend To Discovery)*, p. 122.
7. *Ibid.*
8. See Berlitz, *The Mystery of Atlantis*, especially pp. 51-64 and pp. 78-87; also see *Mysteries From Forgotten Worlds*, pp. 131-156.
9. Much apocalyptical evangelical literature has been published in the United States in the 1960s and 1970s. See, for example, Lindsey, *The Late Great Planet Earth*.
10. See transcript 5748-5 (June 30, 1932) among many others.
11. See Nostradamus' *Epistle to Henry II* and his "1999" quatrain, which reads in part: "In the year 1999 and seven months, from the sky will come a great king of terror." Also see McCann, *Nostradamus*, pp. 412-421.

12. Tompkins, *Mysteries of the Mexican Pyramids*, p. 286, cites December 24, 2011 as the end of the next cycle.
13. See Waters, *The Book of the Hopi*, pp. 333-334.
14. See Cheiro, *Cheiro's World Predictions*, pp. 233-254.
15. Tomas, *The Home of the Gods (Atlantis From Legend To Discovery)*, p. 27.

NOTES
Chapter 17
Through the Looking-Glass

1. De Santillana and von Dechend, *Hamlet's Mill*, p. 119.
2. "Puzzling Out Man's Ascent", *Time*, November 7, 1977, Vol. 110, No. 19, p. 67.
3. Berlitz, *Mysteries from Forgotten Worlds*, p. 170; also see Marshack, *The Roots of Civilization*, various references to bones inscribed with notations dated at 30,000 B.C.
4. De Santillana and von Dechend, *Hamlet's Mill*, p. 383.
5. *Ibid.*, p. 384.
6. Transcript 3976-15.
7. "Pelee" may refer to either Mt. Pelee on the Caribbean island of Martinique or to the Kileua volcano in Hawaii. The native Hawaiians believe that eruptions of this volcano are caused by the god Pelee.
8. Waters, *The Book of the Hopi*, p. 26.
9. See Hapgood, *The Path of the Pole*.
10. Waters, *The Book of the Hopi*.
11. The spiritual entities caused this radical transformation to take place by influencing the body's endocrine glands.

NOTES
Appendix

I

1. For an instructive essay on some of the many irregularities and other factors involved in measurement of the earth, see King-Hele, "The Shape of the Earth", *Science*, June 25, 1976, Vol. 192, No. 4246.
2. Tompkins, *Secrets of the Great Pyramid*, p. 45.
3. Davidson and Aldersmith, *The Great Pyramid: Its Divine Message*, p. 120.
4. Rutherford, *Pyramidology*, Vol. II, pp. 244-245.
5. See Davidson and Aldersmith, *ibid.*, p. 120.
6. *Ibid.*
7. In *Secrets of the Great Pyramid* (p. 209) Peter Tompkins also came close to pointing out the incorporation of a value for equatorial longitude. Indeed, he presents the following illustration:

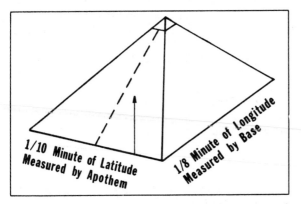

It is captioned to the effect that the Egyptian foot, the royal cubit and other units "all fit perfectly ... into the base and apothem of the Great Pyramid because they are all fractions of a correct geographical degree of latitude or longitude at the equator." It is obvious that Tompkins felt that a longitudinal value is involved, but what he failed to appreciate is that there is a significant difference in length between a degree of latitude and a degree of longitude at the equator. The base of the Pyramid cannot accurately incorporate both a half minute of equatorial latitude and longitude because a half minute of that longitude is about 20 feet (6 meters) longer than that latitude. It is far too loose an approach to the question to say that it does both. Tompkins's colleague Stecchini was apparently very much aware of this, yet he also expected a longitudinal value to be involved. He wrote:

> One would have expected the perimeter of the Pyramid to have been calculated by the length of the degree of longitude at the equator, but the builders instead calculated by the degree of latitude, because their concern was the length of the arc of meridian. *(Secrets of the Great Pyramid, p. 373.)*

Only the perimeter of the sockets matches a longitudinal value, and both Tompkins and Stecchini overlooked them.

8. Actually, the article's figure is 3949.909 miles, but converting 6356.774 km at 39.37 inches to the meter we get 3949.9081 miles. 3949.909 implies a conversion rate of 39.370004. Since 39.37 is used elsewhere in this work, I have chosen to use 3949.9081 miles for the sake of consistency in these calculations. The difference between 3949.909 miles and 3949.9081 miles is 4.752 feet and has no significant effect upon our results.
9. See, for example, Petrie, *Seventy Years in Archaeology*, pp. 36-37.
10. Part IV, p. 12.
11. King-Hele, "The Shape of the Earth", *Science*, June 25, 1976, Vol. 192, No. 4246.

NOTES
Appendix

II

1. See Stecchini's remarks in the appendix of *Secrets of the Great Pyramid*, p. 372.
2. Maragioglio and Renaldi, *L'Archetettura Della Piramidi Menfite*, Part IV, p. 48.
3. *Ibid.*, Part V, p. 100.
4. *Ibid.*, Part IV, p. 12; also see Hassan, *The Sphinx: Its History in Light of Recent Excavations.*
5. Fakhry, *The Pyramids*, p. 105.
6. Maragioglio and Renaldi, *ibid.*, Part IV, p. 66.
7. Edwards, *The Pyramids of Egypt*, p. 235.
8. Other researchers think there may have been only one layer of granite at the base instead of two as supposed by Edwards.
9. Edwards, *ibid.*, p. 228.

NOTES
Appendix

III

1. Transcript 281-25, as in Lehner, *The Egyptian Heritage*, p. 26.
2. The correct or pure form of "mir" is probably "mr", but as we are accustomed to words with vowels in English, I have adopted the spelling "mir". Other writers use "mer".
3. Stecchini, *Secrets of the Great Pyramid*, p. 291.

4. Edwards, *The Pyramids of Egypt*, p. 231.
5. *Ibid.,* p. 238.
6. Tompkins, *Secrets of the Great Pyramid*, p. 209.
7. Stecchini, *ibid.,* p. 320.
8. Smyth, *Our Inheritance in the Great Pyramid*, (1890 edition), p. 215.
9. In one place Tompkins notes that *if* it were calculated on a degree of latitude at the equator, the length of the Greek or geographic foot would be .30715 meters, and that would fit the base almost exactly 750 times. But he does not suggest that there was an historical unit of this length.
10. Derived from Smyth's Pyramid inch values of 412.132, 206.066 and 230.289 respectively and multiplied by 1.001 to yield British inch values. See Smyth, *ibid.,* p. 152-156.
11. Maragioglio and Renaldi, *L'Archetettura Della Piramidi Menfite*, Part IV, p. 48.
12. Tompkins, *ibid.,* pp. 247-248.
13. Neither the royal cubit nor the mir cubit, incidentally, fit the height of the King's Chamber evenly.

NOTES
Appendix
IV

1. Richards, *Note On The Age Of The Great Temple Of Ammon At Karnak As Determined By The Orientation Of Its Axis*, p. 7.
2. *Ibid.,* p. 8.
3. *Encyclopaedia Americana*, 1976 edition, "Ecliptic", Vol. 9, p. 588.

The oldest land.

Bibliography

Anonymous. *The Egyptian Museum, Cairo: A Description of The Principal Monuments.* Cairo: Government Press, 1946.

Earth Changes. Virginia Beach, Va.: A.R.E. Press, 1969.

Berlitz, Charles. *The Mystery of Atlantis.* New York: Grosset and Dunlap, 1969.

Mysteries From Forgotten Worlds. Garden City, N.Y.: Doubleday, 1972.

The Bermuda Triangle. Garden City, N.Y.: Doubleday, 1974.

The Bible, King James and Revised Standard versions.

Blanchard, R.H. *Handbook of Egyptian Gods and Mummy Amulets.* Cairo: Publisher not stated, 1909.

Blavatsky, Helena. *The Secret Doctrine,* 2 vol. edition. Pasadena, Cal.: Theosophical University Press, 1970.

Bord, Janet and Colin. *Mysterious Britain.* St. Albans, Hertfordshire: Granada, 1974.

Breasted, James Henry. *Ancient Records of Egypt.* Chicago: University of Chicago Press, 1927.

A History of Egypt. New York: Charles Scribner's Sons, 1937.

Budge, E.A.T. Wallis. *Books on Egypt and Chaldea: A History of Egypt.* London: Kegan Paul, Trench, Trübner, 1902.

Book of the Dead. London: Kegan Paul, Trench, Trübner, 1928.

A History of Egypt. Kegan Paul, Trench, Trübner, 1928.

Osiris: The Egyptian Religion of Resurrection. New Hyde Park, N.Y.: University Books, 1961.

Cayce, Edgar Evans. *Edgar Cayce On Atlantis.* New York: Paperback Library, 1968.

With Hugh Lynn Cayce. *The Outer Limits of Edgar Cayce's Power.* New York: Harper and Row, 1971.

Cerminara, Gina. *Many Mansions.* New York: Wm. Sloan, 1950.

Charroux, Robert. *One Hundred Thousand Years of Man's Unknown History.* Berkeley, Cal.: Medallion Books, 1971.

The Mysterious Unknown. London: Corgi Books, 1973.

Cheiro, (Count Louis de Hamon). *Cheiro's World Predictions.* London: Herbert Jenkens, 1931.

Cole, J.H. *The Determination of the Exact Size and Orientation of the Great Pyramid of Giza.* Cairo: Government Press, 1925.

Corliss, W.R. *Strange Artifacts – A Sourcebook on Ancient Man,* 2 vols. Glen Arm, Maryland: Corliss, 1976.

Davidson, D., and H. Aldersmith. *The Great Pyramid: Its Divine Message.* London: Williams and Norgate, 1925.

De Santillana, Giorgio, and Hertha von Dechend. *Hamlet's Mill.* Boston: Gambit, 1969.

Donnelly, Ignatius. *Atlantis: The Antediluvian World.* New York: Gramercy Publishing, 1949.

Eddy, John A. "Probing the Mystery of the Medicine Wheels." *National Geographic,* January 1977, Vol. 151, No. 1, pp. 140-146.

Edwards, I.E.S. *The Pyramids of Egypt.* New York: Pitman, 1961.

Eliade, Mircea. *The Myth of the Eternal Return.* Princeton, N.J.: Princeton University Press, 1971.

Encyclopaedia Americana, 1976 edition.

Encyclopaedia Britannica Macropaedia, 1974 edition.

Fakhry, Ahmed. *The Pyramids.* Chicago: University of Chicago Press, 1974.

Fell, Barry (H. Barraclough). *America B.C.* New York: Quadrangle/The New York Times Book Co., 1976.

Ferro, Robert, and Michael Grumley. *Atlantis: The Autobiography of a Search.* Garden City, N.Y.: Doubleday, 1970.

Furst, Jeffrey. *Edgar Cayce's Story of Jesus.* London: Neville Spearman, 1973.

Gardiner, Alan. *Egyptian Grammar,* 3rd edition. Oxford: Griffith Institute, Ashmolean Museum, 1976.

Egypt of the Pharaohs. Oxford: Oxford University Press, 1961.

Hapgood, Charles. *The Earth's Shifting Crust.* New York: Pantheon, 1958.

Maps of the Ancient Sea Kings. Philadelphia: Chilton, 1966.

The Path of the Pole. Philadelphia: Chilton, 1970.

Hassan, Selim. *The Sphinx: Its History in Light of Recent Excavations.* Cairo: Government Press, 1949.

Hawkes, Jacquetta. *Atlas of Ancient Archaeology.* New York: McGraw Hill, 1974.

Hawkins, Gerald S. *Stonehenge Decoded.* Garden City, N.Y.: Doubleday, 1965.

Beyond Stonehenge. London: Hutchinson, 1973.

Herodotus, *The History of Herodotus,* translated by George Rawlinson. London: John Murray, 1862.

Hoyle, Fred. "Stonehenge – An Eclipse Predictor." *Nature,* 211: pp. 454-456, July 30, 1966.

James, T.G.H. *Myths and Legends of Ancient Egypt.* London: Hamlyn, 1969.

Kamil, Jill. *Luxor: A Guide to Ancient Thebes.* London: Longmans, 1973.

King-Hele, Desmond. "The Shape of the Earth." *Science,* June 25, 1976, Vol. 192, No. 4246.

Kingsland, William. *The Gnosis or Ancient Wisdom in the Christian Scriptures.* Wheaton, Ill.: Theosophical Publishing House, 1970.

Knauth, Percy. *The Metalsmiths.* New York: Time-Life Books, 1974.

Kunkel, Edward J. *Pharaoh's Pump,* revised edition. Warren, Ohio: Kunkel, 1973.

Lauer, Jean-Philippe. *Observations Sur Les Pyramides.* Cairo: L'Institut Français d'Archaeologie Orientale, 1960.

Les Pyramides de Sakkarah. Cairo: L'Institut Français d'Archaeologie Orientale, 1972.

Lehner, Mark. *The Egyptian Heritage.* Virginia Beach, Va.: A.R.E. Press, 1974.

Lethbridge, T.C. *The Legend of the Sons of God.* London: Sidgwick and Jackson, 1973.

Lindsey, Hal. *The Late Great Planet Earth.* London: Zondervan, 1970.

Magnusson, Magnus. *Introducing Archaeology.* London: Bodley Head, 1972.

Maltwood, K.E. *A Guide to Glastonbury's Temple of the Stars.* London: James Clark, 1964.

Margary, Ivan D. *Roman Roads In Britain,* 3rd edition. London: John Baker, 1973.

Maragioglio, Vito, and Celeste Renaldi. *L'Archetettura Della Piramidi Menfite.* Rome: Centro per le Antichita e la Storia dell'Arte del Vicino Oriente, 1965.

Marshack, Alexander. *The Roots of Civilization.* New York: McGraw-Hill, 1972.

Maspero, Gaston. *The Dawn of Civilization.* London: Society for the Promotion of Christian Knowledge, 1922.

McCann, Lee. *Nostradamus.* New York: Creative Age Press, 1941.

Mead, G.R.S. *Thrice Greatest Hermes.* London: Watkins, 1964.

Melville, Leinani. *Children of the Rainbow.* Wheaton, Ill.: Theosophical Publishing House, 1969.

Mendelssohn, Kurt. *The Riddle of the Pyramids.* New York: Praeger, 1974.

Merejekowski, Dmitri. *Atlantis/Europe –The Secret of the West.* Blauvelt, N.Y.: Rudolf Steiner Pubs., 1971.

Mertz, Henriette. *Atlantis – Dwelling Place of the Gods.* Chicago: Mertz, 1976.

Michell, John, *The View Over Atlantis.* London: Garnstone Press, 1969.

City of Revelation. London: Garnstone Press, 1972.

The Old Stones of Land's End. London: Garnstone Press, 1974.

Montgomery, Ruth. *Here and Hereafter.* New York: Fawcett World, 1969.

Moore, W.G. *A Dictionary of Geography.* Harmondsworth, U.K.: Penguin Books, 1959.

Morris, Henry, and John C. Whitcomb Jr. *The Genesis Flood.* Philadelphia: Presbyterian and Reformed Publishing, 1961.

Muck, Otto. *Cheops und die Grosse Pyramide.* Olten und Freiburg im Breisgau: Walter Verlag, 1958.

Murray, M.A. *Ancient Egyptian Legends.* London: John Murray, 1920.

National Geographic Society. *Greece and Rome, Builders of Our World,* 3rd edition. Washington, D.C.: National Geographic Society, 1968.

Neugebauer, O. *The Exact Sciences in Antiquity,* 2nd edition. New York: Harper and Brothers, 1962.

Norman, James. *Ancestral Voices: Decoding Ancient Languages.* New York: Four Winds Press, 1975.

O'Riordan, Sean. *Antiquities of the Irish Countryside.* London: Methuen, 1968.

Ostrander, Sheila, and Lynn Schroeder. *Psychic Discoveries Behind the Iron Curtain.* New York: Bantam, 1971.

Petrie, William Flinders. *A History of Egypt.* London: Methuen, 1920.

Religious Life in Ancient Egypt. Boston: Houghton Mifflin, 1924.

Seventy Years in Archaeology. New York: Greenwood Press, 1963.

Plato. *The Dialogues of Plato,* Jowett translation. New York: Random House, 1937.

Ralls, Rawleigh H. "The Golden Treasure of Palmar Sur." *Lapidary Journal,* October 1973, Vol. 27, No. 7.

Reiche, Maria. *Mystery on the Desert, (Geheimnis des Wuste).* 7 Stuttgart 80 (Waihingen), Lutzweg 9: Reiche, 1968.

Peruvian Ground Drawings, (Peruanische Erdzeichen). München e. V.: Kunstraum, 1974.

Reisner, George A., and Wm. Stevenson Smith. *History of the Giza Necropolis.* Oxford: Oxford University Press, 1949.

Richards, F.S. *Note On The Age Of The Great Temple Of Ammon At Karnak As Determined By The Orientation Of Its Axis,* (Survey of Egypt Paper No. 38), Cairo: Government Press, 1921.

Robinson, Lytle W. *Edgar Cayce's Story of the Origin and Destiny of Man.* London: Neville Spearman, 1973.

Rutherford, Adam. *Pyramidology,* 3rd edition in 5 vols. Harpenden, U.K.: Institute of Pyramidology, 1968.

Shortt, H. de S. *Old Sarum.* London: Department of the Environment, Her Majesty's Stationery Office, 1965.

Smith, William Stevenson, *History of Egyptian Sculptures and Painting in the Old Kingdom.* Boston: Museum of Fine Arts, and Oxford: Oxford University Press, 1949.

Smyth, Charles Piazzi. *Our Inheritance in the Great Pyramid.* London: W. Isbister, 1874; Charles Burnet, 1890.

Life and Work at the Great Pyramid, 3 vols. Edinburgh: Edmonston and Douglas,1867.

Stacy-Judd, Robert. *Atlantis: Mother of Empires.* Los Angeles: DeVorss, 1939.

Stanford Research Institute. *Applications of Modern Sensing Techniques to Egyptology.* Menlo Park, Cal.: SRI International, September 1977.

Stern, Jess. *Edgar Cayce – The Sleeping Prophet.* Garden City, N.Y.: Doubleday, 1967.

Stecchini, Livio Catullo. "Notes on the Relation of Ancient Measures to the Great Pyramid", an appendix in *Secrets of the Great Pyramid,* by Peter Tompkins. New York: Harper and Row, 1971.

Stewart, Thomas Milton. *The Symbolism of the Gods of the Egyptians and the Light They Throw on Freemasonry.* London: Baskerville Press, 1927.

Sugrue, Thomas. *There Is A River.* New York: Dell, 1967.

Sykes, Egerton. *The Pyramids of Egypt.* London: Markham House Press, 1973.

Thom, Alexander. *Megalithic Sites in Britain.* London: Oxford University Press, 1969.

Megalithic Lunar Observatories. London: Oxford University Press, 1971.

Thompson, William Irwin. *At the Edge of History.* New York: Harper and Row, 1971.

Time. "Puzzling Out Man's Ascent." November 7, 1977, Vol. 110, No. 19.

Tomas, Andrew. *We Are Not The First.* London: Sphere Books, 1971.

The Home of the Gods (Atlantis From Legend To Discovery). New York: Berkeley, 1974.

Tompkins, Peter. *Secrets of the Great Pyramid.* New York: Harper and Row, 1971.

Mysteries of the Mexican Pyramids. New York: Harper and Row, 1976.

Underwood, Guy. *The Pattern of the Past.* London: Sphere Books, 1972.

Velikovsky, Immanuel. *Worlds in Collision.* New York: Dell, 1967.

Verrill, A. Hyatt. *Old Civilizations of the New World.* New York: Home Library, 1942.

Von Däniken, Erich. *Chariots of the Gods?* London: Corgi, 1971.

Von Dechend, Hertha. See de Santillana.

Wake, C. Staniland. *The Origin and Significance of the Great Pyramid.* London: Reeves and Turner, 1882; Minneapolis: Wizards Bookshelf, 1975.

Waters, Frank. *The Book of the Hopi.* New York: Viking, 1963.

Webre, Alfred L. and Phillip H. Liss. *The Age of Cataclysm.* New York: Berkeley, 1974.

World Almanac and Book of Facts 1977. New York: Newspaper Enterprise Associates, 1977.

Zink, David D. *The Stones of Atlantis.* Englewood Cliffs, N.J.: Prentice-Hall, 1978.

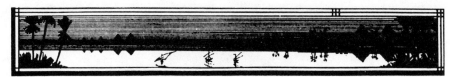

Acknowledgments

The author especially wishes to thank the following for help along the way: David Armstrong, Carolyn Brunton, Edgar Evans Cayce, Gail Cayce, Eileen Deste, Ahmed Abdelmawgoud Fayed, Charles Hapgood, R. Carolyn King, Dianne Ellen Knox, Mark Lehner, Library of the American University in Cairo, Library of the Association for Research and Enlightenment, Library of the Egyptian Museum, John Michell, Walter J. Minton, Sam and Rufus Mosely, Renate Reiche-Grosse, Ebeid Sarofim, Feras Sarofim, Bill and Millie Shaw, Margaret Stevens, Allan Stormont, Carolyn Tanner, Peter Tompkins, Gibson L. Towns, Tim and Alice Willcocks, Linda Wroth, David D. Zink.

WILLIAM R. FIX has degrees in Behavioral Science, History and Philosophy. His interdisciplinary approach has well equipped him to develop his unique insights into the significance of the Great Pyramid.

This innovative, yet totally objective re-appraisal of Egyptological data is an authentic addition to the existing body of knowledge. Easy-to-read and highly persuasive, *Pyramid Odyssey* is indeed "the most important book thus far on the Great Pyramid." It challenges us to re-examine our past — and our future.

Mr. Fix has also written *Star Maps*, a groundbreaking comparison of the initiation practices of the ancient Egyptians with the findings of modern parapsychology. His third book, *The Bone Peddlers*, was published by Macmillan in 1984. It has been called "possibly the most provocative work on the question of human evolution since Darwin's *Descent of Man*".

In the course of his researches and writing, Mr. Fix has travelled extensively and has lived in Canada, Ireland, England and Egypt as well as in the United States. He currently resides near Urbanna, Virginia with his wife and family.

To order PYRAMID ODYSSEY
send $10 per copy ($12.95 plus 5¢ toward postage)
check, cash or money order
to: MERCURY MEDIA, INC.
    BOX 54
    WAKE, VA 23176

Mark envelope "For Odyssey"

Virginia Residents include 4½% Sales Tax

Wholesale rates upon request.